FOR VALOUR

Command and Valour

The Grand Strategy of D-Day & the Battle for Normandy and how 21 heroic deeds helped enable victory.

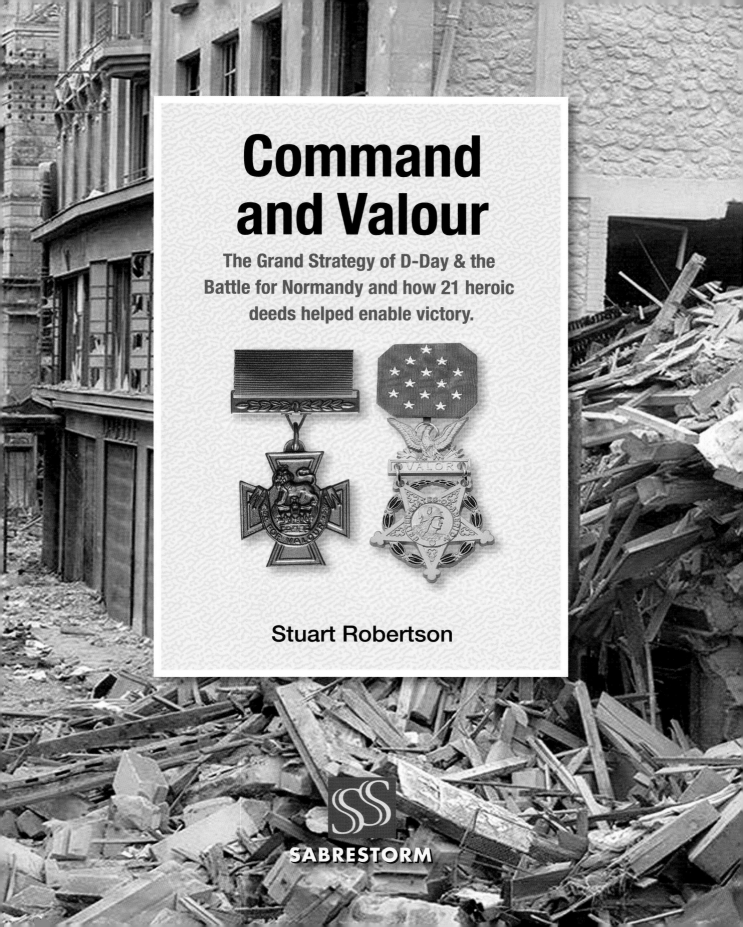

Command and Valour

The Grand Strategy of D-Day & the Battle for Normandy and how 21 heroic deeds helped enable victory.

Stuart Robertson

SABRESTORM

Dedicated to both my Grandfather, Corporal HA 'Jock' Brownbridge, a 'D-Day Dodger' of the Royal Signals (France 1940, North Africa, Sicily and Italy), and my Grandmother, Nurse Muriel 'Woody' Wood, who did more than her bit in providing both medical and emotional support to the wounded of the Second World War during her wartime service at Leeds General Infirmary.

Battles are usually fought, not as they ought to be fought, but as they can be fought; and while the literary man is laying down the law at his desk as to how many troops should be moved here, and what rivers should be crossed there and where the cavalry should be brought up and when the flank should have been turned, the wretched man who has to do the work finds the matter settled for him by pestilence, a want of shoes, empty stomachs, heavy rains, hot suns and a thousand other stern warriors who never show on paper.

CHARLES KINGSLEY 1855.

First published 2019

Designed by Philip Clucas MSIAD

British Library Cataloguing in Publication Data

A catalogue record for this book is available from the British Library

Published by Sabrestorm Publishing,
The Olive Branch, Caen Hill, Devizes,SN10 1RB

Website: www.sabrestorm.com
Email: books@sabrestorm.com

Printed in Europe

ISBN 978-1-78122-011-5

Contents

Preface

Having worked as a full-time battlefield guide for well over a decade, and during that time having accompanied thousands of visitors throughout the Normandy battlefields, the motivation to write this book may well be classed as a cathartic release, born of a desire of setting straight two huge myths that I have found to be inherent within the mainstream portrayal of one of the most famous campaigns within military history.

Known throughout the world simply as *D-Day*, almost every representation within recent popular culture has marginalised a three-month campaign in Normandy, to a story of solely the initial assault. Even then, as popular history interprets 6 June 1944, the limelight seemingly shines almost exclusively upon the struggles faced by American forces. Unbeknown to the majority of observers, the Americans were not in fact the main contributor to the D-Day invasion, but were indeed a junior partner, outnumbered on the landing beaches by their British and Canadian brethren. Indeed, not only did British commanders govern all three branches of Allied forces (land, air and sea), but the Anglo-Canadian contingent contributed the majority of the strength of all three services during the D-Day assault (62 per cent of land forces, 85 per cent of naval vessels crossing the channel, 50 per cent of all supporting aircraft and 50 per cent of all airborne forces were from either Great Britain or Canada). Not just on day one, but throughout the entire Normandy campaign, the Commonwealth forces of Great Britain and Canada took on, and subsequently defeated, one of the largest concentrations of the most fervent and resolute enemy forces to be deployed at any point during the entire war.

Following the publication of my first book, itself a popular narrative limited to the story of D-Day, I would have felt somewhat hypocritical if I had not attempted to take the story on from that incredible day of days, to include the history of the overall battle from a more inclusive perspective of all belligerent nations.

A second myth inherent within the popular portrayal of the battle for Normandy revolves around what exactly was the premeditated Allied strategy, who put together that plan prior to the assault, and then, if there was a deviation from that original planning, what approach was in fact implemented during the subsequent campaign? This history has undoubtedly been distorted, sometimes purposely and shamelessly beyond any recognition of reality. One of the main ambitions of this book is to outline precisely the Allied strategy prior to the launch of Operation Overlord, and how that master-plan was implemented in practice throughout one of the most brutal military campaigns ever endured.

Whilst examining the conduct of both the Allied and the German High Command throughout both the torment and triumphs of the various phases of the battle for Normandy, this book also aims, for the first time within a single volume, to bring together accounts of the incredible acts of valour committed by twenty-one Allied servicemen who, through their actions during the Normandy campaign, would receive their nation's highest decoration for valour.

Alongside the citations and photographs of these recipients of either the Medal of Honor or the Victoria Cross, at the end of the book, for those who have the opportunity of visiting the region, there are directions on how to find locations relevant to these awards.

Below: *Infantry of the 7th Armoured Division advance on the village of Rauray near Caen.*

Acknowledgements

Amongst the many Normandy veterans who have assisted me in my research, it is an honour to be able to acknowledge such individuals as Dr. Ken Tout OBE PhD, Ernie Stringer, Ron Perry, Patrick Thomas, Alfred Green, Bill Bray, Frank Prendergast, Len Corley, Bill Law, Andre Heintz (author of *If I Must Die*), John Roberts, Gordon Newton, Fred Glover, Harry Card, Joe Johnston, Joe Hoadley, Fred O'Toole, Pat Turner, Nick Archdale, George Batts, Gordon May, Don McAdie, Len Smith, Gerry Spencer, Bill Silvester, Maurice Armstrong and Ron Scraggs.

For their inspiration and kindness in sharing of research, I would like to thank the following historians: Dr David Powell and Dr Peter Bell of the University of York St. John as well as Rob Hilton, Mark Zuehlke, James Holland, Neil Barber, Simon Trew and Major General Graham Hollands. I would also like to extend my gratitude to Sarah Palmer, Carl Shilleto, Sean Claxton and Allan Bryson for their suggestions and proof reading of the early drafts of this book and to Neil Barber for his invaluable assistance in the final editing of this book prior to publication. Thanks also to Ian Bayley at Sabrestorm for his continued backing of my work. Finally, I would like to give special thanks to my wife, Jennifer Robertson, without whose constant support, the following of my life's passion, let alone this book, would never have been possible.

Stuart Robertson, Pickering, North Yorkshire
March 2018

Introduction

Tuesday, 6 June 1944 was truly a day without precedent. Upon this day, one of history's greatest ever naval armadas crossed the English Channel before disembarking upon the Nazi-held coastline of mainland Europe, a liberation army drawn from sixteen Allied nations. This, which would eventually become the largest amphibious invasion in history, held the objective of commencing what was hoped would be the final chapter of a global conflict that would ultimately account for over 60,000,000 lives. The combined strength of the Western Allies would pit their might against the forces of a brutal dictatorship which, for the last four years, had held occupied Europe in a vice of evil and despair. Hitler had made slaves of the nations he had conquered; unprecedented brutality had blighted and changed forever the lives of millions of innocent people. By 1944, a coalition like no other had been forged. Millions of fighting men had been brought together to attain one goal, an objective outlined on that unique day by the American General, and the future 34th President of the United States of America, Dwight D. Eisenhower, the Supreme Commander of the Expeditionary Force...

Soldiers, Sailors and Airmen of the Allied Expeditionary Force!

You are about to embark upon the Great Crusade, toward which we have striven these many months. The eyes of the world are upon you. The hopes and prayers of liberty-loving people everywhere march with you. In company with our brave Allies and brothers-in-arms on other fronts, you will bring about the destruction of the German war machine, the elimination of Nazi tyranny over the oppressed peoples of Europe, and security for yourselves in a free world.

Your task will not be an easy one. Your enemy is well trained, well equipped and battle-hardened. He will fight savagely.

But this is the year 1944! Much has happened since the Nazi triumphs of 1940-41. The United Nations have inflicted upon the Germans great defeats, in open battle, man-to-man. Our air offensive has seriously reduced their strength in the air and their capacity to wage war on the ground. Our home fronts have given us an overwhelming superiority in weapons and munitions of war, and placed at our disposal great reserves of trained fighting men. The tide has turned! The free men of the world are marching together to victory!

I have full confidence in your courage, devotion to duty and skill in battle. We will accept nothing less than full victory!

Good luck! And let us all beseech the blessing of almighty God upon this great and noble undertaking.

The following pages record the story of the grand strategy of this unique military campaign, a battle commanded by some of the biggest names in military history. Woven into the narrative of the wider battle are also the stories of individual soldiers who, during the battle for Normandy, would receive their nations' highest accolade.

Right: *The ancient county-town of Saint Lo is left in ruins after it's liberation on 17 July 1944 – four weeks later than General Bradley first anticipated.*

PART ONE

Chapter 1

A History of the Medal of Honor and the Victoria Cross

Above: *Charles Lucas, who in 1854 became the first recipient of the Victoria Cross.*

The history of warfare makes for a complex and multi-faceted study. From the social, economic and political origins of conflict, the preparations and planning of a battle, the logistics from first contact to final extraction, the armaments used, the skills and efficiency of the lowest ranks, to the strategic ability of those within the highest echelon of command, every individual component evokes great debate from academics, seasoned veterans and armchair generals alike. For many, it is the individual soldier's response and conduct under the ultimate strain of battle that conjures an attempt to analyse and understand how the human body and mind respond to the extreme physical and mental challenges of combat. In particular, there is an urge to understand how and why a man will altruistically place his life on the line, often against seemingly insurmountable odds, to carry out an act of extreme valour on the field of battle.

When witnessed, recorded and published, these actions can make legends of men. Often accidental and very rarely, if ever intended, one way of guaranteeing legendary status is to receive your nation's highest award for valour. In the example of the greater part of the Allied forces in Normandy, this would come in the guise, for those who served within the British Commonwealth forces, of the much-fabled Victoria Cross, and for the Americans, the Medal of Honor.

The Victoria Cross is awarded for *'most conspicuous bravery, or some daring or pre-eminent act of valour or self-sacrifice, or extreme devotion to duty in the presence of the enemy.'* Initiated by Royal Warrant in 1856, the covenant was immediately backdated, enabling it to be awarded for actions which took place during the Crimean War of 1853-56. It was the first award that could be bestowed upon any rank of the British armed forces. The medal's origin was undoubtedly influenced by the ever-growing presence of popular media, and in particular the development of a new breed of journalist – the war correspondent.

With the British population becoming increasingly literate, the valour of all combatants, regardless of social background, was brought to the attention of working class readers for the first time. As a result, a sentiment grew amongst the masses that the efforts and sacrifices of all combatants should be acknowledged by the establishment. As such, the Victoria Cross was perceived as a Royal endorsement that acts of valour were to be recognised irrelevant of rank and irrespective of class.

Above: *The Victoria Cross (left), and the Medal of Honor (right).*

The creation of the Victoria Cross is accredited to have been a joint venture between Prince Albert and Queen Victoria herself. Despite such regal origins, the medal's design is extremely modest, taking the form of a simple bronze cross featuring a crown, a lion, and the inscription *'For Valour'*. The medal hangs from a 'V' placed centrally along a bar at the bottom of a crimson ribbon. Folklore states that the metal from which the medal is cast originates from Russian cannons captured by the British during the Crimean War. However, recent research suggests that the old gunmetal is of Chinese origin. One explanation could be that the cannon in question may have been captured by the Russians from the Chinese during an earlier conflict.

The Victoria Cross was first bestowed upon Ulsterman Charles Lucas, a Royal Navy sailor, who in 1854, whilst serving aboard *HMS Hecla*, a wooden battleship that formed part of the British Task Force blockading the Russian fleet, came under fire from Russian coastal artillery overlooking the Baltic Sea. A live shell, fuse still alight, crashed onto the deck of the Hecla before Lucas physically manhandled it overboard, saving both the ship and the lives of its crew. Since this first award, up until the publication of this book, another 1,357 acts of valour have been recognised with the award of the Victoria Cross. Some 182 Victoria Crosses were bestowed during the Second World War, five of which were awarded during the battle for Normandy. On a ratio of men who served, as opposed to those who would receive the medal, the Victoria Cross remains the most scarcely issued of all military decorations awarded for valour during battle.

The highest award within the American armed forces is the Medal of Honor. Initiated in 1861 and awarded for *'acts of valor, above and beyond the call of duty'.*[1] there are today three variations of the award, one for each branch of service (Army, Navy and Air Force). During the Second World War, as the US Air Force was still part of the US Army, there were just two variations (Army and Navy).

The Medal of Honor itself is... *'A gold five pointed star, each point tipped with trefoils, one and a half inches wide, surrounded by a green laurel wreath and suspended from a gold bar inscribed 'Valor' surmounted by an eagle. In the center of the star, Minerva's head surrounded by the words 'United States of America'. On each ray of the star is a green oak leaf... The medal is suspended by a neck ribbon... A shield of the same color ribbon with thirteen white stars, arranged in the form of three chevrons is above the medal'.*[2]

Above: *In 1863, Private Jacob Parrott became the first man to be awarded the Medal of Honor.*

On 25 March 1863, Private Jacob Parrott was the first within a group of six men to be presented with the inaugural award of the Medal of Honor. Eleven months prior to this, during the American Civil War, Parrott was one of a twenty-two man raiding party that breached nearly 200 miles into Confederate territory before carrying out numerous acts of sabotage. Captured, imprisoned and subsequently beaten during interrogation, Parrott escaped captivity to return to Union lines.

In total, at the time of publication, 3,470 awards of the Medal of Honor have been bestowed, 464 were awarded during the Second World War, fifteen (all Army awards), were granted for actions during the battle for Normandy. An additional Medal of Honor was added to this list in March 2014 when President Obama upgraded the Distinguished Service Cross, previously awarded posthumously to paratrooper Joe Gandara of the 82nd Airborne Division. Here, for the first time, Joe Gandara's story is included alongside all the other awards at the pinnacle of recognition for American serviceman who fought in Normandy.

Chapter 2
Operation Overlord

As the Western Allies launched the world's greatest ever amphibious assault, with the objective of commencing the conclusion of the Nazi occupation of mainland Europe, D-Day witnessed the culmination of years of planning and preparation. Operation Overlord, with the assault phase launched under the codename of Neptune, would put ashore 135,000 soldiers disembarking upon five landing beaches, dispersed across almost sixty miles of Normandy coastline. The assault forces were to cross the English Channel aboard more than 5,000 naval vessels and be assisted by over 11,000 aircraft, some 1,500 of which were to fly into battle an additional 20,000 airborne troops - an airborne army that would descend into the night sky on both the eastern and westernmost extremities of the amphibious assault, securing the flanks of the invasion in the immediate hours before the early morning assault upon the five landing beaches.

Below: *The Overlord Area.*

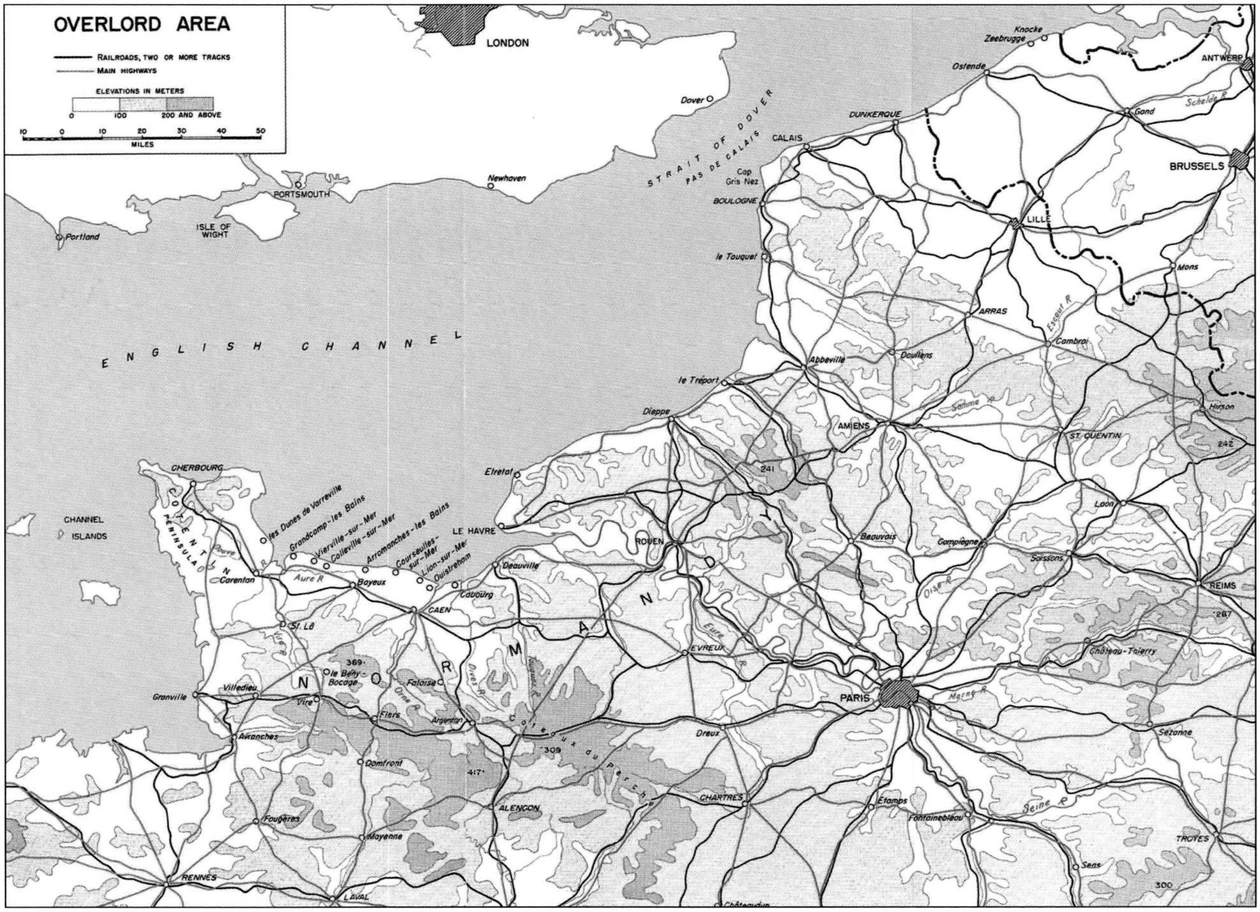

With the flanks secured, albeit tenuously by lightly armed airborne forces, the assault upon the Normandy coastline was to commence at 0630 hours. On the two westernmost beaches code-named Utah and Omaha, General Omar Bradley's US First Army would land just over one third of all amphibious forces on D-Day. Just under an hour later, General Miles Dempsey's British Second Army would put ashore just under two thirds of the D-Day land forces upon three beaches codenamed Gold, Juno and Sword. Having overwhelmed the much feted, yet in truth, much flawed coastal defences, the Allies would advance with an aim of ending the day some five to eight miles inland from their landing beaches. With distance gained between the invasion coastline and Allied frontline by the end of day one, further ground would have to be taken in the days immediately after the initial assault. This space would enable the huge build-up of troops needed to facilitate future operations whilst also repelling what would surely be the inevitable enemy counterattacks.

With an appreciation that the Allies would eventually have to advance from their beachhead in an easterly direction, on to Paris en route to the ultimate objective of Germany, it was foreseen by General Montgomery, the Commander in Chief of all Ground Forces,[3] that the most likely reaction to the assault would be for the Germans to concentrate their main efforts within this eastern sector of the Allied beachhead. With this forethought firmly in mind, on 7 April 1944, then again on 15 May, Montgomery outlined how post D-Day operations should develop. Montgomery's plan determined that, with British and Canadian forces holding the main concentration of enemy reserves to the east, the Americans would build up their strength in the west.

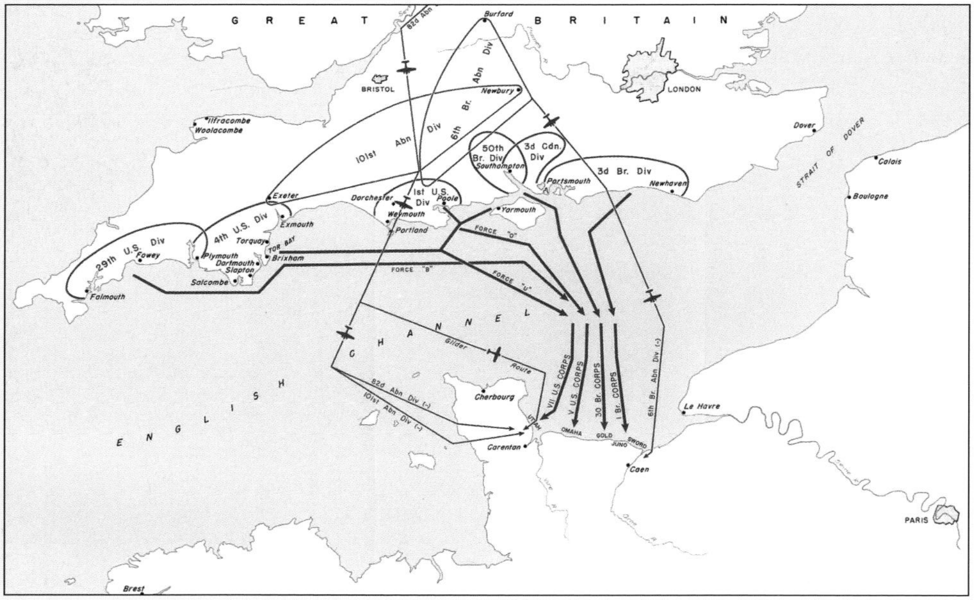

Above: *The Allied Assault Routes.*

Right: *The senior Allied military staff involved in Operation Overlord. Left to right: General Omar Bradley (First US Army), Admiral Sir Bertram Ramsey (Commander all Allied Naval Forces), Air Chief Marshal Sir Arthur Tedder (Deputy Supreme Commander), General Dwight Eisenhower (Supreme Commander), and General Bernard Montgomery (Commander 21st Army Group), Air Chief Marshal Sir Trafford Leigh Mallory (Commander all Allied Air Forces), General Beddell Smith (Chief of Staff to General Eisenhower).*

General Dwight D. Eisenhower 1890-1969

Supreme Commander of the Allied Expeditionary Force

Graduating from West Point in the class of 1915, Dwight David Eisenhower served exclusively on the home front during the Great War. Mentored by General Marshall in the inter-war period, Ike became a firm favourite of the future Chief of Staff of the American Army. Whilst Eisenhower's lack of experience in the field would lead to much cynicism from more experienced personnel, his meteoric progression through the ranks meant that by November of 1943, he had become Supreme Commander of amphibious operations in North Africa, Sicily and Italy.

Although politics would always dictate that the supreme commander of any potential cross channel invasion would have to be an American, the selection of Eisenhower as Supreme Commander for Operation Overlord was still undoubtedly a shock appointment. Although thought by many as simply an administrator, Eisenhower's tact and diplomacy, alongside his easy going and reassuring character were qualities which undoubtedly unified potentially fractious individuals as he oversaw the planning of D-Day and the subsequent campaign in North West Europe. A great delegator, Eisenhower himself entrusted the planning of D-Day and the subsequent Battle for Normandy to the British General, Bernard Law Montgomery.

On 1 September 1944, at the conclusion of the battle for Normandy, a time where there were now far more American troops in the field than their British and Canadian allies, once more politics intervened to ensure an American, and that American being Eisenhower, took over from Montgomery as commander of all Allied land forces in the European Theatre. However, with Eisenhower failing to implement a defined strategy, it could be argued that from this point the North West European Campaign would suffer a lack of direction. Eisenhower's detachment from the battlefield, never having his Headquarters located in the same country as the front line, his policy of a broad front with supplies and the overall line stretched too thinly, is widely recognised as a strategic blunder which many have stated contributed to the Allies being caught off guard in December 1944 as the Germans launched their last-ditch counter-attack known today as the Battle of the Bulge. Although doubts still remain as to Eisenhower's strategic ability, his huge talent in diplomacy, a skill that would later lead him to serve two terms as the 34th President of the United States, undoubtedly contributed greatly to Allied victory in North West Europe.

Dwight D. Eisenhower died at the age of 78 on 20 January 1961. He is buried in his hometown of Abilene, Kansas.

This would eventually lead to the Americans breaking out into Brittany, before enveloping the enemy's main strength at a location somewhere between the Rivers Seine and Loire, therefore forcing either its surrender or annihilation. As the Commonwealth forces held the bulk of the enemy to the east, American forces were to land on the south-east coastline of the Cherbourg Peninsula. Once ashore, these forces would move upon the fortress port of Cherbourg. Once Cherbourg was secured, huge numbers of American troops would fill the peninsula, ready to pounce through the enemy line at its weakest point. From there they would sweep west to liberate and open the sea ports within the Breton (Brittany) Peninsula, simultaneously carrying out a left hook manoeuvre behind the main enemy concentration to the east, encircling the enemy before forcing their surrender. Montgomery had hoped this campaign would be completed within ninety days of the initial assault.

It is worth addressing from the start that many have in the past conveniently forgotten, or perhaps deliberately ignored these briefings during which Monty, having been delegated the responsibility for all strategic planning and implementation of all land operations by General Eisenhower, clearly and concisely outlined plans which beyond doubt confirmed his overall strategy of goading the enemy in the east, in order to keep the bulk of enemy forces away from the American front to the west. This pre-meditated plan is underscored beyond doubt by the words of General Bradley, himself no great supporter of Montgomery, and therefore surely an individual who would not be predisposed in favour of offering an alibi to a potentially self-serving Montgomery...

The Overlord ground strategy formulated months before... called for Monty not to 'break out' but to hold and draw the Germans to his sector, while I 'broke out' in my sector and wheeled to the east. We adhered to that basic concept throughout the Normandy Campaign with no major changes in strategy.[4]

The success of this unprecedented undertaking would only be possible through the skill and determination of the Allied fighting men who would partake in what Eisenhower named *The Great Crusade.*

Below: *Generals Montgomery and Eisenhower.*

Overleaf: *The D-Day assault with the Americans landing to the west and the Anglo-Canadians landing further east.*

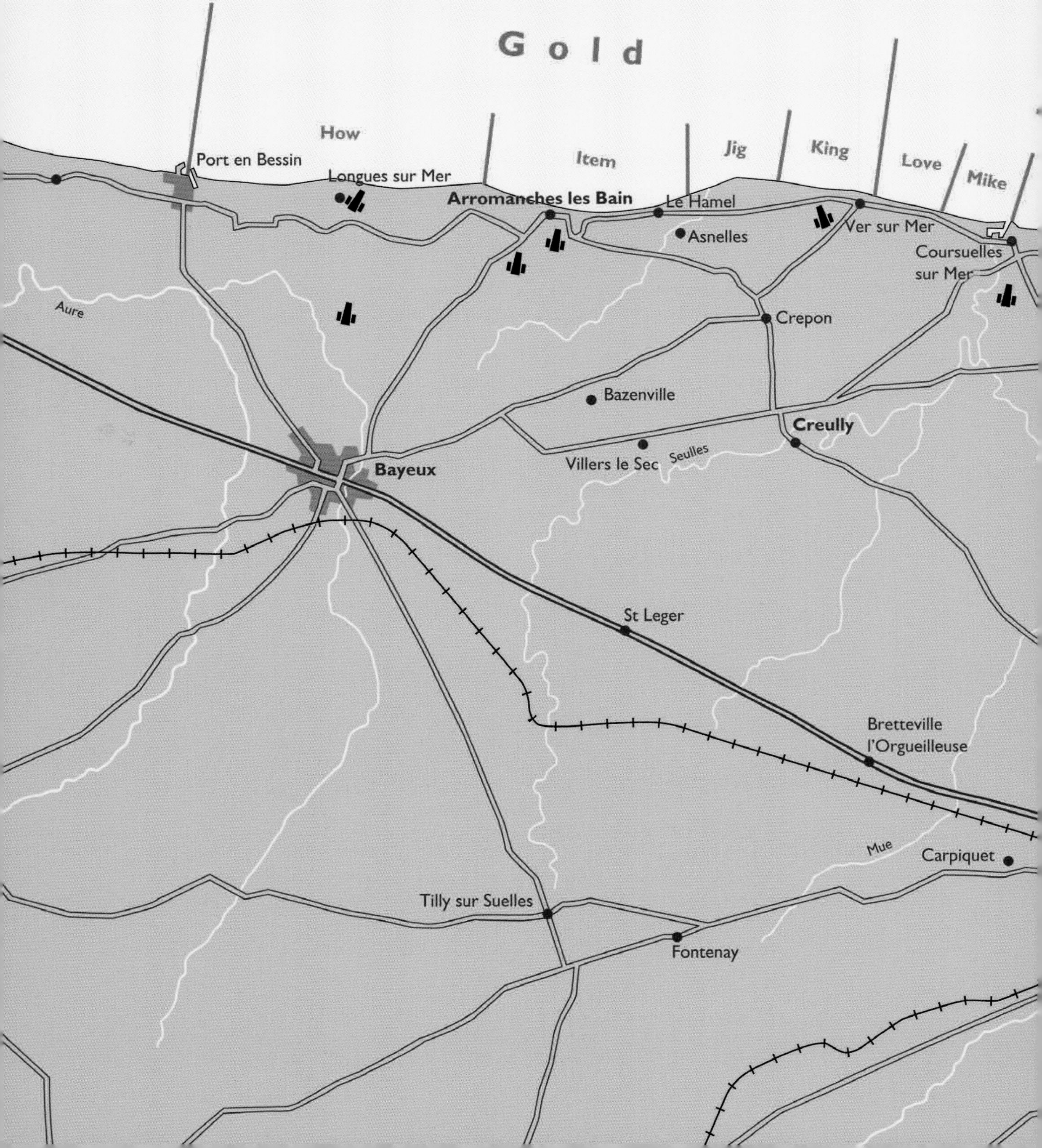

Gold
How
Item
Jig
King
Love
Mike
Port en Bessin
Longues sur Mer
Arromanches les Bain
Le Hamel
Asnelles
Ver sur Mer
Coursuelles sur Mer
Aure
Crepon
Bazenville
Creully
Villers le Sec
Seulles
Bayeux
St Leger
Bretteville l'Orgueilleuse
Mue
Carpiquet
Tilly sur Suelles
Fontenay

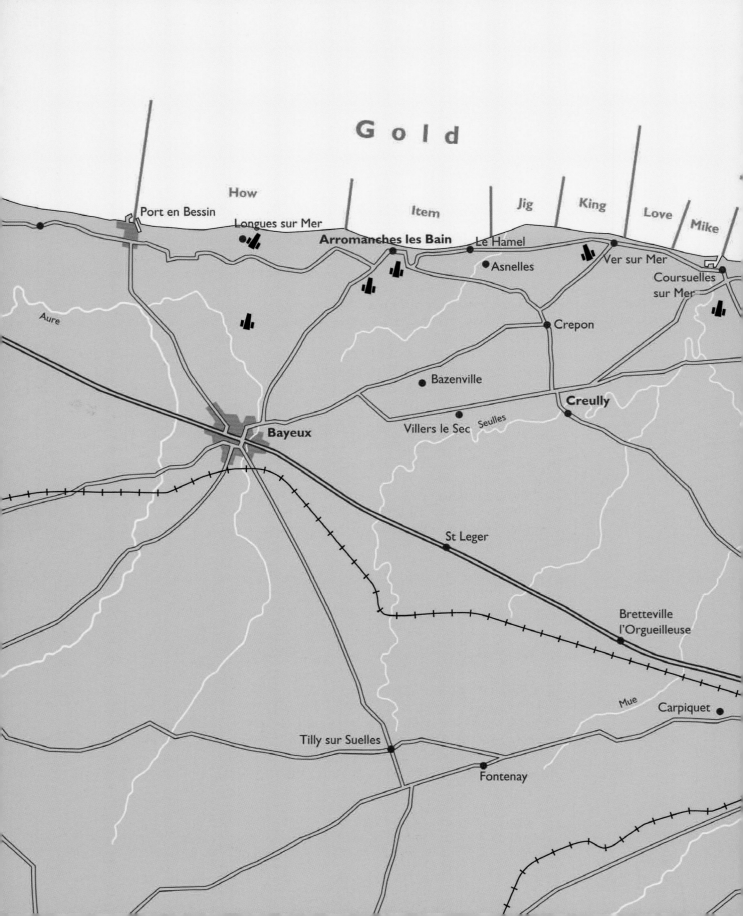

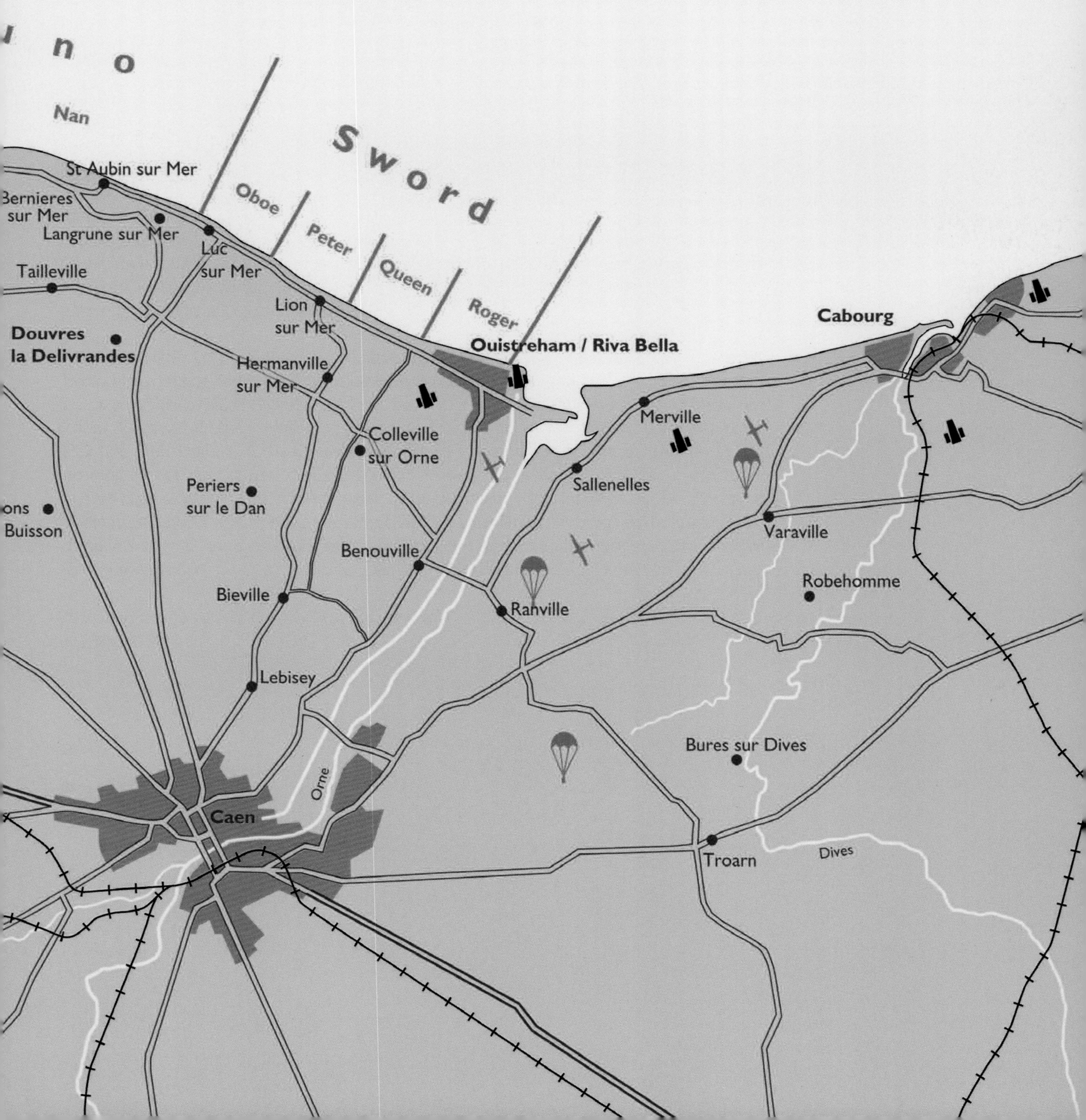

uno
Nan
Sword
Oboe
Peter
Queen
Roger
St Aubin sur Mer
Bernieres sur Mer
Langrune sur Mer
Luc sur Mer
Tailleville
Lion sur Mer
Douvres la Delivrandes
Hermanville sur Mer
Ouistreham / Riva Bella
Cabourg
Merville
Colleville sur Orne
Sallenelles
Periers sur le Dan
ons Buisson
Varaville
Benouville
Robehomme
Bieville
Ranville
Lebisey
Bures sur Dives
Orne
Caen
Troarn
Dives

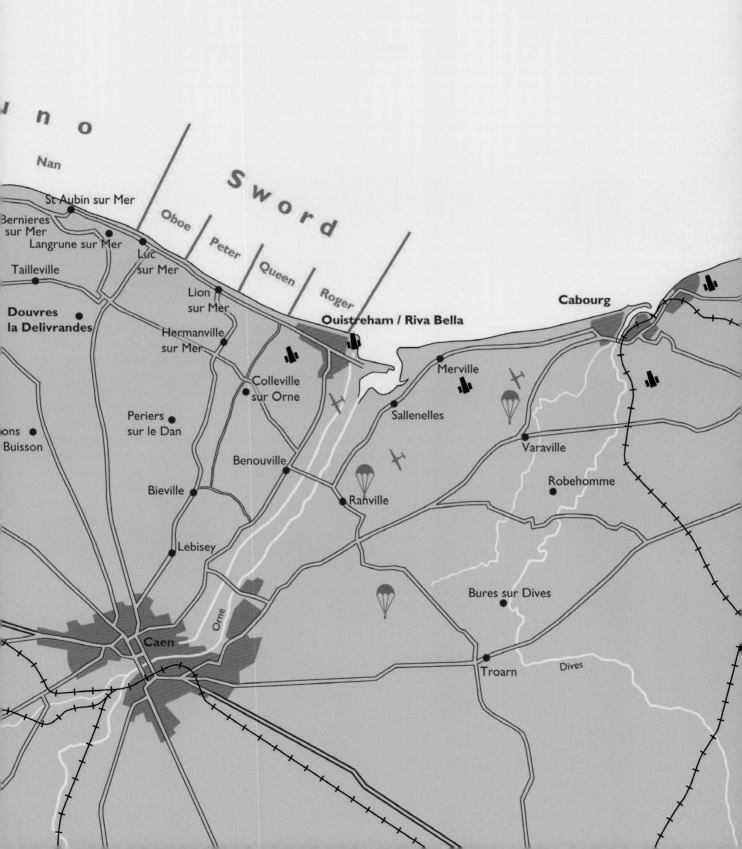

PART TWO

Chapter 3

The President's Son

As the planning and preparations for the invasion gained momentum, the westernmost of the five landing beaches became a great cause of concern for the Allied Command. Located on the south-east coast of the Cherbourg Peninsula, Utah was separated from the other four landing beaches by the estuary of the River Vire. Not only was the Utah Sector dangerously isolated from the other beaches, but any potential advance inland would inevitably be hindered as large expanses of low lying marshland had been purposely flooded by the Germans to prevent free movement in the area.

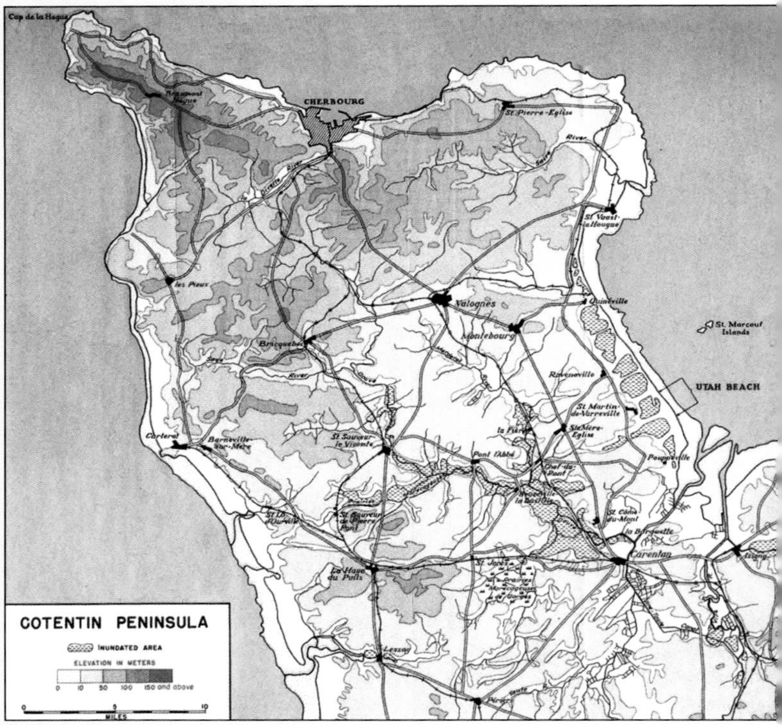

Above: *The Cotentin Peninsula*

The presence of the 91st *Luftlande* Division, positioned within striking distance of the Utah Beach assault, added greatly to Allied anxiety. To counter such vulnerability, it was decided that some 12,000 airborne troops, drawn from the American 82nd and 101st Airborne Divisions, would jump behind Utah Beach in the hours of darkness, five hours before the first wave assault came ashore. In seizing control of four causeways which ran over a flooded corridor located directly behind the beach and securing the immediate area behind the beach at a distance of up to eight miles inland, the airborne would block the march of the 91st *Luftlande* Division. This would pave the way in holding open a buffer zone for the amphibious forces to move into, hopefully encountering as little resistance as possible, at least in the formative stages of the battle.

With the airborne forces easing the pressure, the combined might of unprecedented air and naval bombardments would precede the US 4th Infantry Division's assault on Utah Beach in the hope of neutralising the enemy's limited number of fixed fortifications which had been built within this sector. Whilst the topography confronting the amphibious assault at Utah had worried the planners, one distinct positive was the fact that these physical defences within the Utah Beach sector were, by far, the weakest of all five landing beaches. Having initially emphasised maximising the potential benefits of the lay of the land, the local command, partly through complacency and partially through logistical restraints beyond their control, had failed to develop the

Left: *The draw from Uncle Red sector of Utah Beach leading to Exit number 2 – 9 June 1944.*

tangible strength of the Utah Beach defences. Of over a dozen strongpoints under construction, by D-Day few of these were operational and only two fully so. Therefore, if the airborne forces were successful in achieving their task of denying the 91st *Luftlande* Division a march against Utah Beach, potentially fewer than 100 Germans would oppose the attack of 23,000 American troops drawn from the combined strength of the 4th and 90th Infantry Divisions.

The first wave assault at Utah Beach was scheduled for disembarkation at 0630 hours. In anticipation of this, the Utah defences were to feel the full wrath of what the planners called the *Joint Fire Plan*. This preliminary attack, implemented at all five landing beaches that morning, would subject the defences overlooking the invasion coastline to unprecedented aerial and naval bombardment before the first men hit the beach. Whilst the success of these bombardments would determine the amount of resistance faced by the first wave assaults, in practice the effectiveness of such bombardments would vary greatly from beach to beach and would very much be dependent on how weather conditions affected the accuracy of the bombing within each sector.

At Utah, the two strongpoints capable of resisting the initial assault encountered enormously contrasting experiences. The main enemy strongpoint overlooking the sector where the first wave of the American attack was scheduled to disembark was shrouded by fog and cloud. Consequently the aerial bombardment had little or no impact. In contrast, just over one mile to the south, the second operational strongpoint was visible from the air and hit hard. With almost 300 B26 bombers dropping over 4,400 bombs, any potential for this particular strongpoint to offer anything other than derisory opposition was smashed completely by the US Army Air Force.

In a fortuitous twist of fate, and largely as a consequence of the loss of two guiding vessels, combined with stronger than anticipated channel currents, the first wave of the Utah Beach assault was dragged out of position and touched down over a mile to the south of their intended sector - a navigational error which led the first wave touching down directly in front of the bombed-out strongpoint, neutralised to the extent that it could offer only pitiful resistance. With very few casualties suffered in the initial assault, those commanding the first wave of the Utah Beach landing soon realised they had been put ashore at the wrong location.

On to this stage enters the recipient of the Normandy campaign's most controversial Medal of Honor. The oldest man to land in the first wave on D-Day, 56-year-old

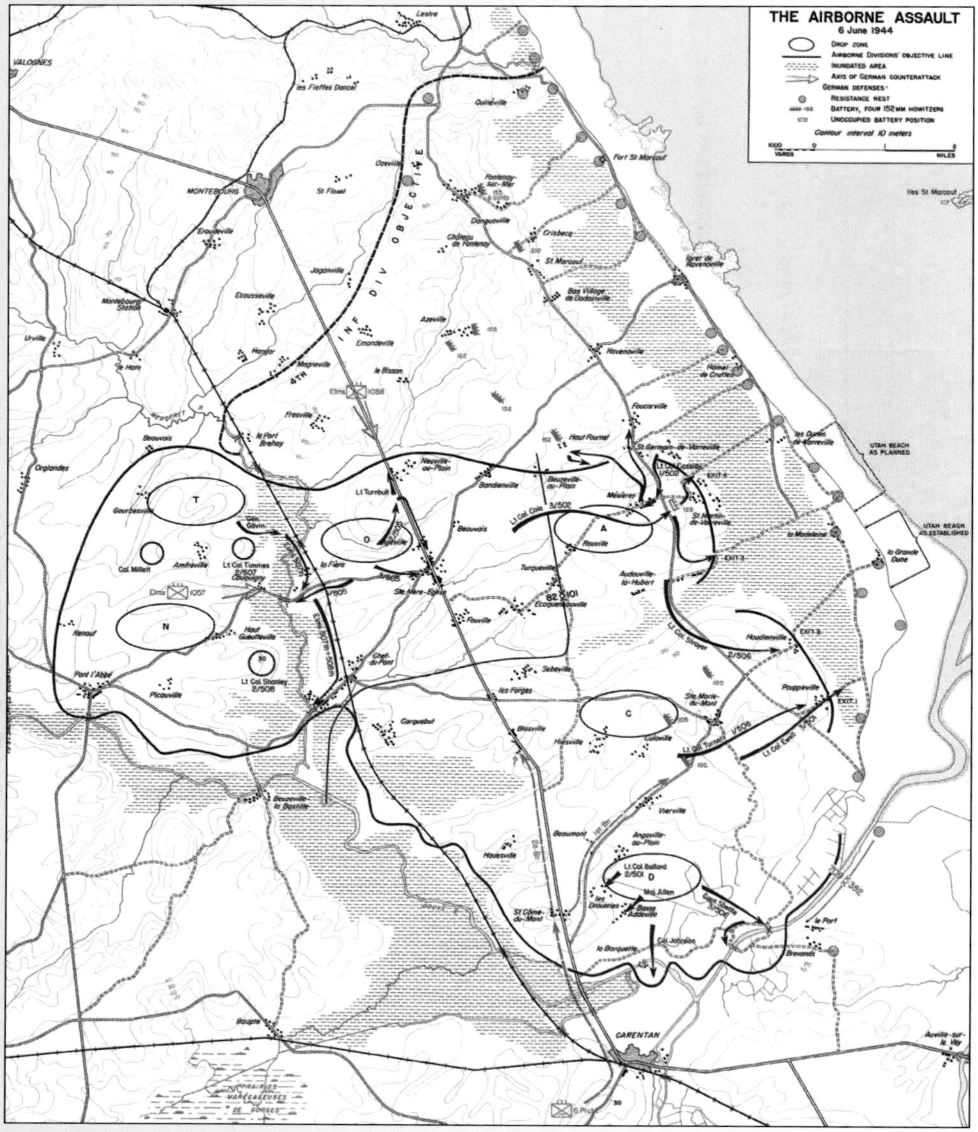

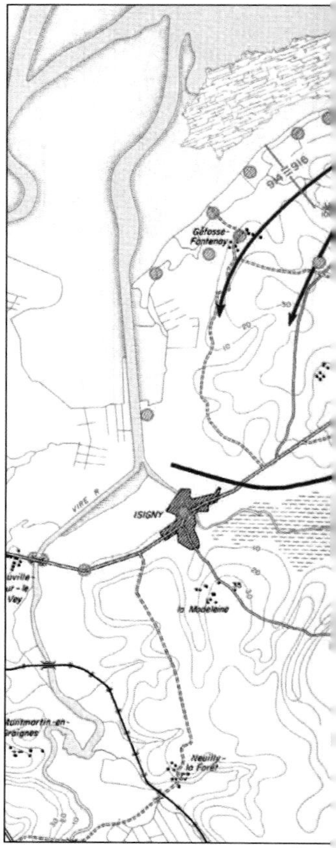

Brigadier General Theodore Roosevelt Jnr, had already overcome great odds to be present at the world's greatest amphibious assault. Half-crippled with arthritis, with a history of heart disease and having only just recovered from a near fatal bout of pneumonia, Roosevelt had been ordered to stay away from the initial battle by his commanding officer, Major General Raymond Barton (Commanding 4th Infantry Division). Refusing to be denied the opportunity of becoming part of history, only through his sheer bloody-mindedness, did the cousin of FDR, and the eldest son of the 26th President of the United States of America, lead ashore the first wave assault onto Utah Beach. Realising the first wave had landed in the wrong place, alongside Colonels Van Fleet (Commanding 8th Regiment, 4th Infantry Division) and Caffey (Commanding 1st Engineer Special Brigade), General Roosevelt improvised a plan of attack which, whilst suffering few casualties, would subsequently overwhelm the enemy defences

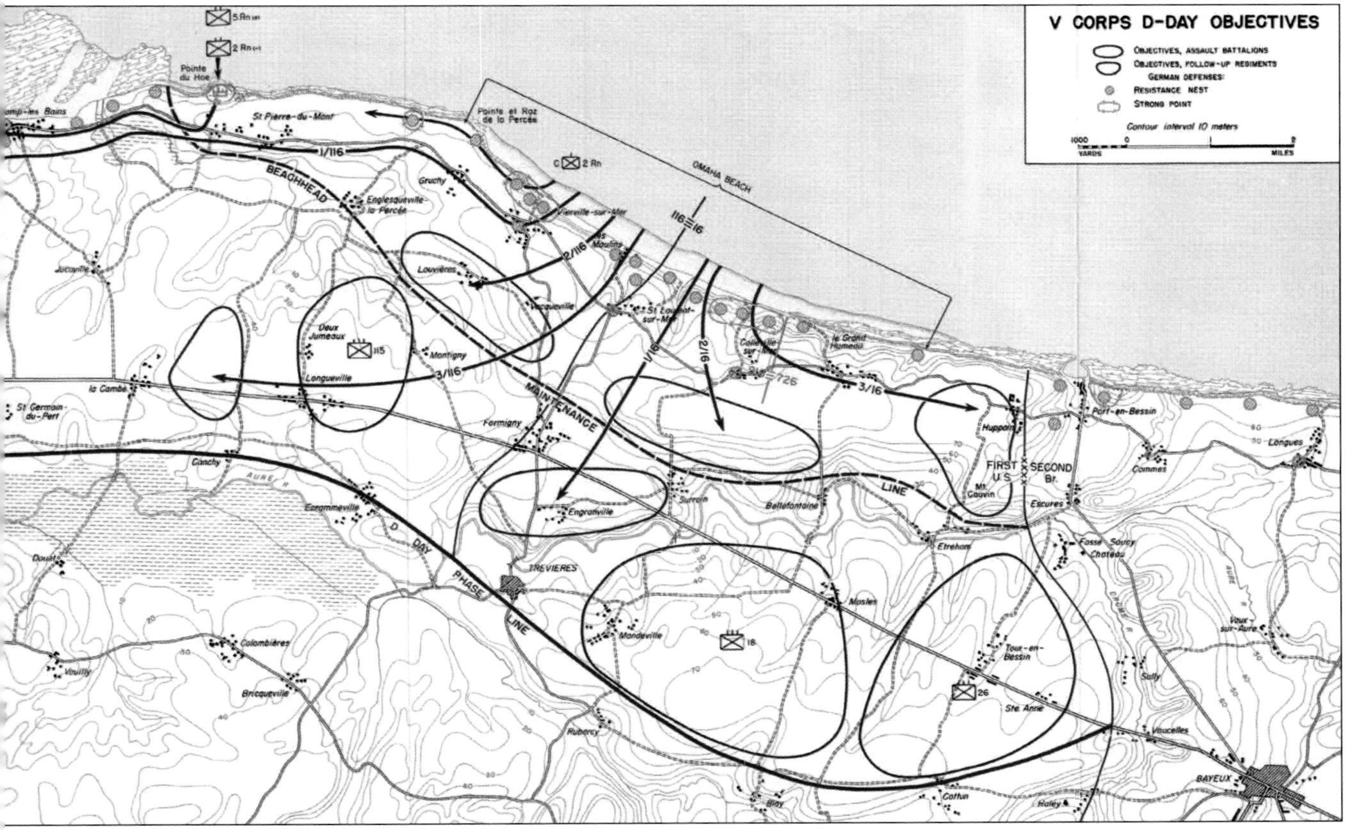

north of the first wave assault, before advancing inland to link up and consolidate with the paratroopers of the 82nd and 101st Airborne Divisions.

The D-Day assault at Utah Beach was undoubtedly an incredible success. The US 4th Infantry Division brought ashore over 16,000 men by the end of the day, suffering fewer than 200 casualties. Much of this success was undoubtedly due to the fortuitous circumstances which so greatly influenced the initial assault. However, well before this good fortune had occurred, the origin of the success of the Utah assault has to be accredited to the improvisation of the airborne troops, who, despite in most cases having been mis-dropped away from their designated drop-zones, had responded magnificently in blocking the potential counterattacks of both the localised enemy forces drawn from the static divisions, as well as that of the mobile 91st Luftlande Division. Facing such a favourable situation, all officers present reinforced the success by taking the log-

Above: *US Army VII Corps D-Day Objectives.*

Opposite page, above: *The US Airborne Assault on D-Day.*

Left: *US infantry advance upon one the causeways leading away from Utah Beach.*

ical, albeit non-sensational decision to improvise the battle from the start line of their involuntary landing. It was these practical, though not unpredictable decisions, made jointly by General Roosevelt and Colonels Van Fleet and Caffey, which led to General Roosevelt being awarded America's highest decoration.

Roosevelt's Medal of Honor was awarded after he succumbed to a heart attack some five weeks after D-Day. For many, the award was the result of political spin, possibly as a consequence of mounting political pressure as another Roosevelt was facing a bitter Presidential Election campaign, but more likely

due to a former President's son having lost his life during a high-profile battle. Roosevelt's citation portrays a General as the barnstorming warrior, who, whilst facing a maelstrom of enemy fire, led his men to a position of victory against great adversity. Such a sentiment is hardly supported by the fact that the 1st Battalion of the 8th Regiment of the 4th Infantry Division put ashore the first 800 men at Utah Beach, before moving up to four miles inland, at a cost of just twenty-nine men killed. Whilst there is no denying that Roosevelt was an exceptional leader who undoubtedly inspired confidence amongst the men he commanded, men who in return displayed nothing but respect and loyalty to a commander they themselves revered in nothing but the highest esteem, it is nevertheless difficult to endorse the notion that General Roosevelt deserved to be awarded America's highest award for valour for his actions on D-Day. This statement is not intended to disrespect the man himself, after all, Teddy Roosevelt did not personally seek to be considered for what was a posthumous award. Who is to say that he himself would not have been embarrassed to have received the honour when so many others did so much more without such recognition.

Today, Brigadier General Theodore Roosevelt Junior is buried at the Normandy American Cemetery and Memorial.

Brigadier General

THEODORE ROOSEVELT JUNIOR

4th Infantry Division

For gallantry and intrepidity at the risk of his life above and beyond the call of duty on 6 June 1944, in France. After two verbal requests to accompany the leading assault elements in the Normandy invasion had been denied, Brigadier General Roosevelt's written request for this mission was approved and he landed with the first wave of the forces assaulting the enemy held beaches. He repeatedly led groups from the beach, over the seawall and established them inland. His valor, courage, and presence in the very front of the attack and his complete unconcern at being under heavy fire inspired the troops to heights of enthusiasm and self-sacrifice. Although the enemy had the beach under constant direct fire, Brigadier General Roosevelt moved from one locality to another, rallying men around him, directed and personally led them against the enemy. Under his seasoned, precise, calm, and unfaltering leadership, assault troops reduced beach strong points and rapidly moved inland with minimum casualties. He thus contributed substantially to the successful establishment of the beachhead in France.

Above left: *Brigadier General Theodore Roosevelt Jnr, pictured next to his jeep 'The Rough Rider', named in reference to the unit which his Father and namesake commanded during the Spanish-American war of 1898.*

Chapter 4
Bloody Omaha

Whilst the presence of the 91st *Luftlande* Division had caused great concern amongst those planning the Utah Beach landing, in contrast, with Allied Intelligence having identified a figure of not exceeding 650 enemy troops positioned within, or directly supporting, the fifteen complexes of fixed fortifications directly overlooking Omaha Beach, with the addition of a mere 1,200 or so enemy troops located within striking distance of the Omaha assault, with no significant reserve force in close proximity, it was clear that the core threat at Omaha came in the form of the immediate crust of defences overlooking the beach.

Analysis of both the terrain and the enemy defences heavily influenced the plan of attack at Omaha. With many planners believing that aerial bombardment would be the key component in overwhelming the bulk of the German fortifications, a plan was formulated where, after a very short but sharp naval bombardment, before the first wave of infantry hit the beach, 450 heavy bombers would drop over one kiloton of bombs, a ratio of almost seventeen tons of high explosives per enemy defender. The promise of such an extraordinary bombardment, the like of which the world had never seen before, provided reassurance and confidence for those troops within the first wave assault at Omaha. As early as February 1944, the hierarchy of the US Army V Corps was already predicting that... *'Every house and other building with observation over the beach will be knocked out. Also, all pillboxes'.*[5]

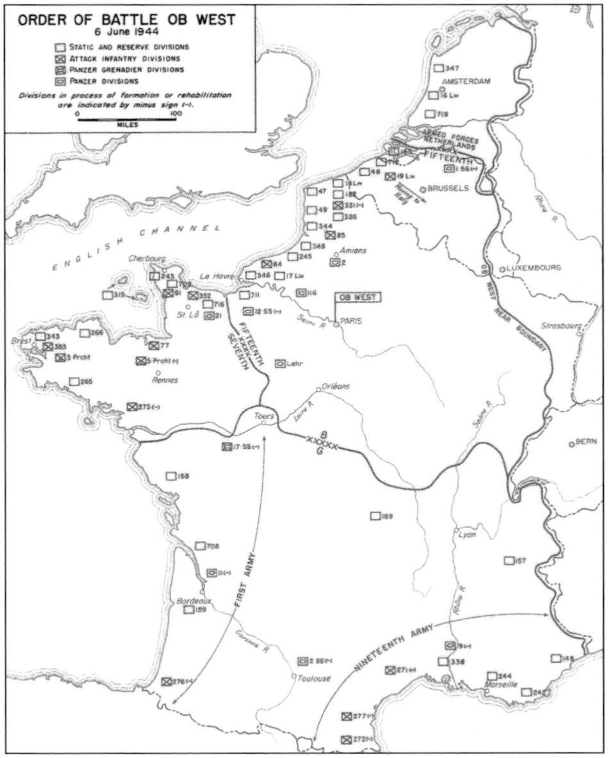

Below: *German Order of Battle : 6 June 1944.*

At face value the plan devised by General Bradley (Commander of the US First Army) sounds impressive and as momentum grew, so did a widespread air of confidence as Bradley and his team devised their tactical assault within a distinct atmosphere of what can only be reflected upon with hindsight as great naivety. In the words of Joe Balkoski, America's premier Omaha Beach historian...

General Bradley was Ike's chief practitioner of the confidence school, but his expectations relating to the application of firepower on Omaha Beach fell conspicuously into the realms of over-confidence.[6]

As the day of reckoning drew ever closer, there were no signs of any slackening of enthusiasm from the highest echelons of the American Command. General Eisenhower had briefed his subordinate commanders and was quoted on record as stating that every man involved in the first wave assault should be *'optimistic and cheerful because*

Major General Omar N. Bradley 1893-1981

Commander of the US First Army (June 6th to July 13th) and 12th US Army Group (from 14 July 1944,under operational command of 21st British Army Group until 1 September 1944)

Born in a log cabin to an impoverished family from Clark, Missouri, in February 1893, in the face of extreme poverty, Omar Nelson Bradley excelled both in the classroom and on the sports field. After graduating from the school at which his Father worked as a teacher, Bradley found temporary employment at his home town's railway yard, working as a boilerman. Despite an initial wish to study law, Bradley was persuaded to apply for West Point, graduating alongside Dwight D. Eisenhower in the class of 1915.

Commissioned to the infantry with the rank of Second Lieutenant, Bradley would serve exclusively on the home front during the Great War. During the inter-war period Bradley served at numerous military academies, one of these secondments being a four-year spell working as a mathematics teacher back at West Point. Attaining the rank of Major-General in March 1942, Bradley's first command was of the 82nd Infantry Division which, in the three months he served as commanding officer, was transferred from regular infantry status into the US Army's first ever airborne division. With General Matthew Ridgway taking command of the 82nd in June 1942, Bradley's next command was of the 28th Infantry Division.

Bradley's first overseas appointment would arrive for the invasion of North Africa, during which he would serve under the command of Generals Patton and Eisenhower. A favourite of Eisenhower, Bradley was fast-tracked into becoming the most senior American commander during the Normandy campaign. Nicknamed the GI's General, a legend was created by the war journalist Ernie Pyle where Bradley would be portrayed as a commander universally respected if not indeed adored by the men he commanded. Such a legacy has since been widely refuted, not least by the US Army's official historian SLA Marshall, who commented that this persona *"was played up by Ernie Pyle...The GIs were not impressed with him. They scarcely knew him... he didn't get out much to troops... the idea that he was idolized by the average soldier is just rot".**

After Normandy, Bradley would go on to command all American forces in North West Europe, a force which eventually numbered over 1,300,000 troops - no other General would ever command a higher number of American troops in the field of battle. After the war, Bradley was appointed Chief of Staff of the American Army and then Chairman of the Joint Chiefs of Staff.

In September 1950, Bradley would become one of just nine men to hold the rank of Five Star General in the US Army, the equivalent of a British Field Marshal. Omar Bradley retired from the military in 1953 and died aged 88 in April 1981. He is buried in the Arlington National Cemetery.

** D'Este - Patton: A Genius For War. Page 467.*

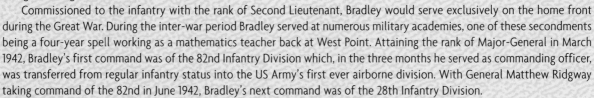

he has behind him the greatest firepower ever assembled on the face of the earth'.[7] Bradley himself had already stood in front of those landing in the first wave declaring to them, *'You men should consider yourselves lucky and are to be congratulated. You have ringside seats at the greatest show on earth'.*[8]

As ever, the devil was in the detail. At Omaha, the naval bombardment was limited to less than half an hour – one third of the duration of that aimed against Utah. In addition, Bradley insisted, against the wishes of the US Army Air Force, on changing the variant of bombs to be dropped on the enemy's defences. Bradley did not want the preliminary bombing to crater the beach and cause obstruction to the exit roads leading inland from the coast. At Bradley's instigation, instant fuses would be used on

some of the smaller fragmentation bombs - anti-personnel bombs which would explode on impact - hardly the type of bunker-busting ordnance which the air force had recommended as being capable of both destroying concrete bunkers and terminating their occupants.

Despite the concerns expressed by the air force long before D-Day that such a bombardment would have little or no effect on the enemy's fixed fortifications, Bradley continued to favour enabling rapid movement inland, rather than thwarting the enemy's ability to resist the initial assault. Given these factors it could be well argued that the initial bombardment at Omaha was doomed to failure from the start. With less than half an hour allocated for the naval guns to aim their wrath against the Omaha defences, fog and cloud masked what would arguably have been in any case an ineffective aerial bombardment.

Above: *With little or no fire support, Omaha Beach would become a battle between American infantry and a largely unseen enemy.*

Inevitably, the preliminary bombing at Omaha completely failed to neutralise the enemy's defences. With the air force unable to visually locate their target, with their orders determining that under such circumstances they should bomb by radar, but at the same time impose a margin of error so that no bombs fell short amongst their own troops making their final run in to the beach, the vast majority of the bombs landed up to two miles inland from Omaha Beach, leaving the vast majority of the defences untouched as the first wave assault made their final run in.

Popular history has been very kind to General Bradley when assessing the Omaha Beach assault. Today's assessments largely identify the origins of the near failure emanating from either the over-exaggeration of the quantity and quality of the Omaha defenders, or errors of judgment within the command of the air force, and not as a consequence of the interference of Bradley, a man who himself ensured the blame be passed away from his own shoulders. In the words of Joe Balkoski…

A bitter General Bradley later professed shock at the 2nd Bomb Division's failure to soften up the beach, blaming the useless result on the airman's timidity. Bradley, however, ought to be more forgiving, for he himself had designed an inflexible landing plan that had positioned thousands of army troops and dozens of landing craft two miles or less from shore when the Liberators would fly directly overhead and release their bombs. Under those conditions - made even more hazardous by the cloud blanket over Normandy on D-Day - one could hardly blame the airmen for being apprehensive, for accidental bomb releases just a few seconds too soon could have caused hundreds of American and British deaths.[9]

Below: *US Army V Corps on D-Day*

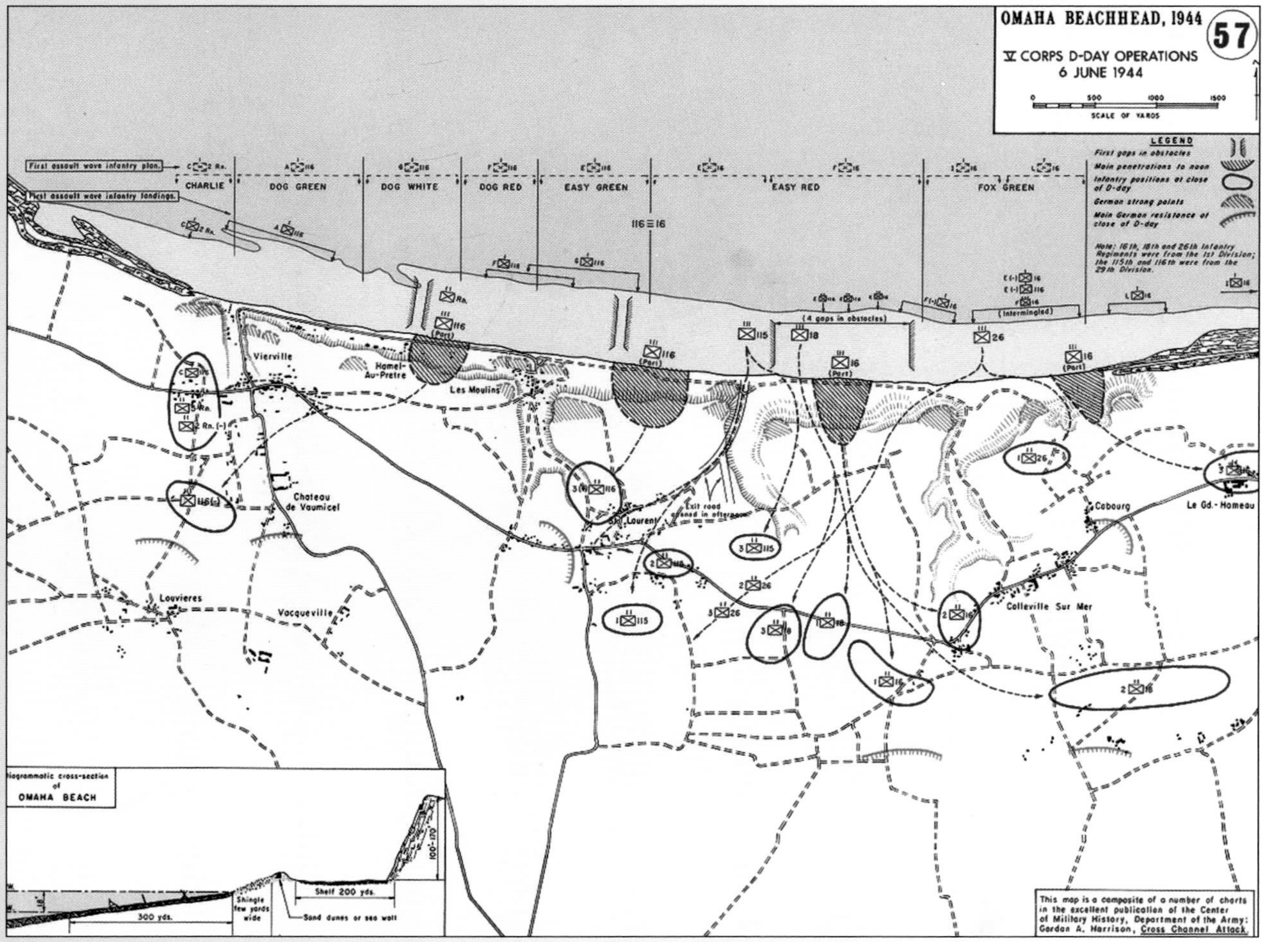

Above: *The dramatic assault of Omaha is vividly captured within this iconic image of D-Day.*

The Omaha bombardment had been a complete failure and now Bradley's Americans were about to learn for themselves the painful lesson which Commonwealth forces had acquired twenty-two months prior to D-Day when, on 19 August 1942, a force of 6,000, mainly Canadian troops, had led a raid against the German-held coastline at Dieppe. With insufficient supporting fire from the sea, air or from the beach itself, foot soldiers were tasked with overwhelming a firmly entrenched enemy who were armed with automatic weapons and enclosed within concrete bunkers. Dieppe was a slaughter, assessed by many as a greatly flawed, ill-conceived and poorly executed operation. Now, on D-Day, let down by their commanders, only the courage of individual and small groups of American soldiers would save the reputation of the US Army Generals and prevent America from suffering the humiliation of their very own Dieppe.

General Bradley's chosen doctrine of an all-out attack against the entire width of Omaha Beach, notwithstanding the apparent strengths or weaknesses of each of the eight sub-sectors, led to a huge contrast in the experiences of the assaulting forces drawn from the 1st and 29th Infantry Divisions. With the enemy's fixed defences positioned almost exclusively next to the five exit roads that ran from the beach, through the elevated ground and beyond, with up to a mile gap between these exit roads, there could potentially be a gap of up to this distance between the enemy's defences. Landing in front of the most strongly defended sectors inevitably meant that the probability of suffering substantial casualties, if not only to be expected, was certainly very high. However, if landing where a gap existed between the strongpoints, fewer casualties would be suffered, a fact emphasised through the experience of the men of the

116th Regimental Combat Team of the 29th Division, who led the invasion ashore on the western half of Omaha Beach. 'A' Company of the 1st Battalion of the 116th Regiment attempted a frontal assault on the most strongly defended sector and endured 173 casualties from a strength of 212 men. Meanwhile, just a half mile to the east, where the enemy's defences were at their weakest, 'C' Company counted in their first wave assault losses of just twenty-two casualties including only six men killed. An hour after the first wave assault came ashore on that same sector, the 5th Battalion of the US Army Rangers landed 500 men and crossed the beach at a cost of only four casualties.[10]

Above: *US infantry take cover during the initial assault on Easy Red sector of Omaha Beach.*

The invasion plan had been based on one main assumption, which failed to materialise. The failure of the aerial bombardment led to the battle of Omaha Beach becoming solely an infantry affair. Bradley had put all his eggs in one basket despite the concerns of his subordinate commanders such as General Charles Gerhardt (commanding 29th Infantry Division) who was convinced, prior to the invasion, that not enough infantry would land on the beach should the Germans resist the initial assault waves. In addition to the concerns of Gerhardt, Colonel George Taylor (commanding 16th Regimental Combat Team) had correctly predicted as early as May that the preliminary bombardment would fail in the aim of terminating the enemy's defenders. A full month before the invasion was launched he was quoted as stating, *'There will be lots of Germans left over after [the navy and air force] gets through the shooting. We'll have to dig them out with bayonets and grenades'.*[11]

Not only did the preliminary bombardment completely fail to achieve its aim, Bradley had also decided that his assault would go in without the vital assistance of both the conventional and specialist armour which was deployed in great abundance in the Commonwealth Sector, a situation recognised within what many consider as the premier history of the campaign in North-West Europe; in the words of Chester Wilmot…

American infantry did not have the necessary armoured support. Yet this support could have been available here, as it was elsewhere, if the Americans had been prepared to accept the advice and assistance of their more experienced allies… It took 3,000 casualties on Omaha to persuade the Americans that gallantry is not enough.[12]

Echoes of such sentiment can be found within General Eisenhower's report to the Supreme Commanders as published in 1946…

Apart from the factor of tactical surprise, the comparatively light casualties which we sustained on all beaches, except Omaha, were in large measure due to the success of the novel mechanical contrivances which we employed, and to the staggering moral and material effect of the mass of armour landed in the leading waves of the assault. It is doubtful if the assault forces could have firmly established themselves without the assistance of these weapons.[13]

It was into the chaos of the enemy's most ferocious resistance that the three American infantrymen who would receive their nation's highest award entered the battle for Omaha Beach.

A little under two hours into the battle, Private Carlton Barrett, a 24-year-old New Yorker, and the only D-Day Medal of Honor recipient to survive the Battle of Normandy, disembarked from his landing craft into the hellhole of Bloody Omaha. By D-Day, Barrett was already a seasoned veteran, having served through previous campaigns in North Africa and Sicily. He was later described by Sergeant Thomas McCann as *'A happy go lucky young man who enjoyed life... [he] reminded me of a bantam rooster, short, stocky, not afraid of anything'.*[14] Now on D-Day, Barrett, part of a reconnaissance party of the 18th Regiment of the 1st Infantry Division, was due to land in advance of his regiment before reconnoitering forward positions prior to guiding his unit inland and to their designated assembly area. Landing on a sector of beach from which two of the five potential exit points led

Private

CARLTON W. BARRETT

1st Infantry Division

For gallantry and intrepidity at the risk of his life above and beyond the call of duty on 6 June 1944, in the vicinity of St Laurent sur Mer, France. On the morning of D-Day Private Barrett, landing in the face of extremely heavy enemy fire, was forced to wade ashore through neck-deep water. Disregarding the personal danger, he returned to the surf again and again to assist his floundering comrades and save them from drowning. Refusing to remain pinned down by the intense barrage of small-arms and mortar fire poured at the landing points, Private Barrett, working with fierce determination, saved many lives by carrying casualties to an evacuation boat laying offshore. In addition to his assigned mission as guide, he carried dispatches the length of the fire-swept beach; he assisted the wounded; he calmed the shocked; he arose as a leader in the stress of the occasion. His coolness and his dauntless daring courage while constantly risking his life during a period of many hours had an inestimable effect on his comrades and is in keeping with the highest traditions of the U.S. Army.

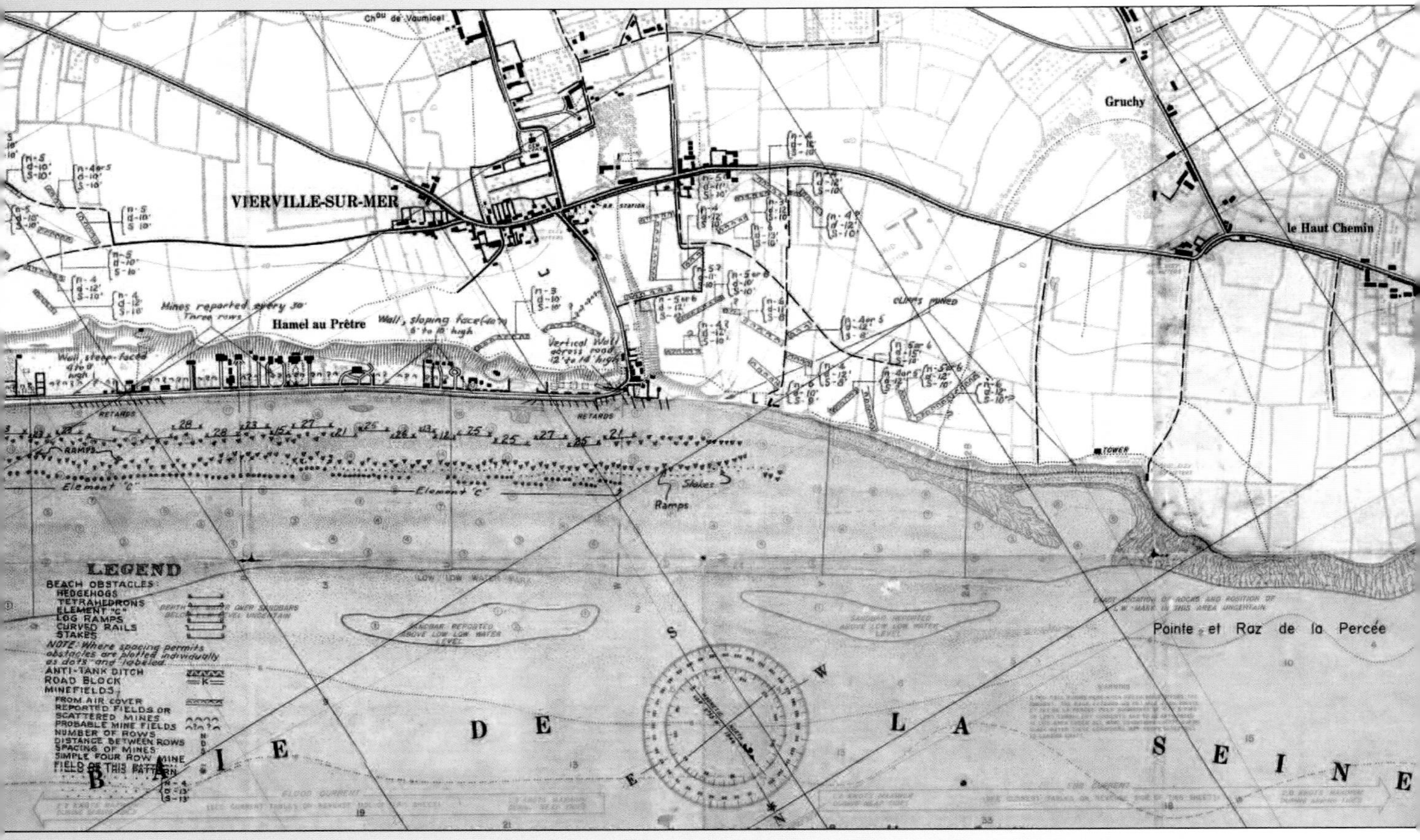

inland, this particular stretch of beach was heavily fortified and resistance particularly strong. With casualties lying all around him, Barrett immediately realised his intended task was impossible, and instead would improvise a role that he judged most beneficial for the greater good.

Above: *A pre-invasion Allied map showing the defences and main features of Omaha beach – west, around Vierville-sur-Mer.*

Making frequent runs across a fire-swept beach, Barrett grabbed wounded men and physically manhandled them either to the relative safety of the high-waterline, or to landing craft offering an escape from danger. After evacuating numerous casualties, under fire, Barrett made further runs, passing messages from one sector to another. Despite receiving minor wounds, Barrett would cheat death time and again in running the gauntlet against intense enemy fire. Lieutenant Foley, of HQ Company of the 16th Regiment of the 1st Infantry Division, was a witness who would himself benefit from Barrett's actions, as Foley states (in the third person) through the following account…

Private Barrett and Lieutenant Foley started to work dragging soldiers from the surf who were in danger of drowning, and assisting them to the meager security that the beach offered… When Lieutenant Foley was wounded, Private Barrett skillfully bandaged his wounds and probably saved his life… Private Barrett then waded out to contact landing boats to get litters [stretchers] to evacuate the casualties, then he assisted in carrying the wounded to the boats. As the last of the wounded were being removed from the beach Lieutenant Foley noticed craft coming in to land. He called

Private Barrett and sent him to contact the boats that were about to beach. Private Barrett was instrumental in furnishing information in regard to the situation. He kept up this work on the beach until he became a casualty, suffering wounds in the left foot, both legs, and hips.[15]

Barrett's Company Commander wrote afterwards...

Moving in and out from one place to another with utter disregard for the shells that were falling around him and the bullets passing by him. He acted as calmly and collectively as if he were enjoying a Sunday afternoon at the beach. Everyone else was pinned down. The calm, collected, efficient figure Private Barrett presented - so out of keeping with the bursting shells, smashed equipment, and wounded and dead men - had an inestimable effect on all those around him, both the unharmed and the wounded.[16]

Barrett would make a full recovery from his wounds before returning home and continuing his service in the US Army for another nineteen years, retiring as a Staff-Sergeant in June 1963.

Carlton Barrett died aged 66 on 3 May 1986. He is buried at the Chapel of the Chimes Cemetery in Napa, California.

Three hundred yards further east, on Fox Green sector, the heroics of Carlton Barrett were emulated by a corporal from the 16th Regiment of the 1st Infantry Division. John Pinder, known as *Joe*, was a talented baseball player from Pennsylvania. Under different circumstances, *Joe* on this day would have been celebrating his 32nd birthday alongside his family. Instead, he had landed almost directly in front of Omaha's largest individual strongpoint, *Widerstandsnest* Number 62, which at that moment was spewing out its wrath of deadly fire upon the American assault. Wounded as soon as he landed, Pinder, like Barrett, would make many selfless runs across the beach. Sergeant Robert Michaud witnessed Pinder's heroics...

Corporal
JOHN J. PINDER
1st Infantry Division

For conspicuous gallantry and intrepidity above and beyond the call of duty on 6 June 1944, near Colleville sur Mer, France. On D-day, Technician 5th Grade Pinder landed on the coast 100 yards off shore under devastating enemy machine gun and artillery fire which caused severe casualties among the boatload. Carrying a vitally important radio, he struggled towards shore in waist- deep water. Only a few yards from his craft he was hit by enemy fire and was gravely wounded. Technician 5th Grade Pinder never stopped. He made shore and delivered the radio. Refusing to take cover afforded, or to accept medical attention for his wounds, Technician 5th Grade Pinder, though terribly weakened by loss of blood and in fierce pain, on three occasions went into the fire-swept surf to salvage communication equipment. He recovered many vital parts and equipment, including another workable radio. On the third trip he was again hit, suffering machine gun bullet wounds in the legs. Still this valiant soldier would not stop for rest or medical attention. Remaining exposed to heavy enemy fire, growing steadily weaker, he aided in establishing the vital radio communication on the beach. While so engaged this dauntless soldier was hit for the third time and killed. The indomitable courage and personal bravery of Technician 5th Grade Pinder was a magnificent inspiration to the men with whom he served.

While leaving the assault boat... *Corporal Pinder was struck by a shell burst. Although the side of his face was left hanging and he could only see from one eye, he held his hanging flesh with one hand and with the other gripped the radio and dragged it to shore. When he reached the shore, Corporal Pinder refused medical treatment, and before he could be stopped, ran back into the heavily mined water to rescue more floating equipment. He continued this work, rescuing much needed equipment in a very calm manner, seeming to disregard the intense fire all about him. Corporal Pinder made several trips to salvage communications supplies, and on one of these, while returning to shore, he was struck by a machine gun strafing the area. Despite his serious and painful wounds, he managed to struggle ashore with the load he was carrying. Even in this condition, he did not stop, but continued to help in setting up communications, exposing himself on the beach without any fear of the constant fire until he was hit again and killed.*[17]

John Pinder is buried at Grandview Cemetery, Florence, Pennsylvania. In May 1949, the U.S. Army barracks at Zirndorf, Germany were renamed 'Pinder Barracks' in *Joe's* honour. Although the barracks have since been demolished, a business estate, known as 'Pinder Park', now occupies the same site.

Whilst the selfless actions of Pinder and Barrett were both truly remarkable and undeniably worthy of the award for which they were both recognised, there was another member of the *Big Red One* who could have been awarded his nation's highest award for any of several remarkable feats he undertook that day. Having been dragged by the currents of the ocean to the east of his unit's intended landing zone, 26-year-old Lieutenant Jimmie Monteith from Low Moor, Virginia, crossed a fire-swept beach before finding the relative safety of the cliffs which flanked the eastern extremity of Omaha. With substantial casualties already suffered in crossing the beach, those positioned around Monteith were reluctant to move. Realising these men needed inspiration, Monteith stepped forward to lead the way. On foot, he led two Sherman tanks across the beach before, on his hands and knees, he cleared the way through a minefield so that the tanks could provide covering fire. He then led a force from the beach to climb the high ground before flanking, attacking and eventually overwhelming the first enemy strongpoint overlooking Omaha to be defeated on D-Day. If these acts were not impressive enough, Monteith would then have to defend this newly taken ground against a German counterattack. Staff Sergeant Aaron Jones (L Company, 16 RCT) explains…

A large group of enemy started an attack on the position and set up machine guns on the flanks and rear. The Germans yelled to us to surrender because we were surrounded. Lieutenant Monteith did not answer, but moved toward the sound of voices and launched a rifle grenade at them from 20 yards, knocking out the machine gun

First Lieutenant

JIMMIE W. MONTEITH JUNIOR

1st Infantry Division

For conspicuous gallantry and intrepidity above and beyond the call of duty on 6 June 1944, near Colleville-sur-Mer, France. 1st Lieutenant Monteith landed with the initial assault waves on the coast of France under heavy enemy fire. Without regard to his own personal safety he continually moved up and down the beach reorganizing men for further assault. He then led the assault over a narrow protective ledge and across the flat, exposed terrain to the comparative safety of a cliff. Retracing his steps across the field to the beach, he moved over to where two tanks were buttoned up and blind under violent enemy artillery and machine gun fire. Completely exposed to the intense fire, 1st Lieutenant Monteith led the tanks on foot through a minefield and into firing positions. Under his direction several enemy positions were destroyed. He then re-joined his company and under his leadership his men captured an advantageous position on the hill. Supervising the defence of his newly won position against repeated vicious counterattacks, he continued to ignore his own personal safety, repeatedly crossing the 200 or 300 yards of open terrain under heavy fire to strengthen links in his defensive chain. When the enemy succeeded in completely surrounding 1st Lieutenant Monteith and his unit and while leading the fight out of the situation, 1st Lieutenant Monteith was killed by enemy fire. The courage, gallantry, and intrepid leadership displayed by 1st Lieutenant Monteith is worthy of emulation.

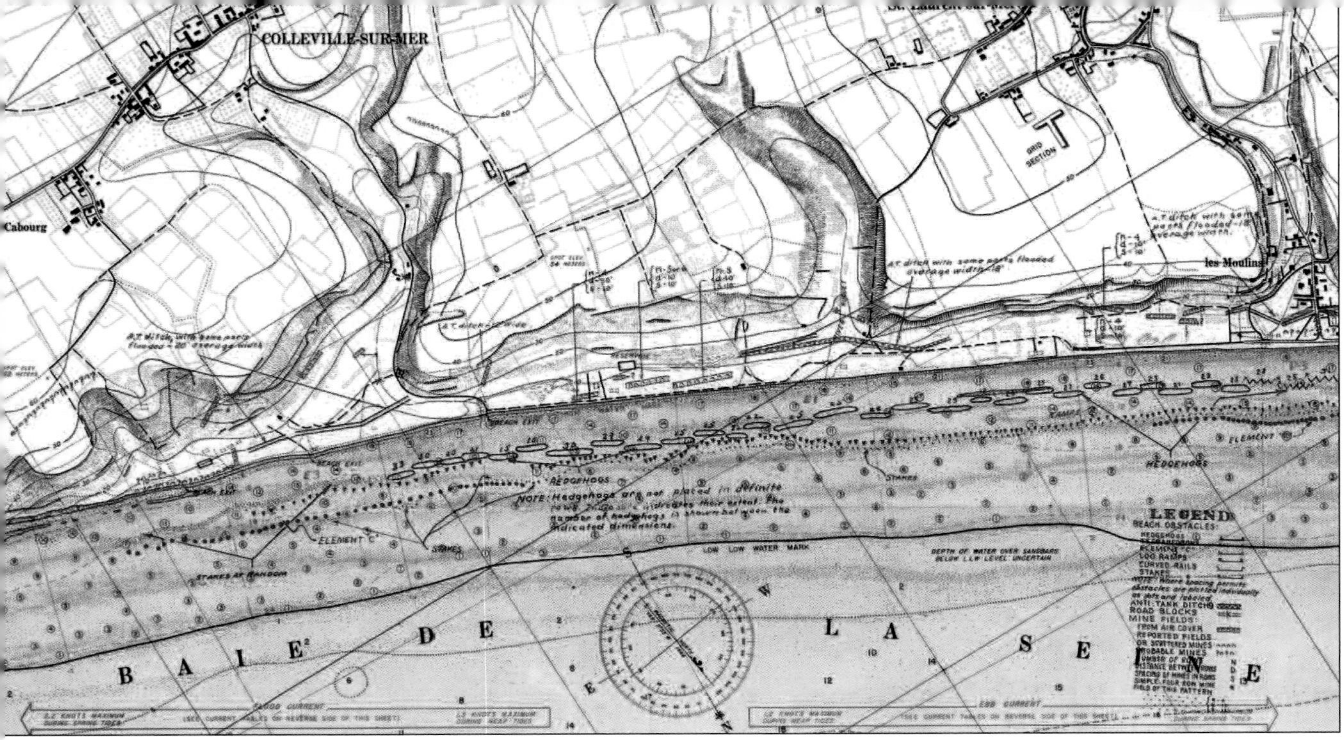

position. Even with a large force the Germans couldn't break through our positions, so they set up two machine guns and started spraying the hedgerow. Lieutenant Monteith got a squad of riflemen to open up on the machine gun on the right flank. Under cover of the fire he sneaked up on the gun and threw hand grenades, which knocked out the position. He then came back and crossed a 200 yard stretch of open field under fire to launch rifle grenades at the other machine gun position. He either killed the crew or forced them to abandon the weapon. Back on the other flank enemy riflemen opened up on us again and Lieutenant Monteith started across the open field to help us fight them off, but was killed by the fire of a machine gun that had been brought to our rear.[18]

Above: *Pre-invasion map of the defences of Omaha beach near Colleville-sur-Mer.*

At first Monteith would be cited for the Distinguished Service Cross. However, thanks to the persistence of an unknown staff officer of the 1st Infantry Division, Monteith's citation was brought to the attention of General Eisenhower. On inspection of such remarkable deeds, Eisenhower himself insisted that the award be upgraded to the Medal of Honor.

Lieutenant Jimmie Monteith Jnr is buried less than a mile from where he fell, in the Normandy American Cemetery at Colleville sur Mer.

There is a saying that victory masks incompetence; it can be equally said that valour is no substitute for supporting fire. Nonetheless, the flaws within the plan of attack at Omaha were offset by the improvisation, courage and selfless determination of the fighting men who landed there. With over 4,000 casualties, including maybe up to 1,700 of these men killed, Omaha was a victory which came at a great cost. Although by the end of the day the German defences were broken, few Americans had advanced more than a mile from the shoreline. With such a tenuous hold, very susceptible to counter-attack, it is fortunate that no considerable enemy presence was placed against such a confined beachhead. Whilst the battle for the beach had been won, it was now vital that the American forces overcame the shock of their initial assault and, from the second day on, advance as quickly as possible, moving not just inland but also to the east and west to enable the link up with the neighbouring beaches.

Chapter 5

The Man They Couldn't Kill

Akin to the American operation to the west, the amphibious assault by General Miles Dempsey's British Second Army upon the landing beaches codenamed Gold, Juno and Sword, would also be preceded by a mass landing of airborne forces. Commencing just after midnight, the objectives of the British 6th Airborne Division included the capturing, intact, of two bridges running over the River Orne and the Caen Canal. Located between the small towns of Benouville and Ranville, these vital crossings would later serve as the lifeline between amphibious forces landing on Sword Beach and the airborne forces located at the eastern side of the two waterways. In addition, to delay, if not prevent enemy counterattacks emanating from a position further again to the east, five bridges and a culvert within the valley of the River Dives would have to be destroyed. The list of primary objectives assigned to the 6th Airborne Division would be completed through the neutralisation of a four-gun coastal artillery battery located south of the town of Merville. Once these immediate missions were complete, the Division would consolidate upon a ridge of high ground within a largely wooded area known as the Bois de Bavent. Possession of this ground would deny an elevated position from which the enemy could observe and direct fire upon the amphibious assault at Sword Beach.

With conditions similar to those experienced by the American airborne forces operating some sixty miles to the west, the 6th Airborne Division suffered terribly from the very start. A combination of less than suitable weather conditions, combined with heavy anti-aircraft fire, dispersed the airborne landings far and wide. One of the worst scenarios was faced by the British and Canadian paratroopers who were scheduled to land upon Dropping Zone 'V'. Of the seventy-two planes designated to drop their human cargo upon this target, only seventeen made it. The rest of the force was dispersed over sixty square miles, with many paratroopers descending into a watery grave within the flooded marshlands.

Despite some units suffering up to 75 per cent casualties, the 6th Airborne Division fought back. General Gale's men captured the bridges over the Caen Canal and the River Orne intact, succeeded in destroying the objectives over the River Dives and, albeit at less than a quarter of their intended strength, and in the process suffering fifty per cent casualties, successfully neutralised the Merville Gun Battery. Within this remarkable feat of arms, the 6th Airborne Division became the only Allied division to achieve all of its primary objectives on D-Day.

With the eastern flank under the control of the airborne forces, the assault on Sword Beach would be led ashore by Major General Tom Rennie's British 3rd Infantry Division. Montgomery had specifically chosen this Division, which he himself had commanded during the Battle of France in 1940, for what was undoubtedly the toughest task assigned to any division on D-Day.

The brief sounded simple - to secure, and then advance beyond, the vital crossroads town of Caen. However, of all D-Day missions, this was the most time sensitive

Above: *Rommel inspects the 21st Panzer Division a month before D-Day.*

and would have to be achieved in advance of the enemy obtaining the opportunity of reinforcing an area which Rommel himself had cited as the gateway to Paris. The brief may sound straightforward but to achieve this goal the 3rd Division would have to defeat coastal defences that included not just the highest weapons density of any of the five landings beaches, but also the *Stutzpunktgruppe Riva Bella* – the largest individual beachfront fortification in Normandy. If this task was not tough enough, the 3rd Division would have to face a unique threat in breaking through a secondary, and then a third line of layered fortifications that contained a combined total of nine additional strongpoints located between one and three miles inland from the beach. These defences would have to be silenced as the Division covered the eight miles separating the coast from a city with a peacetime population of over 60,000 inhabitants.

These objectives, assigned in February 1944, were allocated a month before the Allies detected the arrival of the 21st Panzer Division in close proximity to the city of

Caen. Reassessing the new situation brought about by the arrival of an additional 16,000 German troops and 120 tanks, reluctantly, Montgomery and Rennie decided to retain Caen as the 3rd Division's D-Day objective. Despite Montgomery's supposedly cautious nature, such a plan was deemed by many as being too ambitious, especially given that the forces landing on Sword Beach could potentially face resistance from more enemy forces, both numerically and in terms of quality, than those resisting the other four beaches combined. Despite the improbability of success, the objective remained, a goal born of necessity lest the Sword beachhead be confined to too narrow a foothold. Breathing space was needed to bring ashore the mass logistics of reinforcements and equipment necessary to ensure the Allies would be on the front foot during the formative stages of the ensuing battle.

The attack at Sword Beach commenced at 0725 hours, some fifty-five minutes after the first wave assault in the US Sector. A later landing was necessitated by tidal timings and although the element of surprise would be lost on the British beaches, the delay would at least allow the vast naval armada extra time to vent their fury at the enemy's defences.

Despite the typical lack of an effective aerial bombardment, a combination of prolonged naval fire, alongside a shrewd plan of attack which focused the strength of the British assault upon relative weak spots within the enemy's defences, therefore

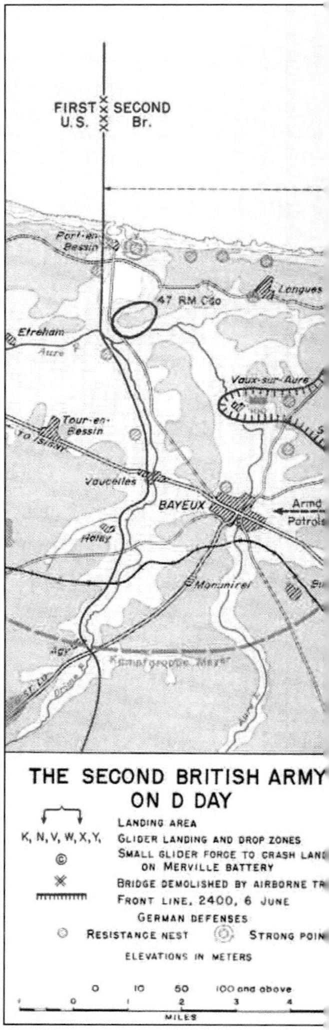

Left: *An Allied bomber flies above Sword Beach.*

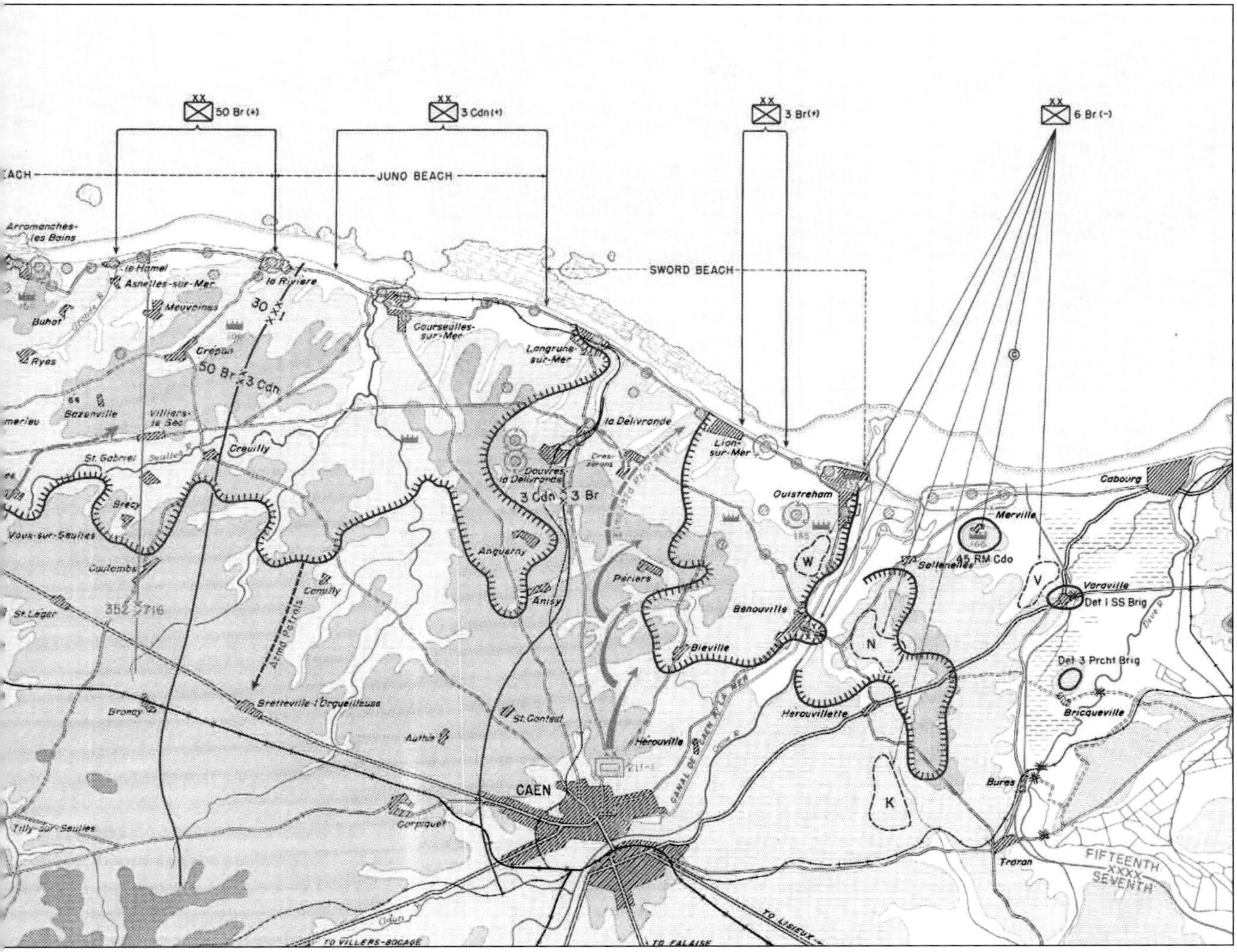

Above: *British Second Army on D-Day.*

avoiding a frontal assault where the defences were at their strongest, enabled a relatively quick breakthrough.

With the 3rd Division pouring through the enemy line at their chosen weak spot, Commandos of the 1st and 4th Special Service Brigades landed on either flank of the main assault in order to manoeuvre and attack the enemy's heaviest defences from the rear. Casualties were substantial, but within ninety minutes of the first wave assault, the secondary defences were engaged as the 3rd Division commenced its push toward Caen.

Early progress was good. Before mid-day the majority of secondary fortifications were overwhelmed at little cost to the attackers - the defenders seemingly lacking the will to fight, mainly as a consequence of the prolonged naval barrage that had drenched their positions in the hours preceding the first wave assault. Methodically, a combination of infantry and tanks worked impeccably together in clearing the mass of concrete bunkers, tunnels and trenches which made up the most elaborate fortifications to be built anywhere in Normandy.

However, this impressive early progress came to a dramatic halt just after midday at a position almost three miles inland from Sword Beach. The 1st Suffolk Battalion of the 3rd Division, having already cleared a four-gun artillery battery two miles behind the beach, came against the final fixed fortification which blocked its drive on Caen. A failure in what was otherwise almost faultless pre-invasion intelligence had dangerously underestimated the strength of the strongpoint positioned between the two main roads that led from the beach to Caen. Codenamed *Hillman*, a fortification thought to consist of just a handful of weapons pits and populated by no more than thirty to forty second-rate troops, was in fact the operational headquarters of the 736th Infantry Regiment. What was anticipated to be of little overall threat to the general advance was in fact a position manned by up to five times the anticipated number of enemy troops, garrisoned within a labyrinth of underground bunkers, dispersed across over fifty acres of high-ground overlooking the wide-open cornfields through which the infantry of the 3rd Division was now attempting to advance.

With automatic fire blocking any potential advance, the threat of stalemate loomed large. Finally, at approximately 1500 hours, some four hours after the Suffolks made their first approach on *Hillman*, the breakthrough was achieved as Private James Hunter commenced a one-man charge against two machine-gun nests, an act that would earn Hunter a Distinguished Conduct Medal (amongst the second tier of British awards), but more importantly, an act which ultimately enabled movement into the heart of the fortress. Another four hours would be needed to secure the site, but even then elements of the strongpoint's garrison did not surrender until the following morning. However, by 1900 hours, with one of the two roads to Caen blocked by the resistance of the *Hillman* strongpoint, the 3rd Division's advance had been depleted to the extent that just one weakened battalion from an anticipated strength of two entire brigades was left in the fight for Caen.

Any hope of Caen being taken on day one was dashed just after 1600 hours as the 2nd Battalion of the King's Shropshire Light Infantry, having advanced to the west of Hillman, and now within two miles of the prized objective, witnessed elements of two of the three regiments of the 21st Panzer Division forming up in front of them in preparation for what would be the German's largest scale counter-attack of D-Day.

Just after 1600 hours the German armour attacked. Although now facing by far the greatest overall threat to the landings, British forces, assisted by remarkably accurate naval fire, not only clashed head on with this huge enemy attack, but in defeating the 21st Panzer Division's attempts to throw the 3rd Division back into the sea, inflicted heavy losses on the most formidable enemy force to be faced by the Allies on D-Day. Impressively, despite facing more German troops than were deployed against the other four beaches combined, and

Below: *A Universal Carrier wades ashore on Gold Beach*

Above: *Queen Sector of Sword Beach on D-Day.*

despite having only been ashore for a matter of hours, the British line held. Reporting losses of 57 of their 120 tanks on day one, the 21st Panzer Division's attempt to defeat the invasion was crushed. Although the German counter had been defeated, the British drive on Caen had failed, a failure that would lead to weeks of attritional warfare as the Germans built up by far their greatest strength against the British and Canadians to the east of the Allied beachhead and around the city of Caen.

Six miles to the west of Sword Beach, Major General Rodney Keller's Canadian 3rd Infantry Division would lead the assault on the central of the three Commonwealth beaches, codenamed Juno. Fighting for the first time on D-Day, but having been garrisoned in England for up to four years in advance of their baptism of fire, Keller's forces were eager to join the fight. Landing on a two brigade front, with two battalions up front for each brigade, the 3rd Division's assault was dispersed over four miles of coastline.

Landing just before 0800 hours, from the off the Canadian assault faced contrasting experiences. Like pretty much everywhere else that day, the much-anticipated aerial bombardment had achieved little or no effect on the enemy's defences, and al-

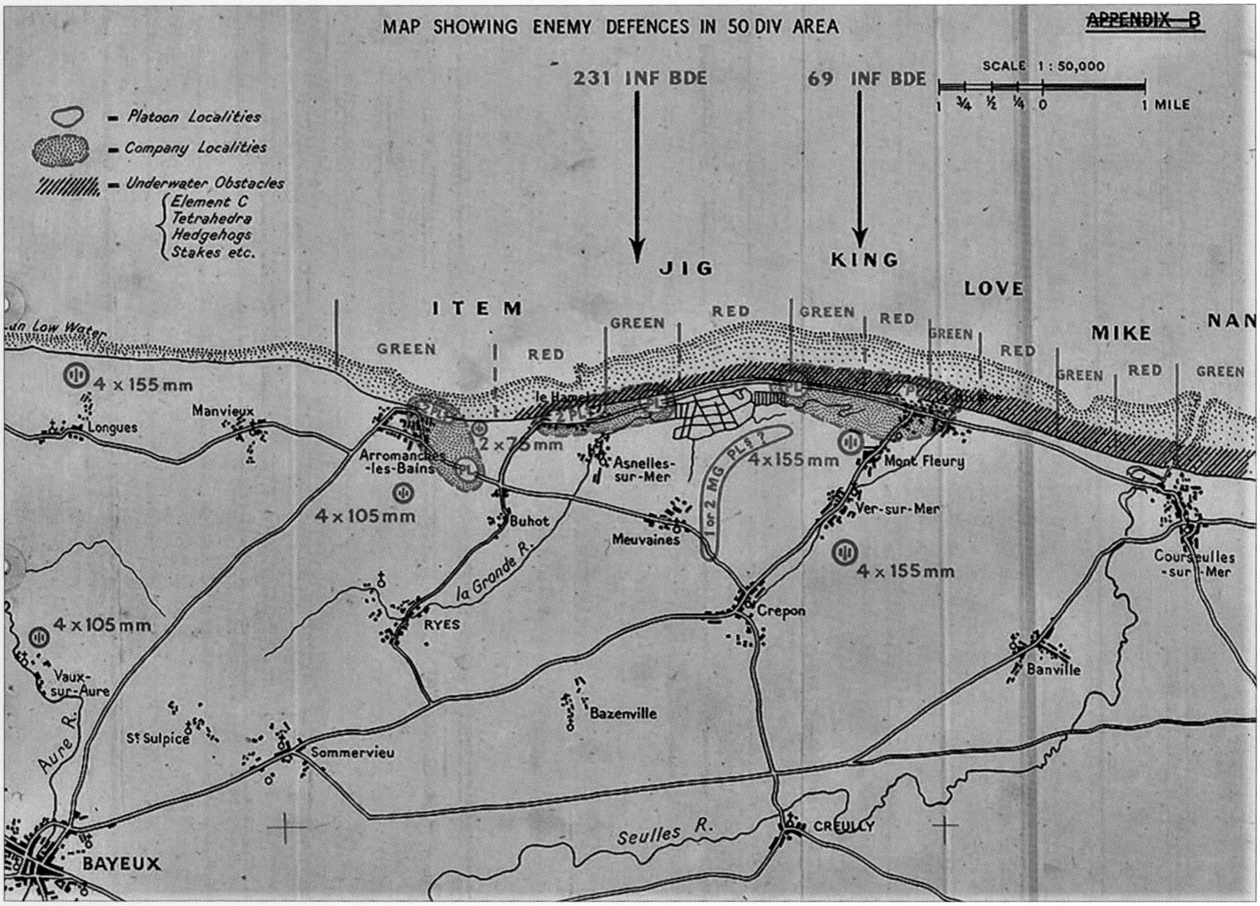

Above: *Gold Beach Defences.*

though the Juno attack had benefitted from the longest duration of any naval barrage, the German fortifications were largely intact as the first wave of the Canadian infantry hit the beach.

Of all Commonwealth forces landing on D-Day, the greatest losses were suffered on Juno Beach to the west of the estuary of the River Suelles at Coursuelles sur Mer. Losing almost 80 per cent of their strength within the first hour of their landing, Captain Gower's 'B' Company of the Royal Winnipeg Rifles did not falter. Under a hail of fire, the *Little Black Devils* engaged and, within an hour, had overwhelmed one of the toughest strongpoints built anywhere along the invasion coastline. Such determination was emulated by the North Shore Regiment on the eastern flank of Juno at St Aubin sur Mer. Attacking an enemy strongpoint many times stronger than pre-invasion intelligence had suggested, the men of 'B' Company of the North Shores were drawn into a six-hour fight. Moving street by street, house by house in a bitter duel against an enemy force superior in number and unyielding in their attempt to hold their line, the North Shores would endure close to 50 per cent casualties before the St Aubin defences fell silent.

With the Queen's Own Rifles overwhelming the central defences of the Juno Beach coastline at Bernieres sur Mer within no more than an hour of disembarkation, overall the Juno Beach assault, although suffering close to 1,000 casualties, had been executed efficiently. By the end of D-Day, the 3rd Division was, although still short of its intended objectives, consolidating at a distance of up to six miles inland from the beach.

Codenamed Gold, the assault on the central of the five D-Day beaches would be led ashore by the British 50th Infantry Division. Despite the common perception that the defences here were the weakest of all the five beaches, although it is true to state that the enemy's defences lacked the concentration of those that existed elsewhere, there were overall a greater number of German strongpoints and more German defenders in the Gold Beach Sector than were present at Omaha. In moving against its D-Day objectives, the 50th Division would have to secure the most square mileage of any unit on D-Day, and would also be most likely to face the German LXXXIV (84th) Corps reserve of *Kampfgruppe* (Battlegroup) Meyer. Consisting of approximately 3,700 men, a mixed force of infantry and self-propelled armour / artillery, *Kampfgruppe Meyer* was garrisoned behind Gold Beach and held a pre-arranged plan of attack, that, if true to form, would see them clash with the British 50th Division as it advanced to its D-Day objectives, which included the town of Bayeux.

The 50th Division had endured its baptism of fire during the battle for Belgium and France in 1940. It had subsequently been evacuated from Dunkirk before forming part of the multi-national force of Commonwealth nations, which under Montgomery's command, had pursued Rommel's much heralded *Afrika Korps* over 2,000 miles of North African desert – thus inflicting upon Rommel the humiliation of the greatest retreat of any army in history. After North Africa, the 50th Division continued its struggle into Sicily. By the start of 1944, the core of the *Northumbrian* Division were, by far, the Allies most battle-hardened troops to fight on D-Day.

Amongst the ranks of the 50th Division was an individual who by D-Day had already distinguished himself in battle on numerous occasions. Through previous campaigns this working-class hero from the north-east of England had survived countless episodes of brutal combat. Through Dunkirk, North Africa and Sicily, having earned the nickname of *The Man They Couldn't Kill*, Company Sergeant Major Stanley Elton Hollis was, on the morning of D-Day, in a rare minority of men who were truly relishing the opportunity of once more taking the fight to the enemy.

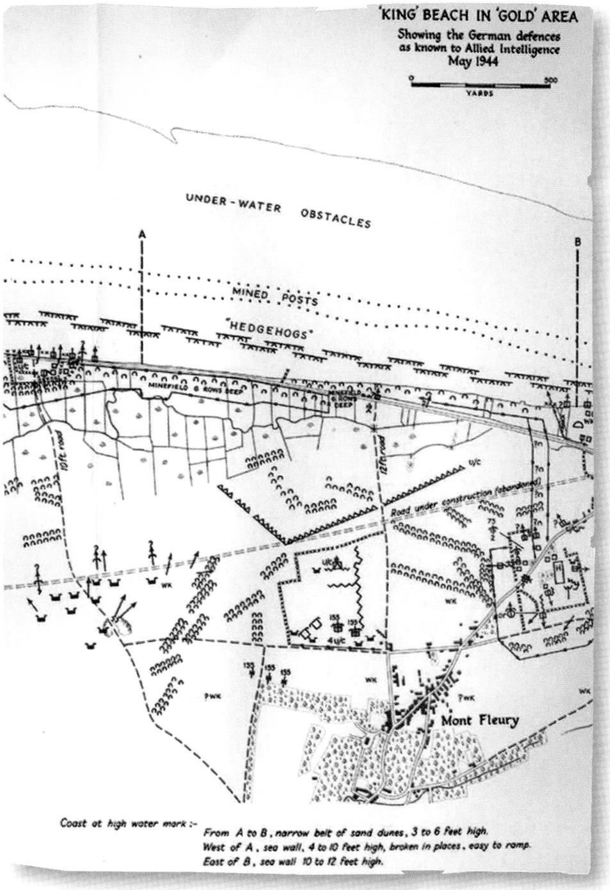

Above: *Gold Beach (King Sector) Defences.*

Born in September 1912, the son of a steelworker from Middlesbrough, North Yorkshire, Stan Hollis' first ambition for serving his country was within that of a seafaring role. Joining the Merchant Navy at the age of 17, Hollis' naval career ended prematurely as a consequence of him developing blackwater fever, a potentially fatal complication arising from malaria. Such a destiny, with hindsight, could easily be interpreted as the Navy's loss and very much the Army's gain. Volunteering to join his local Territorial Battalion of the Regiment of the Green Howards at the outbreak of war, Stan would be within the ranks of the British Expeditionary Force sent to Belgium in 1939. Facing the enemy for the first time during the battle for France in 1940, Hollis distinguished himself in the role of a despatch rider during the evacuation from Dunkirk. His actions quickly gained the admiration of his comrades, as Captain Synge of the 6th Battalion of the Green Howards recalls…

Throughout these days of confusion and hazardous moves, one man will remain in the memory of those who fought with the 6th Battalion at that time. He was Private Hollis, the Commanding Officer's personal despatch rider… He travelled along roads and through towns reported to be held by the enemy and arrived sometimes at his destination only to find that the British troops had gone. Yet he always got through and brought back valuable information. He was always ready to go out again and it was not an unknown sight to see Hollis asleep from sheer exhaustion in the saddle of his motorcycle outside Battalion HQ.[19]

For his role during the evacuation from Dunkirk, Hollis was cited for the Military Medal (this award is within the third tier of the British medal rankings). Whilst it could be stated that there were few if any who deserved the medal more, as a consequence of an altercation in an off-limits public house where, in the immediate aftermath of the Dunkirk evacuation, Hollis was found drinking alcohol at a time when it was forbidden, he would be denied the medal for which he was cited.

Continuing the fight against Nazi Germany in North Africa, another of Stan's comrades, Ernie Roberts, re-tells a tale of how Hollis selflessly put the lives of his comrades before his own personal safety…

Above: *German Countermeasures on D-Day.*

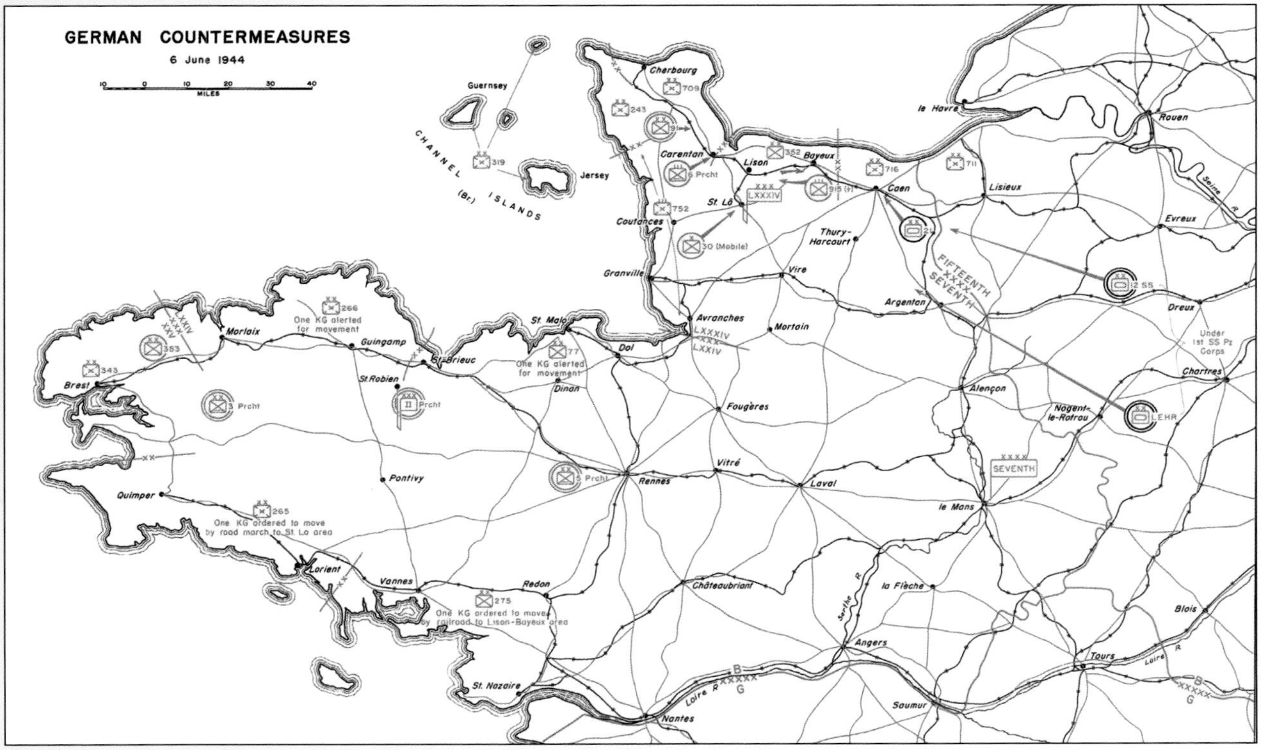

We were in a Bren gun carrier and were under fire, with shells falling around us and we jumped off to find shelter and Stan suddenly yelled at us to "Get down!" He had trodden on this S-mine, one of those evil sorts of devilish contraptions that all the British soldiers feared and hated. Once activated, they jumped up into the air about ten feet high before exploding with devastating effect… Stan kept his foot hard on it and amazingly it went off harmlessly in the ground. It is safe to say he saved the lot of us – and he finished up with just a bruised foot![22]

As the North African campaign progressed, Stan Hollis was remembered by his comrades for yet another act which, although not recognised through the award of a medal, was in itself a feat many would state worthy of Britain's highest award. Jack Strachan remembers…

It happened at Mersa Matruh during the battle of El Alamein… Stan was a Bren Gun Carrier Corporal in HQ Company. When on patrol that night, he drove at a tank full pelt and then leapt out from his Bren Carrier and took out this German Tiger Tank with what we called a sticky bomb. He just slammed it on the side of the tank and roared off and it went off and killed everyone inside the tank. His bravery made the way clear for the Company to advance. It was right at the beginning of the battle when we were sending out reccy patrols to probe Rommel's defences. It was a very dark night and the Tiger Tank fired on our troops with its lethal 88. It was the bravest thing I ever saw. We were very surprised he didn't get a medal for it. In the end he got nothing. It was probably down to the fact that it happened in the chaos of this major battle. The top brass weren't there – but it was witnessed and admired by all his comrades.[21]

After North Africa came the invasion of Sicily, another operation throughout which Stan Hollis would shine. This time a citation for the Distinguished Conduct Medal, in addition to a Mention in Despatches, would recognise Stan's fearless

Company Sergeant-Major
STANLEY E. HOLLIS
50th Infantry Division

In Normandy on 6 June 1944, during the assault on the beaches and the Mont Fleury battery, CSM Hollis' Company Commander noticed that two of the pill boxes had been by-passed, and went with CSM Hollis to see that they were clear.

When they were twenty yards from the pill box, a machine gun opened fire from the slit and CSM Hollis instantly rushed straight at the pill box, firing his Sten gun. He jumped on top of the pill box, recharged the magazine, threw a grenade in through the door and fired his Sten gun into it, killing two Germans and making the remainder prisoners. He then cleared several Germans from a neighbouring trench. By his action he undoubtedly saved his Company from being fired on heavily from the rear, and enabled them to open the main beach exit.

Later the same day, in the village of Crepon, the Company encountered a field gun and crew armed with Spandaus at 100 yards range. CSM Hollis was put in command of a party to cover an attack on the gun, but the movement was held up. Seeing this, CSM Hollis pushed right forward to engage the gun with a PIAT from a house at 50 yards range. He was observed by a sniper who fired and grazed his right cheek, and at the same moment the gun swung round and fired at point blank range into the house. To avoid the falling masonry CSM Hollis moved his party to an alternative position. Two of the enemy gun crew had by this time been killed, and the gun was destroyed shortly afterwards. He later found that two of his men had stayed behind in the house and immediately volunteered to get them out. In full view of the enemy who were continually firing at him, he went forward alone using a Bren gun to distract their attention from the other men. Under cover of his diversion, the two men were able to get back.

Wherever fighting was heaviest, CSM Hollis appeared and in the course of a magnificent days work, he displayed the utmost gallantry and on two separate occasions his courage and initiative prevented the enemy from holding up the advance at critical stages. It was largely through his heroism and resource that the Company's objectives were gained and casualties were not heavier, and by his bravery he saved the lives of many of his men.

courage in the face of the enemy. Seriously wounded, Stan could be forgiven for thinking that he had 'done his bit' and that his wounds may pave a homeward path away from the horrors of war. Yet despite having a steel plate protecting a fractured skull, Stan would have none of it. Refusing to leave his Green Howards brethren, now in their fifth year of war, the invasion of Normandy would be the next challenge for Stan Hollis and his men.

With over half the recipients of the highest award for valour not surviving the encounter for which their decorations were awarded, there exists within this particular example, an exceptional opportunity to have a recipient relive, in their own words, the actions for which they were rewarded. In the case of the only Victoria Cross to be awarded on D-Day, these are the words of Company Sergeant Major Stanley Hollis...

Above: *Generalfeldmarschal Erwin Rommel*

A lot of the boys had been seasick and they were only too glad to get out of those boats. We ran up to the top of the beach and along a ridge. Two platoons came over the minefield to advance... When we got through this hedge we started getting small arms casualties... We knew the fire was coming from up here somewhere but we didn't know exactly where... I saw it. It was very well camouflaged and I saw these guns moving around in the slits. I got my Sten gun and I rushed at it, spraying it hosepipe fashion. They fired back at me and they missed... I got on top of it and I threw a grenade through the slit... I went round the back and went inside and there were two dead, quite a lot of prisoners... I got about eighteen or twenty prisoners... this was the command post for the Mont Fleury gun battery.[22]

Almost unintentionally, CSM Hollis had single-handedly taken his battalion's primary objective of overwhelming the Mont Fleury Gun Battery. As Hollis' unit moved further inland the order was given to clear the village of Crepon. CSM Hollis resumes his D-Day story.

Major Lofthouse ordered the different platoons to search and clear out different farm-houses along the road... We came in the gate. The house was locked, so I broke the door down. I went up the stairs into the various bedrooms, and I burst into one of the bedrooms and there was a small boy about ten or eleven years old... I was covered in blood and he must have been terrified. I am convinced he thought I was going to kill him... I came down again and I decided to have a look to see if there was anything round the back of the house... I went outside, and this was where I was the most frightened I ever was in my life. I looked round this corner and straight away a bullet knocked this lump of stone off the wall. I was very lucky to get away with that. I saw two dogs in a gap in the hedge. They were dancing about, wagging their tails, jumping up and down at somebody, and I knew full well we were forward troops, so I knew there were no mates of ours that were there. On closer inspection I saw a field gun, or what appeared to be a field gun, so I went back and told the Company Commander what I'd seen. He told me that we would see what we could do about it. But before I went back, I told seven or eight of 16 Platoon to dash out and engage whatever was

Generalfeldmarschall Erwin Rommel 1891-1944

Commander of *Heeresgruppe B* (from August 1943 to 17 July 1944)

A schoolmaster's son, Erwin Johannes Eugen Rommel graduated from the Danzig Officer Cadet College in 1911. Wounded three times during Great War campaigns fought in France, Romania and Italy, Rommel would not just be awarded the Iron Cross; First and Second Class, but also Germany's highest award, the 'Pour le Merite'. Subsequent postings as an instructor at the Dresden Infantry School and the war academies of Potsdam and Wiener Neustadt would commence Rommel's inter-war years, a time that also saw him publish the highly rated military manuals *'Infanterie Greift An'* (Infantry Attacks) and *'Panzer Greift An'* (Tank Attacks). In the 1930s, Rommel gave lectures at various *Hitler Jugend* (Hitler Youth) camps, becoming a key figure in the movement which called for the *Hitler Jugend* to be made into a paramilitary youth army.

Appointed as commander of the *Fuhrer-begleit-bataillon* in 1939 (Hitler's personal bodyguard), it was during this time that Rommel gained close contact with Hitler and first befriended Joseph Goebbels, Nazi Germany's Minister of Propaganda. Goebbels became a great admirer of Rommel and would become a key figure in Rommel's career, ensuring that his future exploits would be generously portrayed and greatly celebrated within Nazi propaganda. As Nazi Germany invaded Poland, continuing as commander of Hitler's bodyguard, Rommel's contact with the Fuhrer increased to the extent that, now a *GeneralMajor*, he became part of Hitler's inner circle.

Upon Rommel's request for active service, in February 1940, Hitler gave him command of the 7th Panzer Division, a unit at the spearhead of the invasion of Belgium and France. With Goebbels' propaganda focusing almost exclusively on Rommel's exploits, his celebrity grew within Germany, as did resentment amongst his peers that he was receiving disproportionate glory to the exclusion of those who fought alongside him. With friends in high places, Rommel's reputation was being forged, not necessarily because of his unparalleled skill on the battlefield, but rather due to his unequalled exposure and unrivalled favour amongst the highest echelons of the Nazi regime.

Further fame would arrive for Rommel as commander of the *Afrikakorps*, from 1941 to 1943. The campaign in North Africa witnessed incredible early victories, only for the tide to turn in October 1942 as Montgomery's Eighth Army drove Rommel back over 2,000 miles of desert, inflicting upon him the greatest retreat in military history.

Shortly after illness would rule Rommel out of battle until late 1943 when, as commander of *Heeresgruppe B* (Army Group B), Rommel moved his forces from Italy to France to counter a potential cross channel invasion. Despite some accounts stating Rommel intuitively predicted that the Allied invasion would arrive against the Normandy coastline, there is no evidence to suggest that he thought the attack would arrive anywhere else other than the Pas de Calais region of northern France. Caught off guard and immediately placed on the ropes through the strategy imposed upon him by his nemesis of the North African campaign, Rommel would fail to repel the Allied invasion and would be taken out of the battle for good as his staff car was shot off the road by a spitfire on 17 July 1944.

Only narrowly surviving the wounds sustained in Normandy, Rommel was hospitalised before returning to his home in Herrlingen. It was here on 14 October 1944 that a detachment of SS troops accompanying two Generals from Hitler's headquarters surrounded Rommel's home before informing him that he had been implicated in the July 20 assassination plot. Given a choice of taking poison and having his reputation, and family, remain intact, or otherwise face a court martial, the outcome of which had already been determined, this being a sentence of death, Rommel was driven away from his home in the Generals' staff car. A few minutes later it was reported that Rommel had died of a consequence of his wounds suffered in Normandy. He would be given a hero's funeral and his family provided with a generous pension.

There is no doubt that history has been very kind to Erwin Rommel, portraying him as a good man and a good soldier, albeit fighting for the wrong side. Rommel was undoubtedly a competent commander, but his legacy is surely inflated against his actual achievements. He was also a great manipulator and for him to be portrayed as actively anti-Hitler and anti-Nazi is far from the truth. A great opportunist, Rommel did whatever it took to enhance his career. His ultimate demise belies the fact that there is very little evidence to support the claim that he was an active conspirator in the July 20 assassination plot. Any truth in the speculation that he had hinted that he would have considered becoming a figurehead of any post-Hitler administration can easily be explained through Rommel's thirst for power, whatever the regime.

in the hedge. "Just open up with Bren guns and shoot the hedge up" I said. Well, they ran out of here and immediately all seven or eight of them were killed, stone dead, straight away... I went back... I got my PIAT gun and two Bren gunners, and the three of us crawled through this rhubarb to the forward edge... I poked the PIAT gun through and had a shot... I missed, and then the field gun fired and blew the top off this house... there was sticks and stones and masonry flying all over the place... I crawled back out, walked up the road to join the Company about a hundred yards up the road... Then we heard a terrific racket coming from here and somebody came and told me that the two Bren gunners I had brought in were still in the rhubarb. They were pinned down and couldn't get out. I said to Major Lofthouse, "Well, I took them in, I'll go and try and get them out." So I came back with a Bren gun and I waited behind a wall until there was a lull in the firing, and I ran straight out across the farmyard and sprayed the hedge with the Bren gun. It quietened them down and I was able to shout to the lads to get out and come back and join me, which they were able to do, and we came back and rejoined the Company.[23]

Above: *British troops guard German prisoners while the wounded are cleared from Juno Beach.*

Again, completely disregarding his own safety, Hollis became a one-man army, selflessly risking his own life to save his comrades.

For his actions at both Mont Fleury and Crepon, CSM Stanley Hollis would receive not one, but two nominations for the Victoria Cross. Only as a consequence of the criteria of the award stating that an individual can only be cited for one nomination of the highest award on any given day, did CSM Hollis not receive what could otherwise have potentially been the Victoria Cross and Bar.

Despite suffering a sixth wound in August 1944, Stanley Elton Hollis survived a war during which he is said to have been accountable for over 100 of the enemy. In late 1944 he returned to his native Yorkshire, and it was here as he was lying in a hospital bed in Leeds that he heard he had been awarded the Victoria Cross. He later returned to his family, struggling at first to find work in a bankrupted Britain before finding his niche as the landlord of a pub he later renamed as *'The Green Howard'*. Always uncomfortable with the inevitable exposure which followed the award, Hollis would be reluctant to accept the fame that came with such an accolade. Once, when asked what drove him to undertake such numerous incredible actions, unable to fully explain, *"Because I was a Green Howard"* was the only response he could offer. In one interview Hollis was asked if he thought he was a hero, his response was, *"I was no hero. I did only what I had to do. I just wanted to come home and survive"*.[24]

Stan Hollis died, aged 59, in 1972 and was buried at Acklam near Middlesbrough. His Victoria Cross is displayed at the Green Howards Regimental Museum in Richmond, North Yorkshire. *Hollis Crescent* is named after him at Strensall Army Camp in York and a residential care home for the elderly is named in his honour; *Hollis Court* can be found in Coulby Newham.

In November 2015, a memorial dedicated to Stanley Hollis was unveiled in his hometown of Middlesbrough.

As the 50th Infantry Division continued its D-Day advance, at approximately 1400 hours, the path of the *Double T* would indeed clash with that of *Kampfgruppe Meyer.* Four miles from Gold Beach, *Oberst Meyer* assembled his troops, seemingly unaware of the fact that their every move was being observed. Taking the initiative, the Allies most experienced troops decided to assert their strength before the enemy were themselves battle ready. Driving the enemy attack back over three miles beyond the position of first contact, the majority of *Kampfgruppe Meyer* were killed, wounded or taken prisoner - their hopes of defeating the British dying alongside their commanding officer, as the 50th Division routed the German attempts to defeat the invasion.

At the end of the day, out of an original force of over 3,000, just ninety of Meyer's men were left in the fight, with the 50th Division having inflicted a crushing defeat on their opponents and ending the day overlooking Bayeux. Although falling just short of its objective on day one, Bayeux, the first city liberated in France, would be secured early in the morning of 7 June. This incredible effort was achieved despite the best efforts of the enemy's counter-attack, second in size only to the counter of the 21st Panzer Division against the Sword Beach sector.

It is a tragedy that such a battle barely registers in the annals of popular history, but then not surprising when sources such as the American official historian state that on D-Day the 50th Division was *'advancing against very slight opposition',*[25] a surprising remark given the fact that *Kampfgruppe Meyer* consisted of an equal, if not greater strength, than that of whole of the enemy force which fought within the Omaha Beach sector on D-Day. With Bayeux secure, and intact, the 50th Division's advance continued south, west and east, to the extent that by the end of the first two days of battle, the *'Tyne Tees'* Division held almost twice as many square miles as any other unit to fight on D-Day.

Above: *Stanley Hollis VC.*

D-Day concluded with 155,000 Allied soldiers on Normandy soil. Everywhere but at Omaha had the Allies inflicted a telling defeat on the German defenders. Hitler's much heralded Atlantic Wall of so called impenetrable defences had taken a sound beating. Although the Allies had suffered over 12,000 casualties, this was way below the figure that the Allied High Command had feared prior to the invasion. Despite this, however successful day one had been, D-Day was simply the start of a huge struggle that lay ahead. Only a tiny fraction of the overall German war machine had so far been deployed against the invasion. If managed efficiently, the enemy was still capable of defeating the Allies in Normandy. Three months of continuous bitter fighting followed as hundreds of thousands of men would be pitted against each other in brutal combat. Out of this huge force, another sixteen individuals would receive their nation's highest award.

PART THREE
Chapter 6
Consolidation

The second day of the invasion witnessed steady if not spectacular progress along the whole front. Only the Gold and Juno Beach sectors had been consolidated on D-Day. Gold was then united with Omaha on 7 June, as was Juno with Sword. Albeit still isolated from the rest of the invasion, the amphibious forces at Utah had linked up with the majority of the supporting airborne forces on 7 June, whilst on 8 June, the Commonwealth forces, having faced the arrival of a second armoured division (the 12th SS *Hitler Jugend*), and then immediately after, a third (the *Panzer Lehr* – a unit whose original orders were to attack against the Americans in vicinity to Isigny sur Mer), were holding the bulk of the enemy reserves to the east.

Below: *The 29th Division advance : 7-8 June 1944.*

With the enemy's main strength concentrated against their front, the Commonwealth forces were unable to advance to any significant extent. However, as far as the overall strategic situation was concerned, far more important than the acquisition of territory, the British and Canadians were taking the strain and decisively defeating the foremost German attempts to throw the invasion back into the sea. As the bigger picture

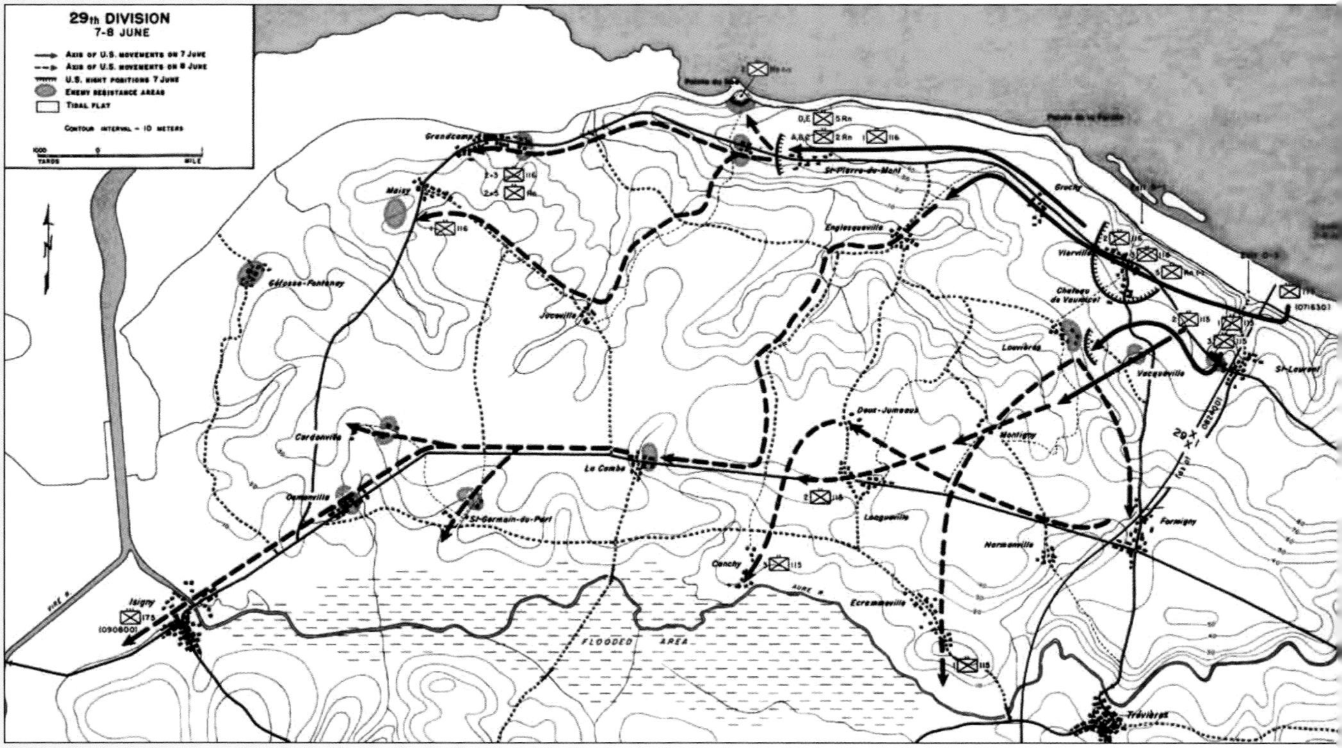

became more apparent, the greatest cause for concern within the Allied Command became the isolation of Utah - the only sector that had yet to be consolidated within the overall lodgment area.

Although no criticism should be aimed at those formations which suffered devastating losses during the initial assault, there can be no denying the very sluggish nature of how the reserve forces, landing on Omaha, either in the afternoon of D-Day, or throughout D+1 - went about the business of organising themselves before taking their advance inland. One obvious explanation was the American commanders' decision to attack upon sectors of beach where the enemy's defences were at their strongest. In addition to this, in setting an objective for these same assault forces to advance several miles inland, too much had been asked of the very first men ashore. Surely, if the American forces had followed the British and Canadian doctrine and had punched through at a chosen weak spot, then used reserve forces landing behind the assault wave to move through their lines to reach a pre-determined objective line, then maybe those units that had led the assault ashore, and therefore most likely to suffer the most severe casualties, would not have been relied upon in realising such ambitious objectives at such an inevitably depleted strength. With no such contingency, and despite facing at worse, minimal opposition, there was little progress inland from Omaha on 7 June.

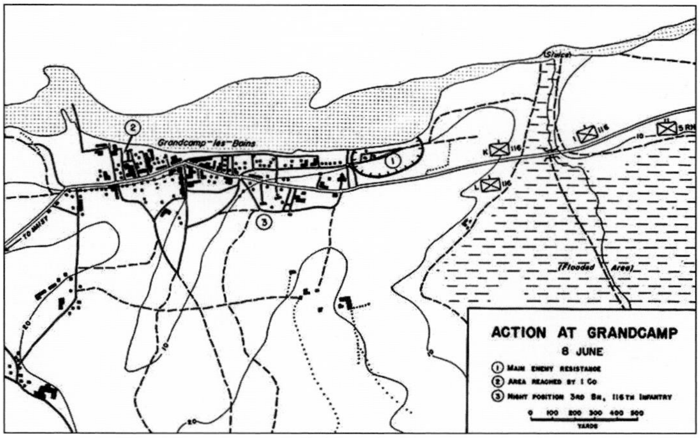

Above: *The route of Peregory's attack at Grandcamp les Bains.*

At long last, on 8 June, the advance of the 29th Division finally gained momentum as infantry, supported by tanks and self-propelled artillery, headed west towards Utah. Once underway, progress was swift as in the early afternoon, the 29ers linked up with Colonel Rudder's Rangers at *Pointe du Hoc*, before, in the early evening, the vanguard approached the small fishing town of Grandcamp les Bains.

Half a mile to the west of Grandcamp les Bains, the advance became restricted to a single road, the land either side being impassable due to flooding. As the first elements attempted to cross the causeway, all hell broke loose as artillery, mortars and automatic fire were aimed against the forward elements of the American advance. A Sherman tank exploded, hit by fire emanating from a strongpoint located on the high ground at the eastern approach to the town. A stand-off developed as the 29ers went to ground and dug in on the eastern side of an incline that led toward a small stone bridge.

With the impasse threatening to descend into stalemate, the impetus of the American advance was restored due to the actions of an individual act of incredible valour. From Charlottesville, Virginia, 28-year-old Technical Sergeant Frank Peregoy had joined the National Guard as a 15-year-old in 1931. On enlistment, the clerk processing his enrollment misspelt his name as Peregory. To correct the error, Peregoy would have had to show his birth certificate. Not being able to, lest he give away his real age, he would forever be known, not by his real name, but by that recorded on enlistment into the US Army. By D-Day Peregory had already received the illustrious *Soldier's Medal* (the highest award the US Army can issue in a non-combat scenario) for saving the life of a comrade during an exercise held prior to his unit leaving America for

Europe, an act described by Carl Proffitt of K Company, 3rd Battalion of the 116th Infantry Regiment...

He was a real dare-devil, you know. He had gotten the Soldier's Medal back in the States for saving a kid's life down in Newbern, North Carolina on manoeuvres down there... This kid was trapped in a weapons carrier... the weapons carrier ran off the road over into an inundated area... real deep... Frank took his bayonet, jumped into the water, cut through the truck canvas and pulled the kid out from drowning.[26]

Three years later, Peregory would now take the battle to the enemy in raging a one-man crusade against a fortification which was blocking the advance of an entire regiment. Leading a solo charge across the stone bridge, he infiltrated German lines before making his way through a labyrinth of trenches and bunkers, killing several of the enemy and taking over thirty prisoners. Within minutes Peregory had single-handedly cleared the way in defeating the enemy strongpoint. For his solo crusade, Peregory would receive the Medal of Honor. However, like so many recipients of this award, he would not be able to accept the medal in person - he was killed at Grandcamp les Bains six days after his incredible exploits.

Technical Sergeant Frank Peregoy (still identified as Peregory) lies at rest in the Normandy American Cemetery at Colleville sur Mer. Ten miles to the west of his final resting place is a memorial dedicated to him located behind a former German machine-gun nest. Now used as a flower bed, but once forming part of the Grandcamp widerstandsnest, some of the last physical remains of the German strongpoint appropriately bear the name of its conqueror.

In 1984, a building complex at Fort Pickett in Virginia was dedicated in his name, as is the Frank D. Peregory United States Army Reserve Center, located in Charlottesville, Virginia.

Technical Sergeant
FRANK D. PEREGORY
29th Infantry Division

On 8 June 1944, the 3rd Battalion of the 116th Infantry was advancing on the strongly held German defences at Grandcamp, France, when the leading elements were suddenly halted by decimating machine gun fire from a firmly entrenched enemy force on the high ground overlooking the town. After numerous attempts to neutralise the enemy position by supporting artillery and tank fire had proved ineffective, Technical Sergeant Peregory, on his own initiative, advanced up the hill under withering fire, and worked his way to the crest where he discovered an entrenchment leading to the main enemy fortifications 200 yards away. Without hesitating, he leaped into the trench and moved toward the emplacement. Encountering a squad of enemy riflemen, he fearlessly attacked them with hand grenades and bayonet, killed 8 and forced 3 to surrender. Continuing along the trench, he single-handedly forced the surrender of 32 more riflemen, captured the machine gunners, and opened the way for the leading elements of the battalion to advance and secure its objective. The extraordinary gallantry and aggressiveness displayed by Technical Sergeant Peregory are exemplary of the highest tradition of the armed forces.

Despite the heroics of Technical Sergeant Peregory, within a day the advance of the 29th Division had once again faltered. With an ever-increasing urgency to link Utah with the rest of the beachhead, the American Command decidedto change emphasis in now prioritising the capture of the crossroads town of Carentan. This task was allocated to the 101st Airborne Division which, in anticipation of the arrival of the 29ers, was given the objective of moving from the north, to head south through the town, to a position upon the banks of the River Douves and the Carentan Canal.

By the evening of 9 June, the American paratroopers had consolidated the majority of their D-Day objectives. Now reinforced and resupplied through the arrival of amphibious forces from Utah Beach, the eyes of the 101st Airborne Division were fixed firmly upon their newly set objective. With Carentan secured, any further counter-

Right: *Despite allegations of heavy handed use of artillery within the British Sector, no operation launched within the US Sector would commence without a comparable or even greater use of supporting fire.*

attack from the enemy could be fended off, whilst the Screaming Eagles awaited the arrival of their compatriots advancing from the Omaha Sector. With haste, Bradley defined the task; nothing should get in the way... "*If it becomes necessary to save time, put five hundred or even one thousand tons of air on Carentan... take the town apart*".[27]

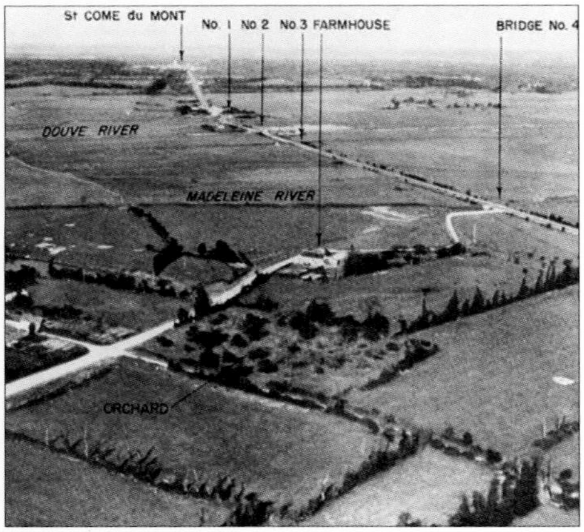

Left: *An aerial photograph highlighting the route of Colonel Cole's attack at Carentan.*

Despite an abundance of supporting fire, with all approaches to the town purposely flooded by the Germans, only one option remained for the Screaming Eagles. Their attack was confined to a single causeway that crossed four waterways, the bridge over one of which had been destroyed by the enemy. In advancing a distance of almost two miles upon an open road, devoid of any kind of cover other than the drainage ditches that ran at either side, to be overlooked by high ground and defended by a well-entrenched enemy, such a task, assigned to the 3rd Battalion of the 502 PIR, under the command of the much-respected Lieutenant Colonel Robert Cole, would be no easy feat.

Below: *The attack on Carentan: 10-11 June 1944.*

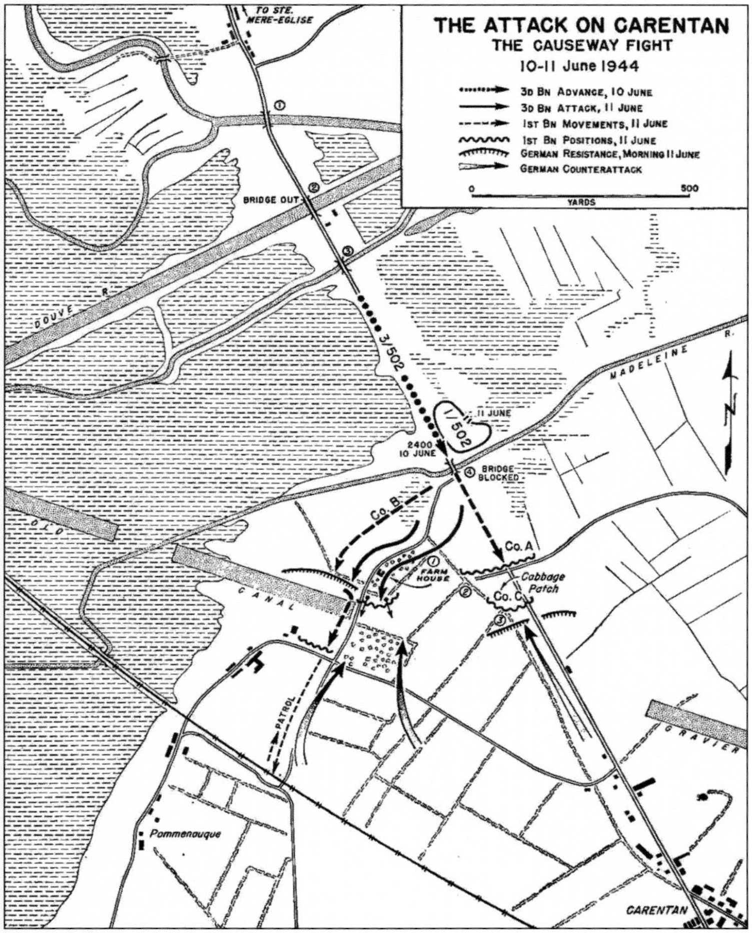

Just after midnight on 10 June, under the cover of darkness, the first elements of Cole's force commenced their attack. The first approach faltered under heavy fire as engineers failed to improvise a crossing of the River Douve, the original bridge having been destroyed by the Germans the previous day. With the attackers forced to retreat to their start line, a reconnaissance party was sent forward just before sunrise on the morning of 10 June and successfully crossed the river by boat before advancing a further half mile toward Carentan. At the crossing of the River Madeleine, any further progression was blocked by an improvised barricade that had been constructed by the Germans. As the first men manoeuvred their way through a gap they had created by sliding a steel barrier across the road, flares were lit and the enemy zeroed in with automatic fire, forcing the attackers back once more to their start line.

Fresh plans were prepared for a third attempt to be made in the afternoon of

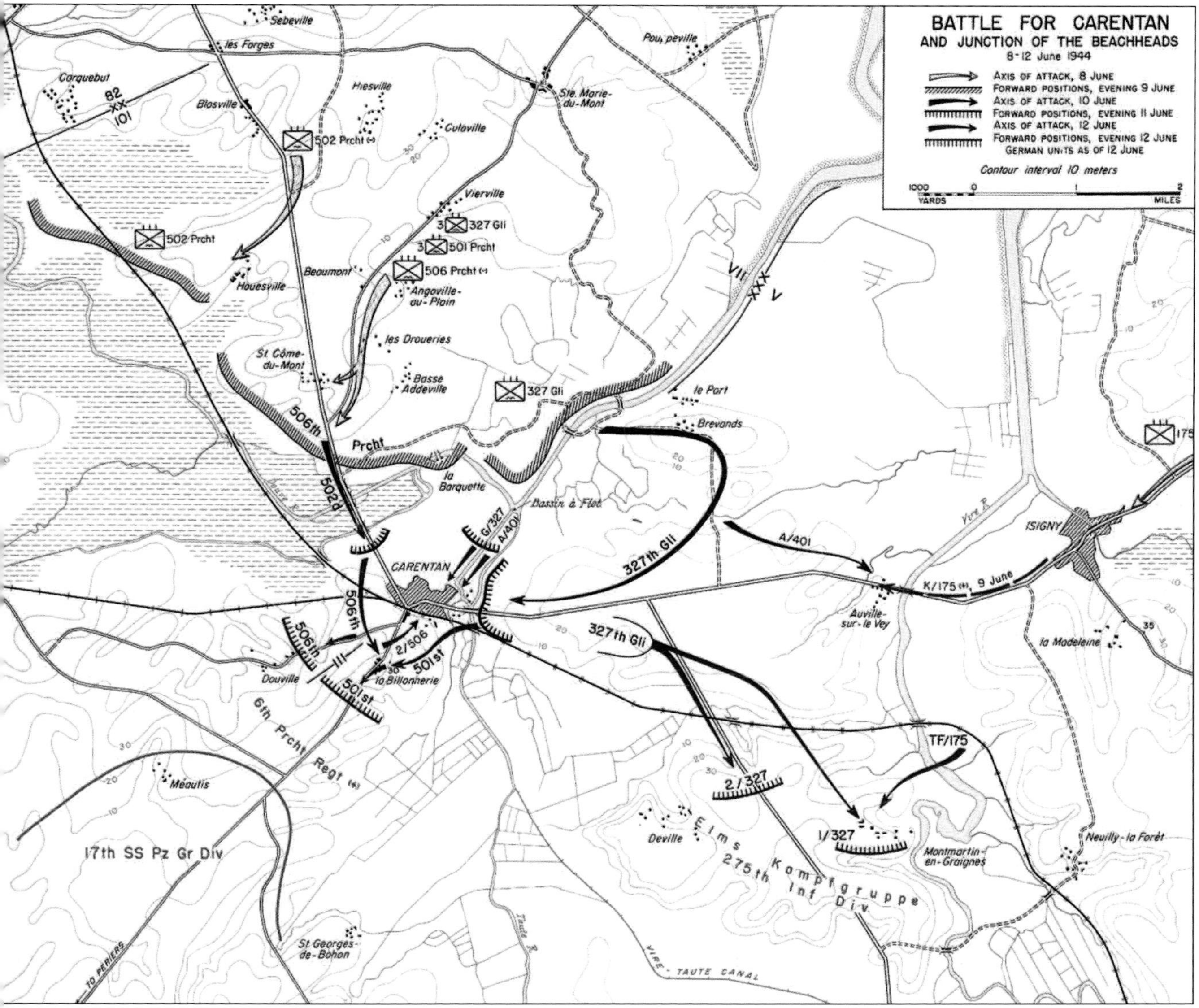

10 June. With wooden planking improvising a crossing over the demolished bridge of the River Douve, with massive artillery and mortar fire in support, a third attack went in and by mid-afternoon, Cole's men had crossed the greater part of the causeway, only to draw fire from a previously undetected enemy presence close to the barricade which still partially blocked the crossing of the River Madeleine. With the enemy covering the only route of advance with automatic fire, stalemate reigned that lasted well into the hours of darkness.

By 0400 hours on 11 June, much of the 3rd Battalion of the 502 PIR had been pinned down in roadside ditches for up to twelve hours. Orders were now passed to resurrect the attack. As a new artillery barrage was requested, Lieutenant Colonel Robert Cole passed word to fix bayonets in anticipation of an infantry charge against the German line.

Above: *Battle for Carentan: 8-12 June 1944.*

Having already suffered considerable casualties, with only 250 men left in the fight, Cole gave the order to attack. Just twenty men followed, the others either seemingly unaware of their orders or unwilling to fight. Standing upright under a hail of fire, Cole beckoned the whole force forward, driving the bulk of the enemy presence into retreat. Exhausted and depleted in strength, having claimed the causeway as their own, Cole's men were relieved by the 1st Battalion who pursued the enemy over open fields as the remainder of the regiment, alongside elements of the 506 PIR, began clearing the town which would eventually form the junction between the two American beaches.

For his fearless command in leading his men across the causeway which would become known as Purple Heart Lane, Lieutenant Colonel Cole would be awarded the Medal of Honor. Tragically, the award would be granted posthumously, as Cole was killed in Holland three months after his heroic actions paved the way for the liberation of Carentan.

Having relinquished Carentan, the German response would arrive in the early morning of 13 June, as elements of the 17th SS Panzer Grenadier Division attempted to reclaim the town. However, as the Screaming Eagles fended off the advances of the SS, the 29th Division now advanced beyond Isigny sur Mer. Finally the Utah and Omaha beachheads were united, providing the Allies with a consolidated beachhead now extended to a width of seventy-five miles.

By the time the two American beaches had been linked, the US V Army Corps had advanced to a distance of fifteen miles inland from Omaha. To the east, and within the sector of the British Second Army, operations were far from fluid as the enemy continued to build up what was, in terms of both quantity and quality, by far their main strength around the city of Caen. However, not only had the British line held in the face of the greatest enemy efforts to throw the invasion back into the sea, but in places Dempsey's men were in fact making inroads against the might of the German war machine.

As the struggle for Caen entered its second week, the Americans commenced the second phase of their grand strategy in making the drive on the port of Cherbourg.

Lieutenant Colonel

ROBERT G. COLE

101st Airborne Division

For gallantry and intrepidity at the risk of his own life, above and beyond the call of duty on 11 June 1944, in France. Lieutenant Col. Cole was personally leading his battalion in forcing the last 4 bridges on the road to Carentan when his entire unit was suddenly pinned to the ground by intense and withering enemy rifle, machine gun, mortar, and artillery fire placed upon them from well-prepared and heavily fortified positions within 150 yards of the foremost elements. After the devastating and unceasing enemy fire had for over an hour prevented any move and inflicted numerous casualties, Lt. Col. Cole, observing this almost hopeless situation, courageously issued orders to assault the enemy positions with fixed bayonets. With utter disregard for his own safety and completely ignoring the enemy fire, he rose to his feet in front of his battalion and with drawn pistol shouted to his men to follow him in the assault. Catching up a fallen man's rifle and bayonet, he charged on and led the remnants of his battalion across the bullet-swept open ground and into the enemy position. His heroic and valiant action in so inspiring his men resulted in the complete establishment of our bridgehead across the Douve River. The cool fearlessness, personal bravery, and outstanding leadership displayed by Lt Col. Cole reflect great credit upon himself and are worthy of the highest praise in the military service.

Chapter 7

Cutting the Peninsula

More than 12,000 men of the 82nd and 101st Airborne Divisions had descended at a distance of between two and nine miles inland from Utah Beach on D-Day. Amongst the paratroopers' objectives was the forming of a defensive shield to fend off potential counter-attacks. Behind this line a buffer zone could be created through which amphibious forces would advance over difficult low-lying and often flooded terrain.

The American airborne operation commenced in a state of complete disarray. On average, fewer than one in five of the paratroopers had hit their designated dropzones and hundreds had drowned in the flooded marshlands that were so abundant in this

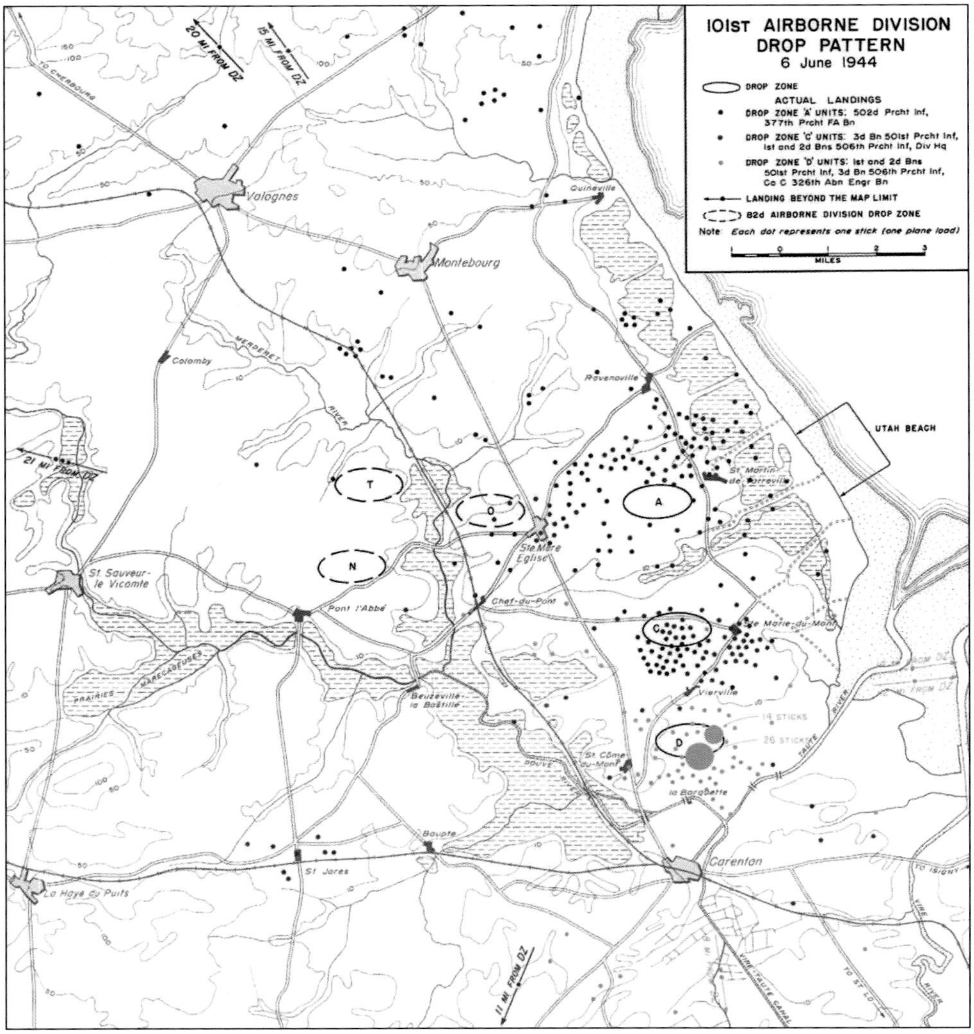

Below left: *The D-Day Drop Pattern of the American 101st Airborne Division.*

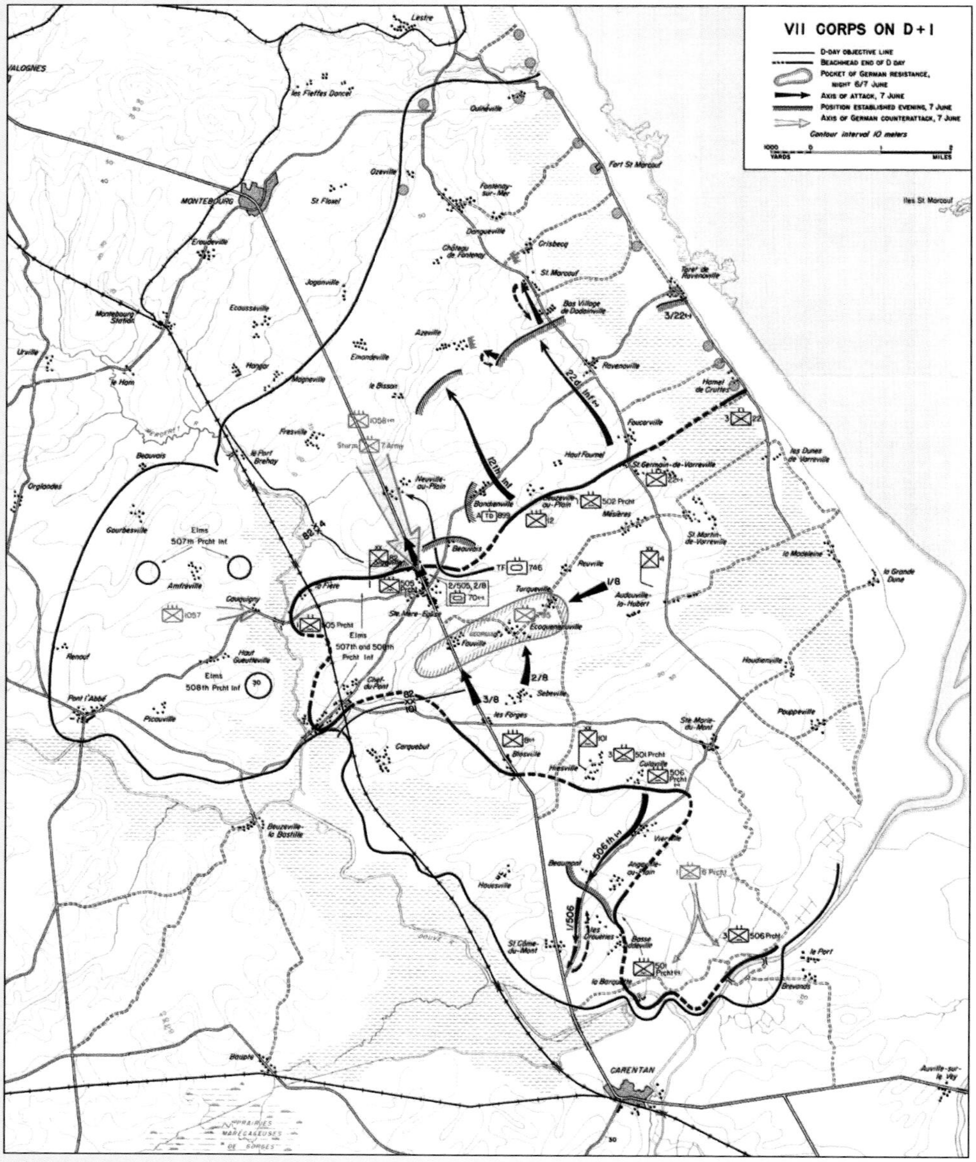

Left: *US Army VII Corps on 7 June 1944.*

sector. Despite such adversity, the American paratroopers, in many cases fighting at a fraction of their intended strength, reacted quickly enough to fend off the enemy's attempts to counter against the amphibious assault.

As the 29th Infantry Division fought their way towards Carentan from the east, the main elements of the US Army's VII Corps headed west from Utah Beach in an attempt to split the Cotentin Peninsula. With the peninsula divided, American forces could starve the enemy located north of the partition of reinforcements and supplies, before making the move on the crucial port of Cherbourg. This strategy differed from the pre-invasion plan which had intended that a single thrust headed by the 4th Infantry Division be made toward Cherbourg in a direct northerly direction. However, despite the lack of any significant resistance, the American advance had stalled

just a few miles north of Ste Mere Eglise, forcing an early deviation from the original plan as the peninsula would first be split east to west, before the northerly approach be made.

With the majority of the 101st Airborne Division linking up with the amphibious forces on day one, for elements of the 82nd Airborne Division, positioned on the whole much further inland, the wait for reinforcements would last for up to three days. The story of the 507 PIR, part of the 82nd Airborne Division, epitomises this struggle. Fewer than sixty of the intended 2,000 men of the regiment had hit their intended landing area. Some touched down over twenty miles from their intended dropzone; hundreds had landed in the flooded valley of the River Merderet. As a consequence of this disastrous start, the 507 PIR would never fight at anywhere near its full strength during the whole of the campaign in Normandy.

Isolated, disorientated and heavily outnumbered, time and again, ad-hoc groups of paratroopers, engaged an enemy many times their own strength. This kind of situation was especially prominent on the western banks of the River Merderet, where paratroopers were drawn into a desperate struggle for survival. Few in number and ill-equipped due to little or no re-supply, not until the evening of 8 June did reinforcements appear and the situation finally stabilise.

Throughout this time, elements of the 82nd Airborne Division had been holding a bridge over the River Merderet close to a hamlet called La Fiere. The flooding of the low laying marshes inland from Ste Mere Eglise had led to the river bursting its banks and inundating approximately 600 yards of ground immediately to the west of La

Above: *Behind every hedgerow, within every farmyard, the enemy is seemingly everywhere.*

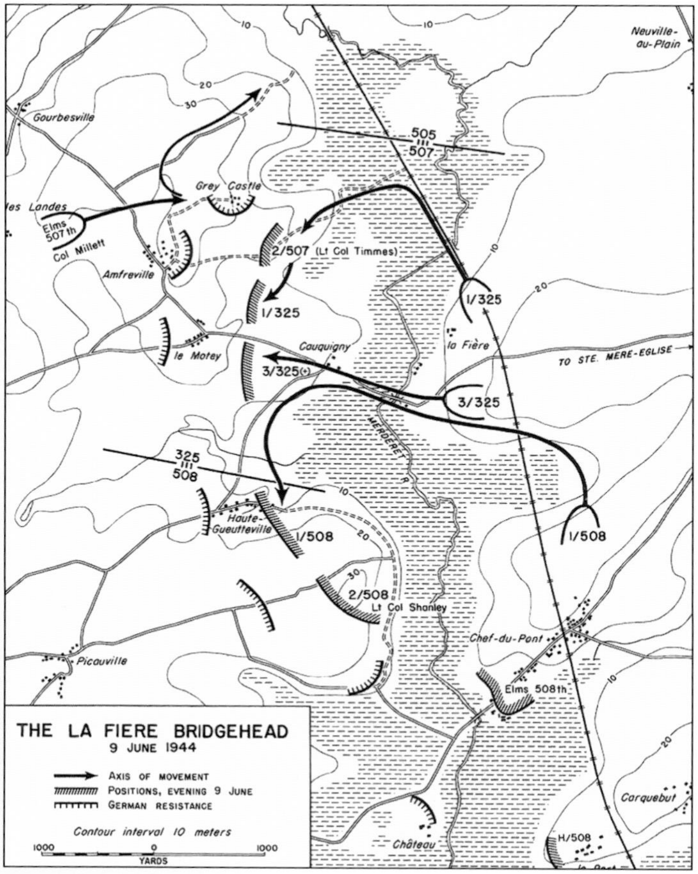

Above: *The La Fiere Bridgehead, on 9 June 1944.*

Above right: *The Normandy Bocage.*

Fiere. Consequently the crossing of a narrow causeway which ran through the valley was one of few, if not the only existing option, that could carry the American advance to the west.

On 6 and 7 June, the Germans had failed on numerous occasions to launch their own counter-attack through this route. Although outnumbering the American defenders, their attempts to move through such a confined approach had been halted by the airborne forces overlooking the causeway from the relative high ground to the east of the river. On the western banks of the Merderet small isolated pockets of American paratroopers were interspersed amongst elements of the 91st *Luftlande* Division. The enemy, although now outnumbered within the peninsula overall, was still dominant in this crucial zone and held in strength the critical position to the west of the causeway around the hamlet of Cauquigny.

On the evening of 8 June, a nocturnal reconnaissance led by the 325th Glider Infantry Regiment (GIR) was instructed to assess the enemy's strength and standing on the western banks of the river. By last light this force had crossed the river by wading through a shallow ford, before entering a myriad of sunken lanes within the infamous bocage (hedgerow country). In the confusion of these dark and featureless tree-lined lanes, cohesion of movement alongside any order of command broke down. Tension increased as the patrols ventured deeper into enemy held ground. At approximately 0400 hours on 9 June, one small group of disorientated paratroopers ran into an ambush. Raymond T. Burchell remembers what happened as the group ran into heavy fire emanating from three sides…

We were greatly outmanned, had walked into a trap and were taking very heavy casualties. Some of our company was surrendering, when Charlie DeGlopper stood up with his BAR blazing away hollering to us, 'Get out! Get Out! Pull Back!' Charlie stood in that road, putting clip after clip into his BAR.[28]

Standing six feet seven inches tall, 23-year-old Charles DeGlopper from Grand Island, New York, deliberately drew fire so that the rest of the group could escape what would surely have otherwise been certain death. Firing his automatic rifle, he not only inflicted significant losses on the enemy, but also bought time for his brothers in arms to escape the deadly ambush. DeGlopper himself would be killed, but due to his heroism others would survive to fight another day. For his selfless actions and incredible valour, DeGlopper would be posthumously awarded the Medal of Honor in March 1946.

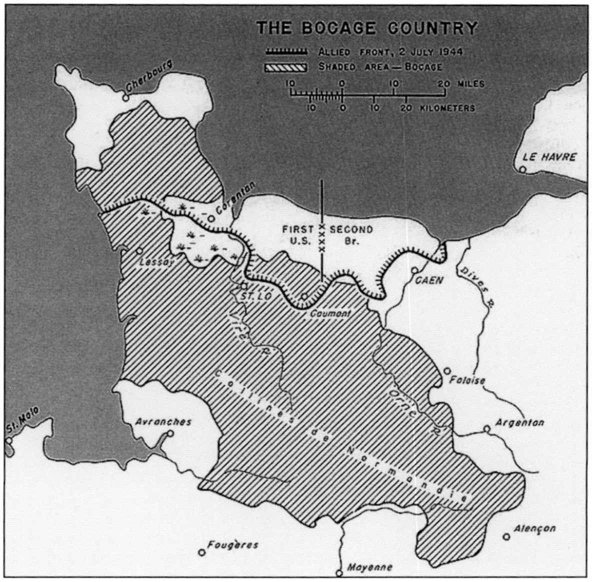

In December 1947, the US Army Transport Ship *Elgin Victory* was renamed the *Private Charles N. DeGlopper.* The following year a road at Fort Bragg, North Carolina was named in his honour. In 1958, the US Army Reserve Training Centre in Tonawanda was named the *Charles DeGlopper Centre*. In January 2015, the Air Assault School at Fort Bragg, North Carolina was renamed *The DeGlopper Air Assault School*. He is today buried at Maple View Cemetery, Grand Island, New York.

At the same time that Charles DeGlopper was making his last stand, another incredible act of selfless valour was taking place only a few hundred yards away. Pinned down under heavy fire and unable to advance, 20-year-old Californian, Private Joe Gandara, took the initiative to change the face of battle. As the citation for his Distinguished Service Cross records...

Private Gandara, a member of Company D, was with a party led by Captain Smith, who was withdrawing on Division orders to the east bank of the Merderet River. This group of men was approximately 150 strong and they were operating in an area held by the 1058th German Infantry. At about 1000hrs, D plus 3, this party ran into a body of Germans strongly fortified in a farm on the banks of the river north of Flaux. The enemy was evidently prepared to prevent withdrawal at all costs, and disperse or force the surrender of the column. For four

Private First Class

CHARLES N. DEGLOPPER

82nd Airborne Division

He was a member of Company C, 325th Glider Infantry, on 9 June 1944 advancing with the forward platoon to secure a bridgehead across the Merderet River at La Fiere, France. At dawn the platoon had penetrated an outer line of machine guns and riflemen, but in so doing had become cut off from the rest of the company. Vastly superior forces began a decimation of the stricken unit and put in motion a flanking manoeuvre which would have completely exposed the American platoon in a shallow roadside ditch where it had taken cover. Detecting this danger, Pfc. DeGlopper volunteered to support his comrades by fire from his automatic rifle while they attempted a withdrawal through a break in a hedgerow 40 yards to the rear. Scorning a concentration of enemy automatic weapons and rifle fire, he walked from the ditch onto the road in full view of the Germans, and sprayed the hostile positions with assault fire. He was wounded, but he continued firing. Struck again, he started to fall; and yet his grim determination and valiant fighting spirit could not be broken. Kneeling in the roadway, weakened by his grievous wounds, he levelled his heavy weapon against the enemy and fired burst after burst until killed outright. He was successful in drawing the enemy action away from his fellow soldiers, who continued the fight from a more advantageous position and established the first bridgehead over the Merderet. In the area where he made his intrepid stand his comrades later found the ground strewn with dead Germans and many machine guns and automatic weapons which he had knocked out of action. Pfc. DeGlopper's gallant sacrifice and unflinching heroism while facing insurmountable odds were in great measure responsible for a highly important tactical victory in the Normandy Campaign.

hours, Private Gandara and his companions were unable to find an issue from this desperate situation. Finally, Private Gandara stepped erect into the enemy lines and, firing a machine gun from the carry position, knocked out three enemy machine guns and opened a gap through which Captain Smith was able to lead his force to safety. Private Gandara was killed in the midst of this heroic act.

The upgrade of Gandara's Distinguished Service Cross to the Medal of Honor would not be made until almost seventy years after his death, and only then as a consequence of President Obama initiating an inquiry into medals that had been purportedly downgraded due to the ethnicity of the recipient. With the original Distinguished Service Cross now upgraded to the highest award, Gandara's Medal of Honor was presented to his niece in March 2014. After the presentation, Major General John Nicholson, Commanding Officer of the 82nd Airborne Division, spoke of Gandara's sacrifice...

Despite his young age when he died, [Gandara] knew full well what would happen when he exposed himself. He knew he was likely to die and he did it anyway. He died protecting his comrades, but he also died to end the oppression of the French people and prevent the oppression of his countrymen. This cause and these people were worthy of his sacrifice.[29]

Gandara's story now stands for posterity alongside the most remarkable legends of ultimate valour committed by those who liberated Normandy from Nazi tyranny. He lies at rest at Woodlawn Cemetery, Santa Monica, California.

Below: *The attritional battle fought within the Normandy bocage suited neither friend nor foe.*

Sadly, the actions of DeGlopper and Gandara achieved little in weakening the enemy's stranglehold on the western banks of the River Merderet. By the morning of 9 June, it had become clear that it would be down to the remainder of the 325th GIR, supported by mis-dropped paratroopers, primarily of the 507th PIR, to force a crossing of the La Fiere causeway. Resistance was bitter and the situation chaotic as the airborne forces ran the gauntlet of fire upon the causeway before close quarter fighting broke out against the enemy within the hamlet of Cauquigny. Albeit at a great loss, the Americans did however succeed where the Germans had previously failed in forcing the causeway, and by the evening of 9 June, the 82nd Airborne Division had consolidated a foothold on the western banks of the River Merderet.

With the west bank of the River Merderet now secure, and with the 9th Infantry Division now at their side, the 82nd continued their westerly advance through Pont l'Abbe. This manoeuvre had originally been intended as one led by the US 90th Infantry Division. However, despite a huge numerical advantage, against an ever-diminishing foe, the *'Tough Ombres'* consistently failed to make headway and rapidly became a cause of great concern to the American Command, a situation outlined by General Bradley…

Almost from the moment of its starting attack, the 90th became a 'problem' division. So exasperating was its performance that at one point the First Army staff gave up and recommended that we break it up for replacements.[30]

Private

JOE GANDARA

82nd Airborne Division

The President of the United States takes pride in presenting the Distinguished Service Cross (posthumously) to Joe Gandara (39561681), Private, U.S. Army, for extraordinary heroism in connection with military operations against an armed enemy while serving with Company D, 2nd Battalion, 507th Parachute Infantry Regiment, 82nd Airborne Division, in action against enemy forces on 9 June 1944, in France. When his detachment came under devastating enemy fire from a strong German force, pinning the men to the ground for a period of four hours, Private Gandara advanced voluntarily and alone toward the enemy position. Firing his machine gun from a carrying position as he moved forward, he destroyed three hostile machine guns before he was fatally wounded. By his selfless devotion to duty and outstanding valour, Private Gandara prevented heavy casualties to members of the detachment. His intrepid actions, personal bravery and zealous devotion to duty at the cost of his life, exemplify the highest traditions of the military forces of the United States and reflect great credit upon himself, the 82nd Airborne Division, and the United States Army.

The situation escalated so quickly that just forty-eight hours after first engagement, the 9th Infantry and 82nd Airborne Divisions were reallocated the lead role as the 90th was placed in reserve, pending the appointment of a new Commander.

The foremost problem faced within the American sector was neither the number, nor the quality of the enemy's forces. With the exception of the 91st *Luftlande* Division, joined in the second week of the invasion by the 17th SS, the overall standard of the German soldier within the American sector was pretty much as low as it got. As General Marcks commented, his forces consisted of…*'a large number of men in uniform with hardly a soldier among them.'* The quality of such divisions had been evident to the command of the German's elite formations for a long time, as stated by General Fritz Bayerlein, commanding *Panzer Lehr*…

Their condition was extremely bad. They had been in France for two to three years, and were completely spoiled. France is a dangerous country, with its wine, women, and its pleasant climate. Troops who are there for any length of time become bad soldiers. They had done nothing but live well and send things home. It is very painful to have to say it, but this was the opinion of all the troops which suddenly were transferred to France from the Russian Front. The troops in France had been in the rear zone for years and, when thrown into combat, failed utterly. Furthermore, the best troops recruited had gone to the Luftwaffe, Paratroopers, and the SS, and no good replacements were ever sent to the infantry divisions.[31]

In great contrast to the Anglo-Canadian forces, who were facing the enemy's elite SS forces during the battle for Caen, the main problem for the Americans was the region's

Below: *Securing the North Flank : 8-14 June 1944.*

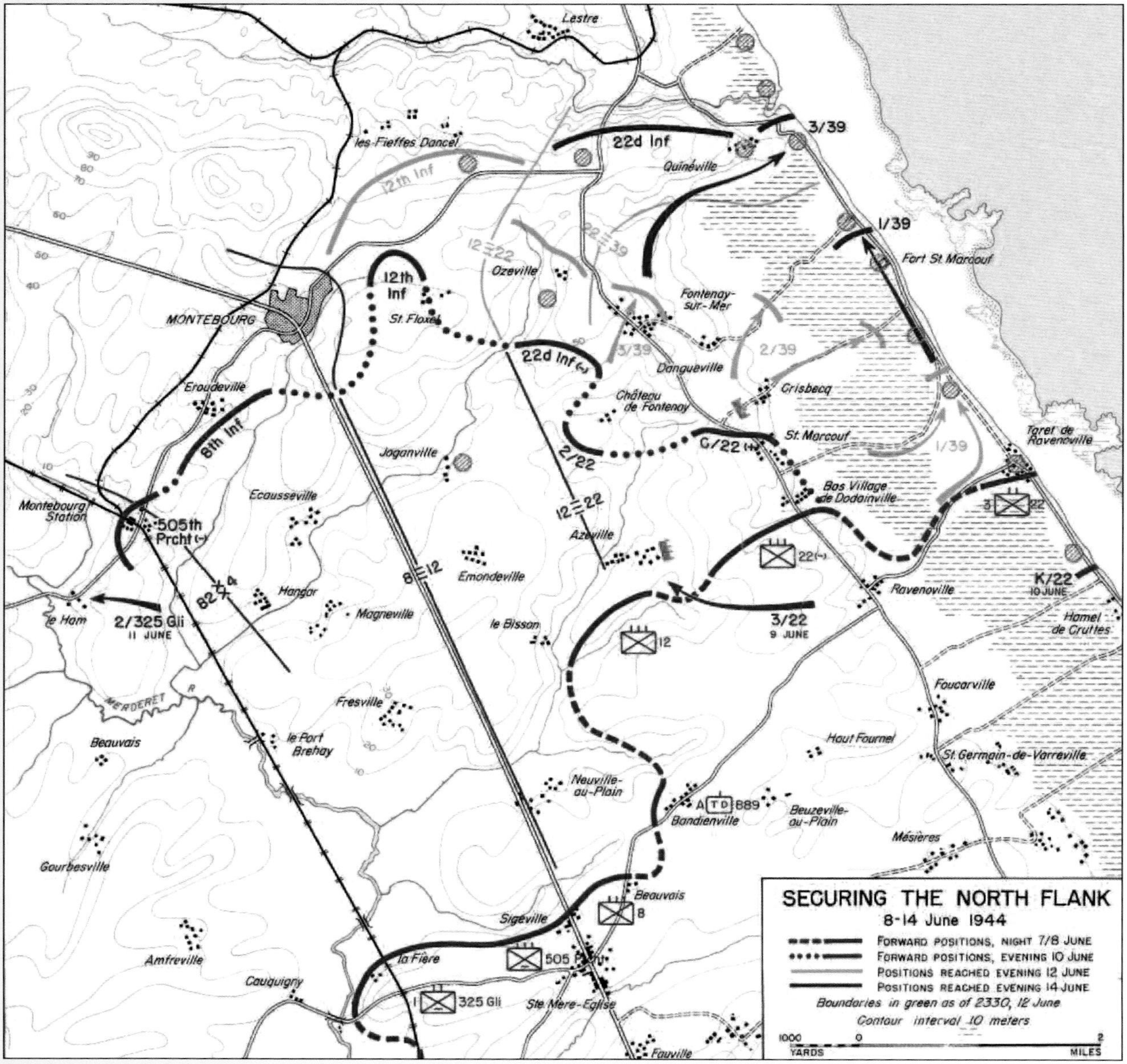

terrain, a combination of inundated low lying floodplains, and a patchwork of small fields, enclosed by the thick foliage of the ancient *bocage*. First appearing over a thousand years ago, the *bocage* terrain of Normandy is bordered by tree-lines built on steep earthen embankments. A system first used to create a windbreak to protect crops growing in fields was, as time progressed, also used to enclose cattle and to mark off property boundaries. Although man-made, this natural feature, often referred to as the Normandy *hedgerows*, is very prominent within, although not exclusive to, the Cherbourg Peninsula.

Above: *US infantry face the enemy in the infamous Normandy bocage.*

It has been argued that such terrain offered every advantage to the defender, although it could equally be argued that the Germans themselves were facing a double-edged sword and may have been better placed not to have broken up their strength piecemeal and be drawn into a bitter scrap for every square yard of ground, but instead withdraw to an overall more beneficial defensive line. Whichever of the two tactics are considered most effective, there is no doubt that this environment certainly hindered free movement and created a very claustrophobic and psychologically challenging situation, a scenario described by a veteran who himself fought through this restrictive terrain...

The Normandy Farmers had done their work diligently over the centuries to enclose the small patches of green pasture and apple orchard and protect their livestock. A single twelve-mile tract might have as many as four thousand of these small enclosed fields, each surrounded on four sides by imposing, impenetrable hedgerows... Steep high banks, their soil compacted by centuries of rain and sun, and with thick roots, rose like ridges on a monstrous waffle around each tiny field. Tall, thickly entwined hedges surmounted each bank. Their branches could reach as high as twenty feet, forming a canopy over the narrow, sunken lanes that hugged the perimeters of the fields. Sharp ditches on both sides made the roads too narrow for military vehicles to navigate and too deep for man to traverse.[32]

Above: *Men of the 8th Infantry Division approach La Haye du Puits during the splitting of the Cotentin Peninsula.*

Soon enough, the least experienced American troops, fighting what was predominantly an unseen enemy, hidden within the Normandy hedgerows, became edgy before morale collapsed entirely. Eventually the US Army would establish training camps in the Cherbourg Peninsula to train newly arrived troops on how to adapt to such conditions. However, with the British and Canadian forces fighting for their lives against the enemy's elite, the training of American troops, who surely should have already been battle ready, was a rare luxury which many would say was afforded only through the torment and sacrifice of the British and Canadian forces who were carrying the weight of the main battle to the east.

Struggling to make headway, as division after division of the enemy's infantry and armour arrived on the Commonwealth front, the Americans continued their slog through hedgerow country against a much weaker enemy which, nonetheless would fight tenaciously in exploiting every advantage the terrain would offer them. With inexperienced units failing to make headway, the situation descended into what the official American historian described as *'virtual paralysis',*[33] a bitter slog *'from field to field, from hedgerow to hedgerow, measuring progress in yards'.*[34]

As the struggle continued, the performance of the American infantry provided the Allied Command with even greater cause for concern, General Bradley once more explains; *'after three more spiritless weeks the 90th again fell on its face when two companies surrendered to the enemy and a battalion position fell... By now the division's morale had been shaken and its confidence gone'.*[35] With the American infantry failing to make headway, the American advance became ever more reliant upon the paratroopers of the 82nd Airborne Division, who, as victims of their own success, were once more called upon to succeed where the regular US Army Divisions had failed. Impressively, within just a week of taking over the advance from the 90th Infantry Division, the 82nd Airborne and the 9th Infantry Divisions advanced as far as Barneville on the peninsula's west coast, completing the partition of the peninsula.

Another Medal of Honor with its origins at this time, but not actually bestowed until decades after the battle, was that awarded to Captain Matt Urban of the 9th Infantry Division. Born to Polish immigrants as Matthew Louis Urbanowicz,

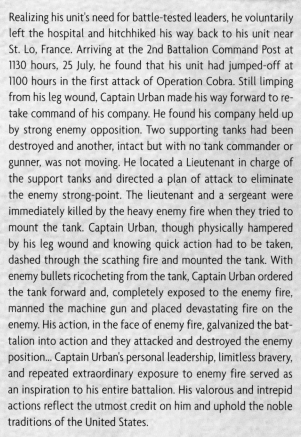

Captain
MATT URBAN
9th Infantry Division

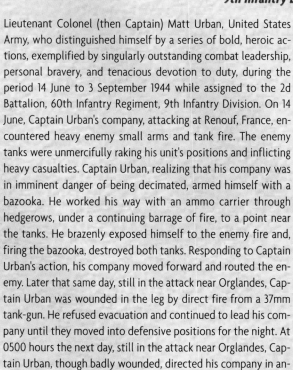

Lieutenant Colonel (then Captain) Matt Urban, United States Army, who distinguished himself by a series of bold, heroic actions, exemplified by singularly outstanding combat leadership, personal bravery, and tenacious devotion to duty, during the period 14 June to 3 September 1944 while assigned to the 2d Battalion, 60th Infantry Regiment, 9th Infantry Division. On 14 June, Captain Urban's company, attacking at Renouf, France, encountered heavy enemy small arms and tank fire. The enemy tanks were unmercifully raking his unit's positions and inflicting heavy casualties. Captain Urban, realizing that his company was in imminent danger of being decimated, armed himself with a bazooka. He worked his way with an ammo carrier through hedgerows, under a continuing barrage of fire, to a point near the tanks. He brazenly exposed himself to the enemy fire and, firing the bazooka, destroyed both tanks. Responding to Captain Urban's action, his company moved forward and routed the enemy. Later that same day, still in the attack near Orglandes, Captain Urban was wounded in the leg by direct fire from a 37mm tank-gun. He refused evacuation and continued to lead his company until they moved into defensive positions for the night. At 0500 hours the next day, still in the attack near Orglandes, Captain Urban, though badly wounded, directed his company in another attack. One hour later he was again wounded. Suffering from two wounds, one serious, he was evacuated to England. In mid-July, while recovering from his wounds, he learned of his unit's severe losses in the hedgerows of Normandy. Realizing his unit's need for battle-tested leaders, he voluntarily left the hospital and hitchhiked his way back to his unit near St. Lo, France. Arriving at the 2nd Battalion Command Post at 1130 hours, 25 July, he found that his unit had jumped-off at 1100 hours in the first attack of Operation Cobra. Still limping from his leg wound, Captain Urban made his way forward to retake command of his company. He found his company held up by strong enemy opposition. Two supporting tanks had been destroyed and another, intact but with no tank commander or gunner, was not moving. He located a Lieutenant in charge of the support tanks and directed a plan of attack to eliminate the enemy strong-point. The lieutenant and a sergeant were immediately killed by the heavy enemy fire when they tried to mount the tank. Captain Urban, though physically hampered by his leg wound and knowing quick action had to be taken, dashed through the scathing fire and mounted the tank. With enemy bullets ricocheting from the tank, Captain Urban ordered the tank forward and, completely exposed to the enemy fire, manned the machine gun and placed devastating fire on the enemy. His action, in the face of enemy fire, galvanized the battalion into action and they attacked and destroyed the enemy position... Captain Urban's personal leadership, limitless bravery, and repeated extraordinary exposure to enemy fire served as an inspiration to his entire battalion. His valorous and intrepid actions reflect the utmost credit on him and uphold the noble traditions of the United States.

Urban was a history and government graduate of Cornell University. Originally cited for the Medal of Honor in July 1944, Urban's original citation was lost as the nominating officer was killed in action. Not until 1979 was the citation found and successfully remitted, leading to Captain Urban being presented the Medal of Honor by President Carter in 1980.

The award was given for a combination of actions that took place over numerous campaigns, one of which occurred on the road to Orglandes on 14 June. Under attack from both infantry and armour, Captain Urban, armed with a bazooka, single-handedly took out two armoured vehicles before leading his unit into destroying the main part of the enemy force. Later the same day Urban would be wounded but would refuse to leave his men. Further acts of valour followed, both in France and later in Belgium. Incredibly, Urban survived all that the enemy could throw at him and is today recognised as one of the most heavily decorated American veterans of the Second World War. Matthew Urban died on 4 March 1995 aged 75. He is today buried at the Arlington National Cemetery.

Despite the very dubious start, the cutting of the peninsula was achieved by 18 June and marked the conclusion of the first half of the US Army VII Corp's second phase of operations. The verve and vigor of the 82nd Airborne, advancing alongside the 9th Infantry Division, themselves veterans of previous campaigns in North Africa and Sicily, had given the American advance renewed momentum. This successful partnership was evaluated by Colonel Kauffman who commanded the 2nd Battalion of the 60th Regiment of the 9th Division...

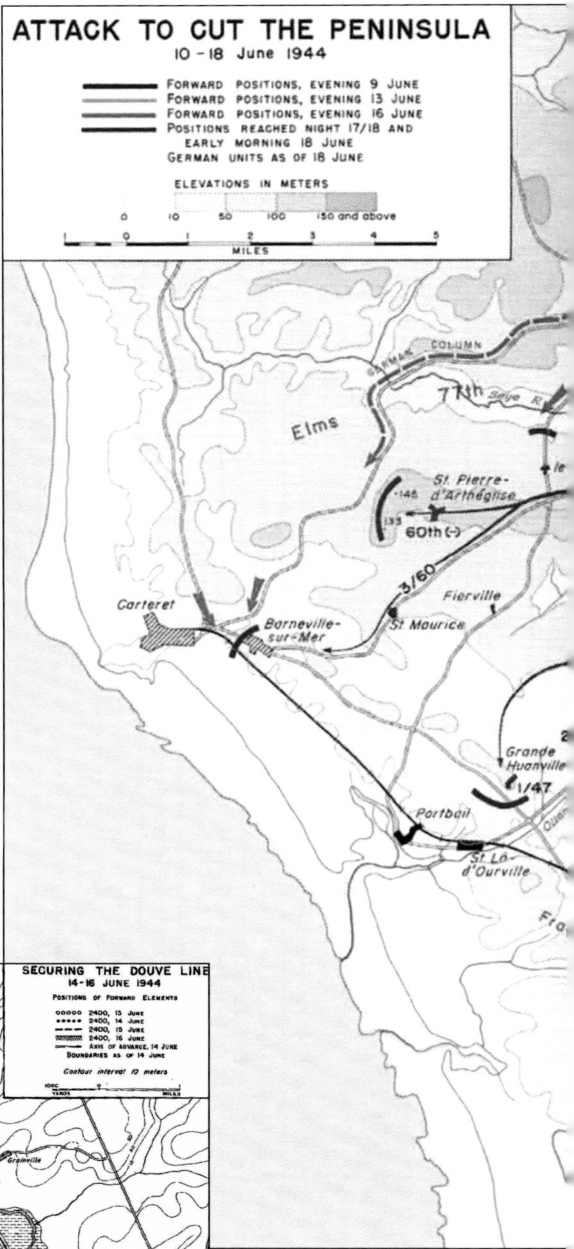

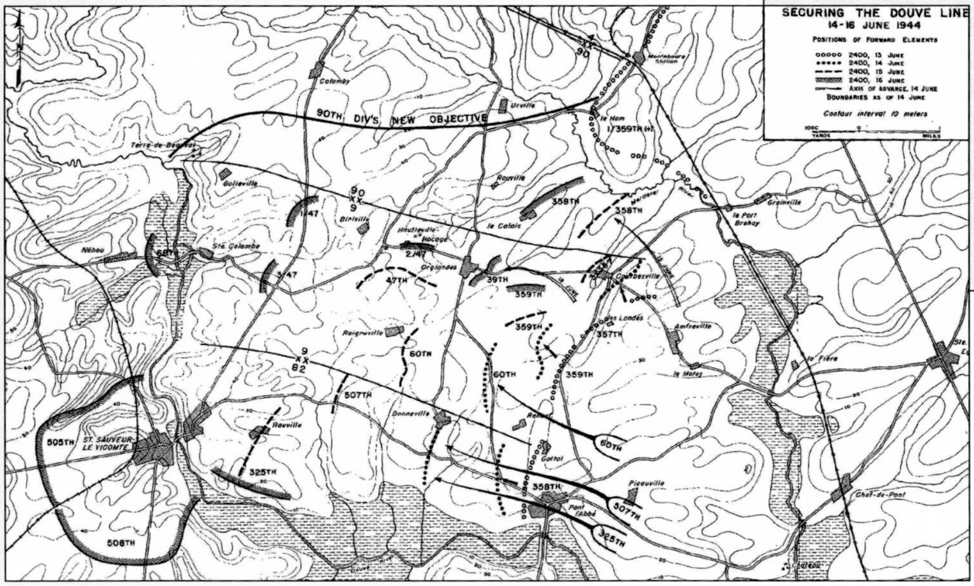

Left: *Securing the Douvres Line: 14-16 June 1944.*

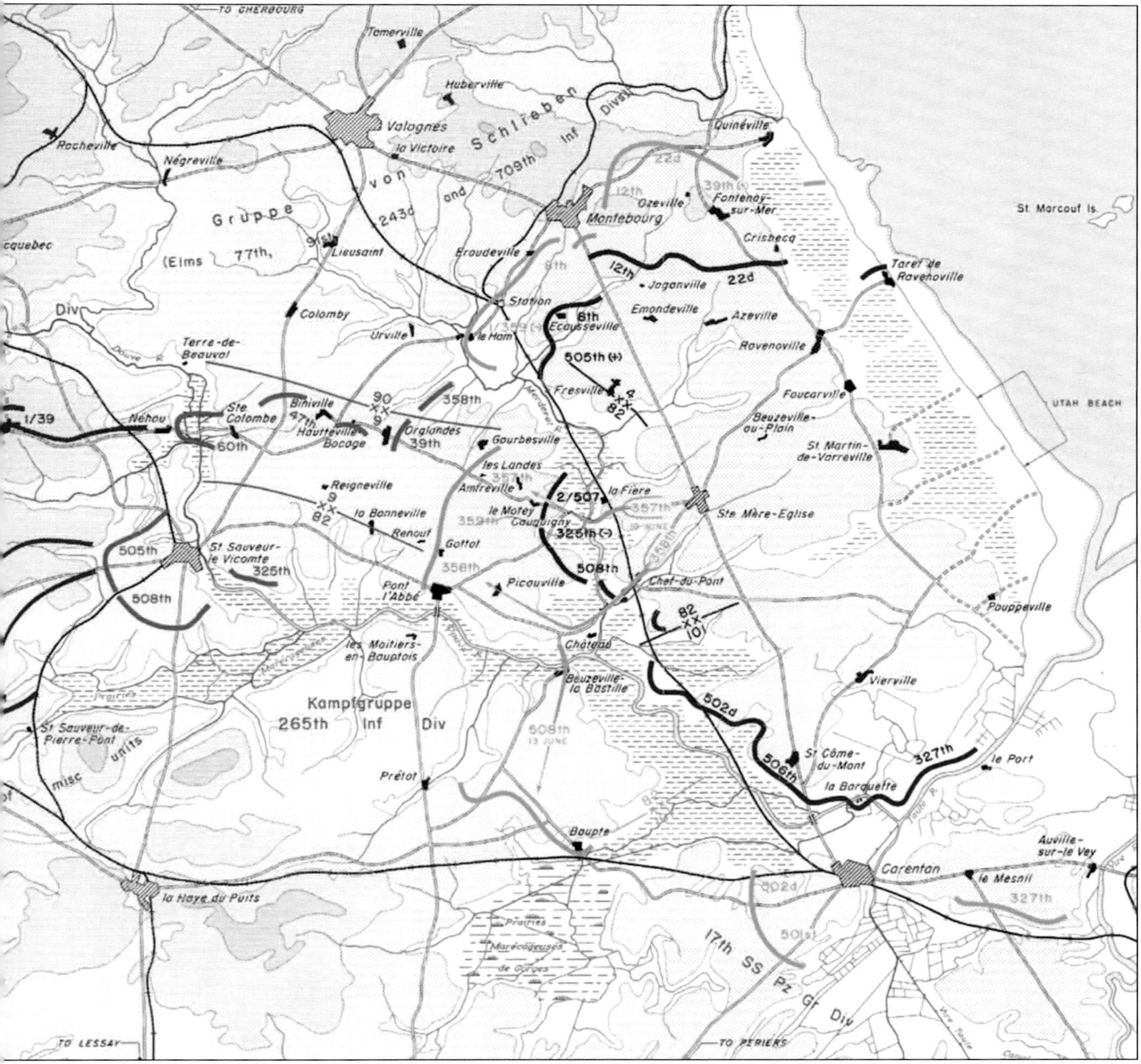

Above: *Attack to Cut the Peninsula: 10-18 June 1944.*

How did the 9th succeed so quickly where the 90th had failed? Because they did not let mortar and small arms fire pin them down; because they took their casualties and kept pushing ahead; because they were willing to ignore snipers and small pockets of resistance and to push onto the main objectives, leaving these minor if annoying matters to be cleared up later.[36]

The next stage of battle for VII Corps, fought alongside General Troy Middleton's VIII Corps, would be the approach to, and capture of the fortress port of Cherbourg.

Chapter 8

Objective Cherbourg

Having cut the peninsula, General Joseph Lawton Collins' VII Corps would now turn ninety degrees north to commence their drive upon Cherbourg. Advancing on their right would be General Troy H. Middleton's newly arrived VIII Corps. From this point the American advance would be lacking the hitherto invaluable spearhead of paratroopers, and from the off, their presence was sorely missed. Without the impetus of the elite airborne vanguard, once again the US Army's advance towards Cherbourg would struggle to make headway through the dense bocage. Encountering exactly the same problems faced earlier by Collins' men, it was now Middleton's men who were feeling the strain. This time the green troops of the 79th Division provided the gravest cause of concern, as Major Harry Herman of the 9th Infantry Division remembers...

They were almost a cruel laugh. They had one regiment attacking through our assembly area whose commander could not read a map, and they lost more men then I have ever seen through damn recruit tricks. It is quite evident that they are not prepared for combat.[37]

Below: *The Attack on Cherbourg: 22-26 June 1944.*

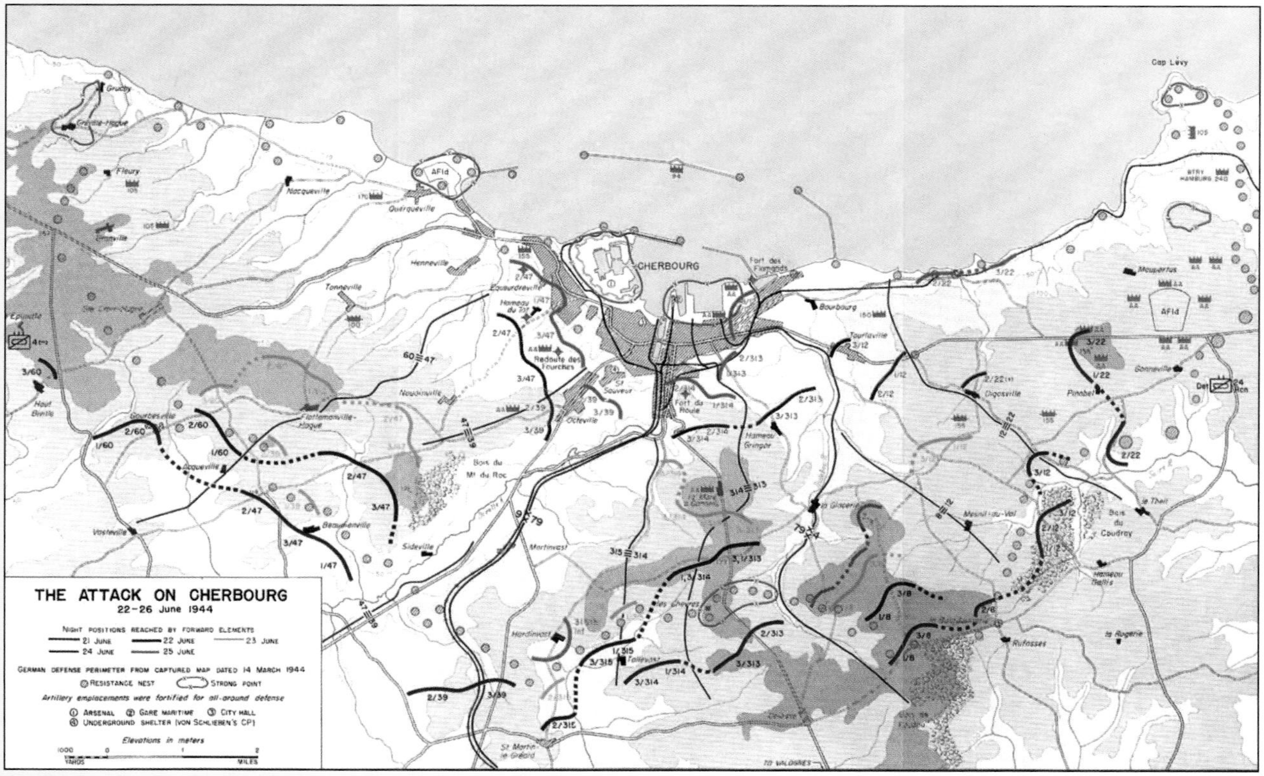

Major General Joseph Lawton Collins 1896-1987

Commander of the US Army VII Corps.

Born in New Orleans, Joseph Lawton Collins graduated from West Point alongside the likes of Matthew Ridgway, Mark Clark and Norman Cota in the class of 1917. Advancing to the rank of Major, Collins served in various capacities during the Great War, albeit exclusively on the home front. Collins' inter-war years were spent in France, Germany and then in 1933, to Manilla, returning to America in 1934. Graduating from the US Army War College in 1938, Collins then became an instructor there, a position he held at the outbreak of the war in Europe in 1939.

As America entered the war in 1941, Collins became the US Army's youngest divisional commander as he took charge of the 25th *Tropic Lightning* Infantry Division. Fighting against the Japanese on the islands of Guadalcanal and New Georgia, it was during this time that Collins became known by the nickname of *Lightning Joe*. Becoming one of very few Generals who would see action in both the Pacific and European Theatres, having impressed both Generals Eisenhower and Bradley, Collins was handpicked at 47 to become the US Army's youngest Corps Commander as he headed the US Army VII Corps during the D-Day assault. Serving with distinction, although not a General who would court the media, and therefore maybe lacking the celebrity of others, he became almost universally respected by his superiors and subordinates alike as he led VII Corps from Normandy to the end of the war in Europe.

After the war, from 1949 to 1953, Collins became the US Army's Chief of Staff, a position he held for the duration of the Korean War. Appointed as the US representative to NATO between 1953 and 1956, this position was fragmented through a brief secondment, as in 1954 he became the US representative with ambassadorial status in Vietnam. After almost 40 years serving in the US military, Collins retired in 1956. Thirteen years later he would watch his nephew, Major General Michael Collins, pilot the command module which, as part of the Apollo 11 mission, would put the first men on the moon.

General Joseph Lawton Collins died in Washington DC in 1987. He is buried in the Arlington National Cemetery.

Struggling to find their feet, the American advance gained momentum through an abundance of supporting fire. Buoyed by the seemingly unlimited amount of high explosives delivered in front of the American front line, courtesy of land, sea and air, the Americans edged north towards Cherbourg, their advance resisted by the already exhausted and much depleted remnants of the enemy's 77th, 91st, 243rd and 709th Infantry Divisions. With the route ahead saturated by artillery, the towns and villages along the American advance were raised to the ground, leaving ancient towns such as Montebourg and Valognes, nothing but burning pyres of shattered ruins.

Above: *Generals Eisenhower, Bradley and Collins photographed after the fall of Cherbourg.*
Top left: *Generals Bradley and Collins.*

Approaching the village of Flottemanville-Hague, the advance of the veteran 9th Infantry Division became blocked by a heavily fortified position on a ridge of high ground. Taking the lead, 21-year-old New Yorker, Lieutenant John Butts, would pave the way in the attempt to clear the enemy resistance centred upon the main road leading to Cherbourg from the west. Lieutenant Butts, one of six brothers, five of whom served in the war, had enlisted in the National Guard in 1939 whilst still studying at high school. In November 1942, he was commissioned as a Second Lieutenant, becoming the youngest commissioned officer in the US Army Ground Forces.

For Butts and the rest of the 9th Division, campaigns in North Africa and Sicily had already been endured. Amongst the most experienced American forces to fight in Normandy, such experience would surely tell as they approached the fortress port of Cherbourg. Already wounded during the struggle to cut the peninsula, on 23 June, Lieutenant Butts was part of a force hit by machine-gun fire. Despite his wounds, he crawled back to the relative shelter of a hedgerow in order to brief the rest of his unit as to the layout of the enemy defences before them. Wounded to the extent that he was forced to hold in his own internal organs, firing his carbine from the hip, Butts took the attention of the enemy away from the main attack as he led a solo diversionary charge. Mortally wounded just ten yards short of the German forward positions, Butt's incredible self-sacrificing solo charge had preoccupied the enemy to the extent that the main attack ultimately succeeded in flanking and eventually overwhelming the enemy strongpoint.

Killed approximately seven miles from Cherbourg, Lieutenant John Butts was first buried in the provisional Military Cemetery at Ste Mere Eglise. In 1948 his remains were repatriated to the United States. On 7 July 1948, with full military honours, Lieutenant Butts was buried in the St Mary's Cemetery in Medina, New York. Today, his Medal of Honor is displayed at the excellent Utah Beach Museum.

Second Lieutenant

JOHN E. BUTTS

9th Infantry Division

Heroically led his platoon against the enemy in Normandy, France, on 14, 16, and 23 June 1944. Although painfully wounded on 14 June near Orglandes and again on the 16 June while spearheading an attack to establish a bridgehead across the Douve River, he refused medical aid and remained with his platoon. A week later, near Flottemanville Hague, he led an assault on a tactically important and stubbornly defended hill studded with tanks, antitank guns, pillboxes, and machine gun emplacements, and protected by concentrated artillery and mortar fire. As the attack was launched, 2nd Lieutenant Butts, at the head of his platoon, was critically wounded by German machine gun fire. Although weakened by his injuries, he directed 1 Squad to make a flanking movement while he alone made a frontal assault to draw the hostile fire upon himself. Once more he was struck, but by grim determination and sheer courage continued to crawl ahead. When within 10 yards of his objective, he was killed by direct fire. By his superb courage, unflinching valour and inspiring actions, Lt. Butts enabled his platoon to take a formidable strong point and contributed greatly to the success of his battalion's mission.

As the American forces closed in on Cherbourg, Montgomery sent a communique to Bradley which included the oft-quoted declaration that *'Caen is the key to Cherbourg.'* Ridiculed by many Americans at the time and ever since, when taken in context, such a remark can be vindicated irrefutably when considering that, within 72 hours of the Allied invasion arriving on the beaches of Normandy, the main American effort, this being the advance on Cherbourg, had indeed progressed without interference from the numerous elite enemy divisions - initially scheduled to engage within the US sector, but instead switched to the Caen front. Despite the bulk of the enemy strength being deployed against the Anglo-Canadian sector in close proximity to Caen, not until the last week of June, two and a half weeks after D-Day, and ten days later than Bradley first anticipated, the American advance finally closed in on Cherbourg.

As the US forces drew ever closer, resistance stiffened as enemy troops of the fortress port manned fixed defences covering every main approach to the town; a layered system of defence as described by the US Army's official history...

On a rough semicircle, from four to six miles out from the port, the Germans had constructed a belt of fortifications varying in depth and type. Always on commanding ground, these fortifications covered all approaches. Defensive lines were often tied in with streams, which served as obstacles to tanks and self-propelled weapons. Where

Right, above: *The final occupants of the Cherbourg 'Fort du Roule' complex come out in surrender.*

Right, below: *Having taken Cherbourg, the route of the American advance was left in a state of devastation. Here Valognes, once monikered 'The Versailles of Normandy', lies in ruins.*

ALWAYS RUTH
IA-298-F

natural barriers did not form a continuous obstacle, they were supplemented by ditches, and roads were blocked with steel gates or bars... The defences were of various types. In some areas there were permanent structures of concrete, with machine-gun turrets and mortars, underground personnel shelters, and ammunition storage rooms. In other places the fortifications consisted mainly of trenches and ditches from which the Germans could fight delaying actions. Hedges were frequently cut to permit a better field of fire, and wire enclosed the fortified area. Within this ring of defensive works were many anti-aircraft positions, and as the Americans approached the Cherbourg defences the enemy made full use of these weapons for ground fire. Most German positions were clearly and accurately shown on the large-scale defence overprints issued to all commanders, but exact information on the strength of the enemy in these positions was lacking. Prisoners continually reported that their units had suffered complete disorganization.[38]

Right: *Bangalore torpedoes are used to clear wire obstacles. The same tactic was used by John Kelly during the action which subsequently led to the award of his Medal of Honor.*

Below: *Enduring such devastation, the civilian death toll would stand at up to 20,000 fatalities.*

The opposition encountered during the drive up the peninsula had to this point been relatively sporadic and offered on the whole by the remnants of an already shattered second rate enemy with little inclination to make anything but token gestures of resistance. On 24 June, as the American advance moved into the suburbs of the city, the face of battle changed as the Cherbourg garrison drew the American forces into bitter house-to-house fighting.

The fiercest resistance was centred around both the Naval Arsenal to the west of the city's harbour and also Fort du Roule, an old Napoleonic fortress, cut into the cliffs which dominate the city from the east. Although originally built in Napoleonic times, the Germans had upgraded the 19th century site into a seemingly impenetrable fortress. The Fort du Roule complex included, not just the usual array of minefields protecting the mélange of mortars and machine guns covering any possible approach, but also a myriad of subterranean tunnels within the cliff itself. This facility accommodated a military hospital, troop barracks, ammunition chambers and a headquarters for command and communications as well as a battery of four 105mm guns, capable of firing at a range of up to ten miles from embrasures cut into the cliff-face, all topped by a battery of anti-aircraft guns positioned 300 feet above the town's port.

It was against Fort du Roule, on 25 June, that two Americans would partake in two separate but related struggles which would lead to them both receiving their nation's highest award. Twenty-one-year-old Corporal John Kelly from Cambridge Springs, Pennsylvania, had joined the army two years to the day before he landed at Utah Beach. Now, two weeks after arriving in Normandy, he and his unit were pinned down under machine-gun fire emanating from the southern approach to the Fort du Roule strongpoint. With seemingly no way forward, Kelly braved heavy fire in order to connect ten-foot long pole charges to blocks of high explosives at the

Corporal

JOHN D. KELLY

79th Infantry Division

For conspicuous gallantry and intrepidity at the risk of his life above and beyond the call of duty. On 25 June 1944, in the vicinity of Fort du Roule, Cherbourg, France, when Cpl. Kelly's unit was pinned down by heavy enemy machine gun fire emanating from a deeply entrenched strongpoint on the slope leading up to the fort, Cpl. Kelly volunteered to attempt to neutralize the strongpoint. Arming himself with a pole charge about 10 feet long and with 15 pounds of explosive affixed, he climbed the slope under a withering blast of machine gun fire and placed the charge at the strongpoint's base. The subsequent blast was ineffective, and again, alone and unhesitatingly, he braved the slope to repeat the operation. This second blast blew off the ends of the enemy guns. Cpl. Kelly then climbed the slope a third time to place a pole charge at the strongpoint's rear entrance. When this had been blown open he hurled hand grenades inside the position, forcing survivors of the enemy gun crews to come out and surrender. The gallantry, tenacity of purpose, and utter disregard for personal safety displayed by Cpl. Kelly were an incentive to his comrades and worthy of emulation by all.

base of an enemy pillbox. With the first charge failing, and a second attempt only partially effective, Kelly made a third solo run to place charges at the base of the pillbox, an act which ultimately enabled him to storm the ensuing positions. With a combination of hand grenades, cold steel and even colder blood, Kelly forced the surrender of the remaining enemy troops within this position.

John Kelly would survive the battle for Normandy, only to be fatally wounded in November 1944. He is buried at the Epinal American Cemetery, France.

First Lieutenant

CARLOS C. OGDEN

79th Infantry Division

On the morning of 25 June 1944, near Fort du Roule, guarding the approaches to Cherbourg, France, 1st Lieutenant Ogden's company was pinned down by fire from a German 88mm gun and 2 machine guns. Arming himself with an M1 rifle, a grenade launcher, and a number of rifle and hand grenades, he left his company in position and advanced alone, under fire, up the slope toward the enemy emplacements. Struck on the head and knocked down by a glancing machine gun bullet, 1st Lieutenant Ogden, in spite of his painful wound and enemy fire from close range, continued up the hill. Reaching a vantage point, he silenced the 88mm gun with a well-placed rifle grenade and then, with hand grenades, knocked out the 2 machine guns, again being painfully wounded. 1st Lieutenant Ogden's heroic leadership and indomitable courage in alone silencing these enemy weapons inspired his men to greater effort and cleared the way for the company to continue the advance and reach its objectives.

On the same day, and during the same battle, less than a mile away from where Corporal Kelly carried out his inspirational act of valour, another incredible individual feat of arms was undertaken by 27-year-old Lieutenant Carlos Ogden of Barton, Illinois.

Approaching the heights of the Fort du Roule complex from the west, pinned down under fire and with his Company Commander lying dead beside him, Lieutenant Ogden took the initiative in a one-man charge against two machine-gun nests protecting a concrete casemate containing an 88mm gun. Leaving a position of cover, armed with rifle grenades, he doggedly advanced against the enemy. In his own words…

We were tied down and were going to get killed, and I thought I might as well get killed going forward as back… Two bullets went through my helmet… They grazed my head and knocked me down.[39]

Moving forward, Ogden destroyed both machine-gun nests and the 88mm gun. Although seriously wounded during this action, Ogden would survive the war and live until 2001, before succumbing to cancer aged 83. He is buried at the Arlington National Cemetery, Virginia.

The struggle for Cherbourg would continue within the heart of the town for four long days. By 26 June, as artillery and bombs pounded the ground above and beside them, hundreds of personnel drawn from every branch of the German forces were confined to the dark tunnels and subterranean caves within the Fort du Roule complex. Only as American tanks were positioned directly at the entrance to the fort, did General Karl Dietrich von Schlieben surrender the Napoleonic fortress that harboured 800 of his men. Although the surrender was signed on 26 June, resistance from die-hard fanatics making their determined, yet inevitably futile, last stand around the main port and the naval arsenal would continue for another 72 hours.

Although Cherbourg was fully in American hands by the end of June, the Germans had carried out such a thorough demolition job of the port facilities that it would not be until September, by which time the advance had moved on to Belgium, that the port of Cherbourg became anywhere near fully operational.

Above right: *German prisoners escorted out of the fortress port of Cherbourg.* **Below right:** *The taking of the Fort Roule complex would lead to the award of two Medals of Honor.*

CHERBOURG

Chapter 9

How the West was Won

Albeit later than anticipated, in taking Cherbourg, General Collins secured the headlines for ensuring the Allies' first tangible post D-Day victory. Meanwhile, in the British Commonwealth Sector, within thirty-six hours of the first Allied troops landing in Normandy, whilst maintaining his core-strategy, Montgomery immediately changed his tactical approach. The 21st Panzer Division was already holding a firm grip on Caen from the east and north, when on 7 June, the fanatical 12th SS *Hitler Jugend* Division joined the fray. Although first intending to combine with the 21st Panzer Division in counter-attacking against the British and Canadian troops to the east of the Allied bridgehead, attacks from the Commonwealth forces obliged the German elite into adopting a blocking strategy from the north and immediate west.

On 8 June, the Panzer Lehr Division, having been forced to abandon its own planned offensive, was likewise forced onto the back foot in attempting to contain the British forces who were approaching Caen from the west. Making it clear that a frontal assault would not just prove incredibly costly in terms of casualties, but also very unlikely to gain ground, Montgomery judged that Operation Perch, a flanking manoeuvre which threatened Caen from the south and west, would provide the necessary amount of pressure to keep both existing, and any newly arriving units, fixed to the Caen front, where he wanted them, away from the Americans to the west.

Having liberated the city of Bayeux on 7 June, the British 50th Division encountered fierce opposition on its subsequent approach to the town of Tilly sur Suelles. This enemy resistance would be the British forces first contact with the most elite regular German Army formation to fight in the entire war.

The Panzer Lehr was formed in January 1944 and drew its strength solely from the elite of Germany's tank commanders and instructing staff. These outstanding individuals, representing the cream of the crop of the German Wehrmacht, had been brought together from numerous staff colleges to form a single fighting formation. Although the following appraisal of the Panzer Lehr was made by its own Commanding Officer, General Fritz Bayerlein, an individual whose evaluation may not be the most objective, it is worthwhile to consider the cadre of this and the other formations engaged during the battle for Caen…

The Panzer Lehr *Division was the best equipped Panzer Division that Germany ever had. It was 100% armoured; even the infantry was completely armoured so that in case of counter-attack they would not suffer casualties from splinters and shrapnel, artillery, or infantry weapons. The armoured infantry travelled in Schuetzenpanzerwagen (halftracks). All this was because of our unique mission of throwing the invading Allies back into the sea. It was planned to make this the best panzer division that existed.*[40]

Bayerlein's *Panzer Lehr* joined the battle for Caen on 8 June, twenty-four hours after the arrival of the 12th SS *Hitlerjugend* Division, which had recruited the fittest and most fervent members from the Hitler Youth movement. Often referred to as *The*

Class of 1926, much of the rank and file of the 12th SS were 18-year-old boy soldiers, brimming with the dogma of National Socialism that had indoctrinated them from the age of seven. Such fanaticism was entrenched through the Division's NCOs and ranking officers, the majority of whom were former members of the 1st SS *Leibstandarte* Division (originally formed as Adolf Hitler's personal bodyguard). The amalgamation of the 12th SS fighting alongside *Panzer Lehr* embodied the cream of the German Army to fight in Normandy, if not the whole of the war, and represented the Germans most determined, and indeed most likely, option for defeating the Allies in Normandy.

Meeting the enemy's elite head on, the British and Canadian forces, fighting through some of the same restrictive bocage terrain faced by the Americans to the west, not just defeated the enemy's most determined attempts to break the invasion, but also made inroads into an enemy line, which in the following weeks would be

Below: *British forces fight their way through the bocage south of Bayeux.*

held, not just by the largest build-up of German armour since the battle for Kursk, but also the greatest concentration of Waffen SS Forces to face the Western Allies during the whole of the Second World War.

The month of June progressed and, as per Montgomery's strategy, the British and Canadian forces continued their crucial, yet seemingly thankless task. The 716th Infantry Division and 21st Panzer Division were first engaged on D-Day, however by the time Cherbourg had fallen, the enemy had also committed to the Caen sector the 346th and 711th Infantry Divisions, the 1st SS, 2nd SS, 9th SS, 10th SS and 12th SS *Panzer* Divisions, the 2nd *Panzer* Division and the *Panzer Lehr* Division. These elite formations were supplemented with the arrival of the 3rd Flak-Corps, the 7th, 8th and 9th *Werfer* Brigades and the infamous Tiger tanks of the 101st and 102nd SS Heavy Tank Battalions; all first deployed against the British and Canadians within just a few miles from the city of Caen. In the same timeframe, on a front more than three times the width, only the 3rd *Fallschirmjaeger* Division, the 17th SS *Panzer Grenadier* Division and the 77th and 275th Infantry Divisions had been deployed against the American sector.

To draw, and indeed hold, the clear majority of the enemy's reserves to their sector, the British and Canadians would not just defend the eastern half of the beachhead, but also mount offensive operations designed to tie down and glue those forces to their front and away from the American sector. This reality is far from the circumstances as portrayed by the likes of the American popular historian Stephen Ambrose who once put into print '*Montgomery had said he would take the city on D-Day, but he had not, nor did he do so in the following ten days. Nor was he attacking*'.[41]

Left: *Lane by lane, hedgerow by hedgerow – Bradley's forces face their bitter slog through the Normandy hedgerows.*

Although Ambrose died in 2004, there has been no shortage of American pundits who are seemingly predisposed, if not downright determined in picking up the baton and continuing the regurgitation of such myths. In recent years, the Pulitzer prize-winning Rick Atkinson, not a trained historian but a former journalist, now famed for his self-titled 'Liberation Trilogy', a collection of works now largely regarded in America as the definitive history of America's War, describes the British performance during the battle for Caen as 'feeble' and 'clumsy'. [42]

Above: *Men of the British 49th Infantry Division inspect a knocked-out Tiger tank.*

Such ludicrous and frankly offensive accusations, so commonplace amongst the ranks of a certain breed of popular historian, have, even in recent years, infiltrated the world of academia. Olivier Wieviorka, eminent Professor of History at the École Normale Supérieure Paris-Saclay, who has had books on the subject published by institutions such as the University of Yale Press and the Harvard University Press, can be quoted as stating…

Realising that Montgomery was able, neither to take Caen, nor break down the German defences… Disappointed with this [British] inability to complete an important strategic move, the Americans took over control of operations around Caen.[43]

The Americans took over operations around Caen? The German defences remained unbroken? Such deluded remarks hardly reflect the reality of the battle, yet are touted as fact by one of France's leading academics.

Yet another example of distorted history, touted in France as being the definitive documentary telling the story of D-Day and the Battle for Normandy, the 2014 French production *La lumière de l'aube* (The light of dawn) does nothing but add to the myth…

After five weeks of failure the British finally take the D-Day objective of Caen. Inevitably Monty took the plaudits - in the world of the blind, the one-eyed man is king! [44]

Such ignorance has only served to detract from the efforts of the forces who liberated those, who themselves may be wise remembering, were unable to help themselves. Indeed, not only were the British and Canadian forces foiling the enemy's principal and most concentrated efforts of defeating the invasion, by doing so, the Commonwealth forces were tying down well over three quarters of the enemy's reserves in of-

Below: *The situation on 30 June 1944.*

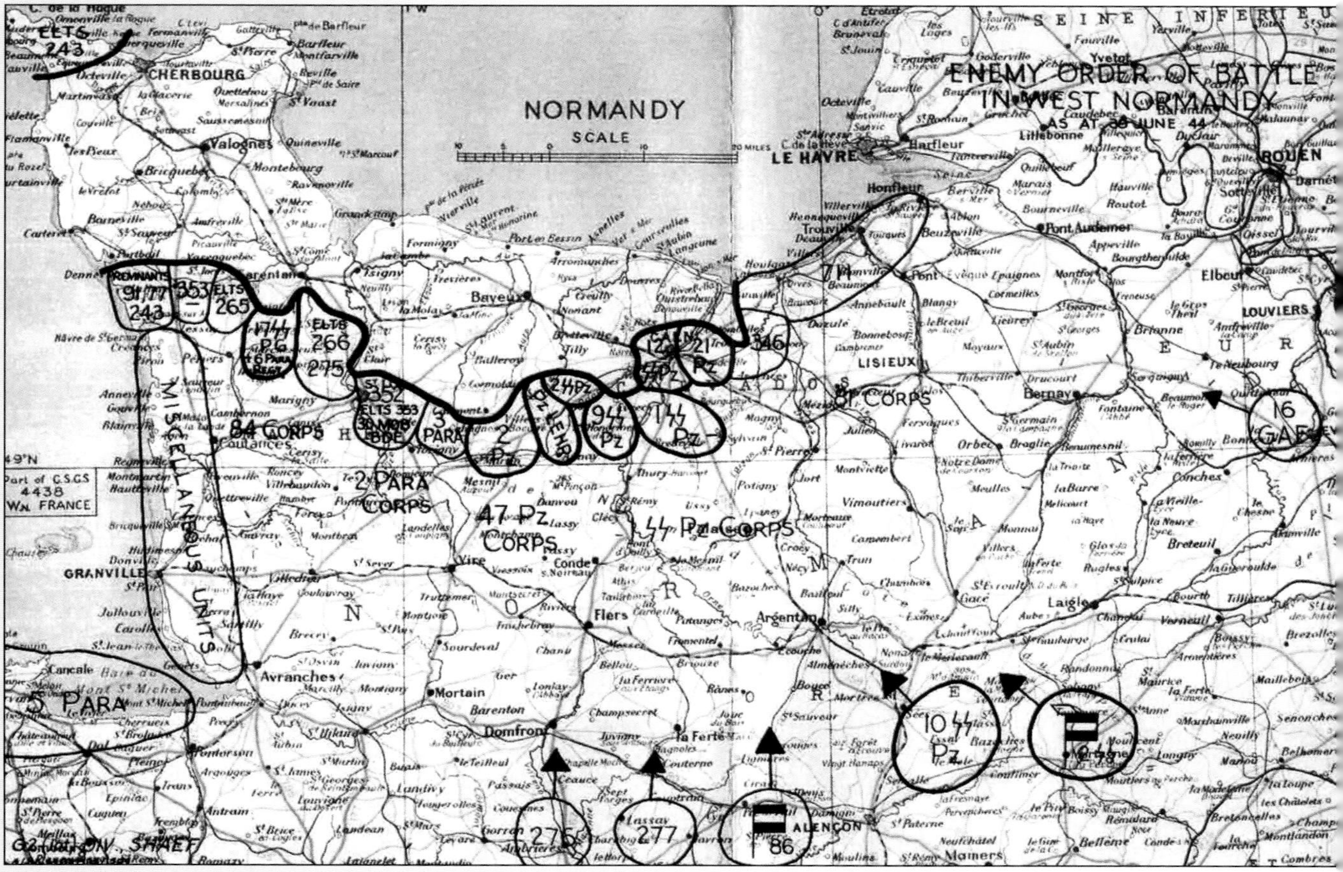

fensive actions so that they were unable to move against the Americans. This fact was observed by General Fritz Bayerlein when remarking on the condition of his own forces just five days after D-Day, comments which prove the accusations by the likes of Ambrose, Atkinson and Wievoirka to be truly absurd...

The British counter attacked... My chance to drive to the sea was lost... We had lost about 100 tanks to the British. Half my striking force was gone.[45]

All hope the Germans had in defeating the invasion had been crushed, not by the Americans fighting in the hedgerows of the Cotentin peninsula, but by the Anglo-Canadian coalition fighting between Bayeux and Caen, as Colonel Helmut Ritgen who served with the *Panzer Lehr* in Normandy stated...

[By 10 June] ... *the only classic armoured attack conducted by the Panzer Lehr Division in Normandy was at an end. At the same time, the attempt to thwart the enemy... and regain the initiative finally failed.* [46]

Above: *The young soldiers of the 12 SS Hitler Jugend defend the western approach to Caen.*

Montgomery's premeditated plan, of holding the bulk of the Germans to the east, to enable the breakout to the west, was a strategy outlined months before D-Day. As the battle progressed, those unaware of the masterplan became disillusioned with what appeared at face value to be nothing more than stalemate in the making. Consequently, a huge myth was born. Amazingly, and scandalously, this myth still exists today. The Allies could never correct such a falsehood at the time, lest risk giving away their grand strategy. Yet, despite numerous explanations offered either shortly after the battle, or in the immediate years after the war, still, almost eight decades after Montgomery delivered victory in Normandy, misinformation blights and degrades the history of his reputation and those who fought under him. Any such controversy could and should have been put to bed decades ago if only historians could have referred to the archives, or taken on the words such as these from General Bradley's 1951 autobiography entitled *'A Soldier's Story'...*

While Collins was hoisting his VII Corps flag over Cherbourg, Montgomery was spending his reputation in a bitter siege against the old university city of Caen. For three weeks he had rammed his troops against those panzer divisions he had deliberately drawn towards that city as part of our strategy of diversion in the Normandy Campaign. Although Caen contained an important road junction that Montgomery would eventually need, for the moment the capture of that city was only incidental to his mission. For Monty's primary task was to attract German troops to the British front that we might more easily secure Cherbourg and get into position for the breakout... In this diversionary mission Monty was more than successful, for the harder he hammered towards Caen, the more German troops he drew into that sector.

Too many correspondents however, had overrated the importance of Caen itself, and when Monty failed to take it, they blamed him for the delay. But had we attempted to exonerate Montgomery by explaining how successfully he had hoodwinked the German by diverting him toward Caen from the Cotentin, we would have also given our strategy away. We desperately wanted the German to believe this attack on Caen was the main effort.

Monty's success should have been measured in the panzer divisions the enemy rushed against him whilst Collins sped on toward Cherbourg. Instead, the newspaper readers clamoured for a place name called Caen, which Monty had once promised but failed to win for them.

In the minds of most people, success in battle is measured in the rate and length of advance. They found it difficult to realise that the more successful Monty was in stirring up German resistance, the less likely he was to advance. For another four weeks it fell to the British to pin down superior enemy forces in that sector while we manoeuvred into position for the US breakout.[47]

Even if Bradley's memoirs were not enough to silence the doubters, by the time of their publication, Monty's strategy had already been endorsed in print by General Eisenhower, who in his 1946 official report on Operations in North West Europe, stated...

Our strategy, in the light of these German reactions, was to hit hard in the east in order to contain the enemy main strength there while consolidating our position in the west. The resulting struggle around Caen, which seemed to cost so much blood for such small territorial gains, was thus an essential factor in ensuring our ultimate success. The very tenacity of the defence there was sufficient proof of this. As I told the press correspondents at the end of August, every foot of ground the enemy lost at Caen was like losing ten miles anywhere else.[48]

It has been argued that after the war, Montgomery contrived to adapt his premeditated plan to fit the eventual outcome of the battle. Again, such an accusation can be instantly discredited by inspecting the communiqués published at the time. For example, on 8 June, Monty wrote to Alanbrooke (Chief of the British Imperial General Staff)...

The Germans are doing everything they can to hold on to Caen. I have decided not to have a lot of casualties by butting up against the place; so I have ordered Second Army to keep up a good pressure at Caen, and to make its main effort towards Villers Bocage and Evrecy and thence SE towards Falaise.[49]

To state, as Ambrose does, that the British were not launching offensive actions during this time simply belies the most basic inspection of the reality of the battle, as Monty wrote to his assistant Freddy de Guingand on 9 June ...

If the Germans wish to be offensive and drive into our lodgment area between Caen and Bayeux, the best way to defeat them is to be offensive ourselves and the plan given will checkmate the enemy completely if we can pull it off.[50]

Long before the invasion was launched, Montgomery held an appreciation of how his grand strategy would develop and recorded in his diary two weeks before D-Day...

Above: *The 15th Scottish Division advance during Operation Epsom.*

So long as Rommel has to use his strategic reserves to plug holes, then we have done well.[50]

Such a strategy undoubtedly achieved the desired effect. On 10 June Rommel reported… *'The enemy has complete control over the battle'.*[51] Such dominance was further emphasised on 21 June by *Brigadefuhrer* Kurt Meyer of the 12th SS H*itler Jugend*…

Without talking about it openly we knew we were approaching a catastrophe. The static type of fighting in the murderous bridgehead north of the Orne would inevitably lead to the destruction of the panzer divisions deployed there... The tactical 'fixing' along the battlefield had cost us the irreplaceable blood of our best soldiers.[53]

Despite having been in contact against the British and Canadians for less than four days, Meyer's report confirms the desperate situation that the I SS Panzer Corps was facing, a situation outlined by *Generalmajor* Fritz Kraemer (Deputy Commander of the I SS Panzer Corps)…

By 11 June the three divisions controlled by Corps had been considerably weakened… In percentages, the losses were as follows…

21st Panzer Division: [at this point having been engaged exclusively within the Commonwealth Sector for no more than 5 days] *killed, wounded and missing in action – about forty per cent; put out of action – guns, about thirty per cent; tanks, about fifty per cent. The number of Type IV and V tanks fit for action, held by the division, was approximately 30/40* [The archive of the 21st Panzer Division states that on 1 June, the division held a strength of 98 Type IV and Type V tanks [52] – this means approximately forty per cent of the division's armour had been lost in the first five days in their struggle fought exclusively against British or Canadian troops].

12th SS Panzer Division: [at this point having been engaged exclusively within the Commonwealth Sector for just 4 days] *killed, wounded or missing in action – about twenty-five per cent; put out of action – guns, about ten per cent; tanks, about twenty per cent. About sixty Type IV and V tanks were fit for action* [The 12th SS archive states that on 1 June, the division held a strength of 146 Type IV and Type V tanks[55] – this means approximately forty per cent of the division's armour had been lost in the first four days in their struggle fought exclusively against British or Canadian troops].

Panzer Lehr Division: [at this point having been engaged exclusively against the Commonwealth Sector for just 3 days] *killed, wounded or missing in action – about twenty-five per cent; put out of action – guns, about ten per cent; tanks, about twenty per cent. About sixty Type IV and V tanks were fit for action* [The Panzer Lehr archive states that on 1 June 1944, the Division held a strength of 237 tanks and assault guns[56] – this means approximately sixty per cent of the Division's armour had been lost in the first three days in their struggle fought exclusively against British or Canadian troops].[57]

By the end of the first week of operations, Monty's masterplan was already in full effect, a fact confirmed by General Bradley...

By the evening of 12 June, we (1st US Army) had celebrated our first week ashore without a single threatening counter-attack on the American Beachhead. Only the British had been hit by panzers in their advance towards Caen.[58]

British and Canadian offensive actions to the east were not just blunting the ability of the Germans to counter the invasion, but were doing so in a way which greatly impressed the enemy's high command as to the efficiency and dexterity of movement shown by the coalition of Anglo-Canadian troops. In the words of Rommel's Chief of Staff...

There was no determined (German) counter-offensive on the days following the 11 June and the Panzer forces under steadily increasing pressure from the British armored divisions were forced into the defensive...[59] *The British divisions were switching the weight of their attack with lightning rapidity.*[60]

Throughout the first month of operations the British and Canadians held everything the Germans threw at them. Despite not being able to gain much in the way of ground, Montgomery's strategy of tying down the bulk of the enemy in the east continued to assist the Americans as they manoeuvred their way into position for breakout. Operations such as Perch, Martlet, Epsom, Charnwood and Goodwood would all be launched with the strategic aim of not just holding the majority of the enemy to the Caen Sector, but ensuring any new arrivals were drawn there too.

Above: *Hans von Luck (commander of the 125th Panzer Grenadier Regiment of the 21st Panzer Division) is briefed during the battle for Caen.*

Whilst all of these operations set tactical objectives of advancing to positions that may not have been reached, which could therefore lead them to be credibly adjudicated as tactical failures, there is no doubt, as the German strength remained glued to the front held almost exclusively by the British and Canadians, that these operations were overall, outstanding strategic successes. Looking at contemporary sources it is also clear to see that tactical failures were acceptable, and indeed likely, and that this could be readily accepted as long as the main strategy remained intact. Indeed, much later in the campaign, on the eve of Operation Bluecoat and the American breakout in the west, Montgomery's orders stated, *'along the whole front now held by the First Canadian and Second British Armies it was essential that the enemy be attacked to the greatest degree possible.'* Realising the strength of the enemy within this sector, Montgomery went on to state that *'any large-scale operations by us in that sector are highly unlikely to succeed.'*[61] Once again, tactical success was irrelevant as long as the main strategy prevailed. Unfortunately, there were at the time, and

have since continued to be, far too many commentators determined to focus on tactical failure, rather than admit that as long as operations were strategically successful, then the tactical outcome is essentially irrelevant. Given the fact that the Americans were facing only a minority of the enemy's might, it was always going to be the case that they would be make greater territorial gains in the west compared to the Commonwealth forces in the east. It is unfortunate that those without an understanding of Montgomery's strategic intent, or those who wish to manipulate the situation for ulterior, perhaps chauvinistic motives, give the impression that American forces succeeded where the Commonwealth operations failed. However, let the words of General Bradley not be forgotten...

In the minds of most people, success in battle is measured in the rate and length of advance. They found it difficult to realise that the more successful Monty was in stirring up German resistance, the less likely he was to advance.[62]

In the words of Brigadier General Denis Whitaker, himself a Normandy veteran...

It was on the Caen front that the British and Canadian troops were not only struggling against much of the fiercest opposition, at an enormous sacrifice of lives, but they – and Monty – were getting nothing but biting criticism in return. SHAEF (Supreme Headquarters Allied Expeditionary Force) commanders, the media, and, later, historians all denounced the British and Canadians for their "slow, feeble performance."[63]

This is not to say that Montgomery was completely without fault. As far as he was concerned, he had supreme confidence in his strategy; this had been defined and was clearly understood by Bradley, as it was Dempsey. In fact, no subordinate commander within Montgomery's immediate circle of command had any negative issue with the way the battle was being fought. Those who did have the problem were those who were detached from the battlefield, mainly within the administrative hierarchy of SHAEF, an organisation whose desk Generals were still primarily headquartered back in England. It has to be said that whilst Monty liaised extremely effectively with his subordinates in the field, there can be no denying there was a distinct lack of communication up the chain of command. Some have argued, with great credibility, that this was due to a lack of respect. As far as Monty was concerned keeping the *'higher ups'* in the picture did not matter; the less they knew, the less they would interfere. It is therefore not surprising, and not insignificantly down to Montgomery himself, that it was at this time, tensions amongst the coalition increased.

An additional factor which did not help the Allies in getting about their work without unnecessary interruption was the fact that the American media were focusing on this particular battle with an unprecedented vigour. One former officer stated that it was only the America journal 'Dog World' which had missed out on dispatching a correspondent to the Normandy battlefields.[64] Ignorant to the strategy, and with the Allies unable to provide an explanation, less they give away their intent, the American media started to portray a situation where it was solely the Americans who were taking the lead in defeating the enemy. Reports circulated that whilst British and Canadian forces were lying idle, drinking tea and suffering far fewer casualties, it

Left: *The fanatical young soldiers of the 12th SS Hitler Youth Division would prove to be some of the most determined foe any Allied force would face during the Second World War.*

Major General Troy Middleton 1889-1976

Commander of US Army VIII Corps.

Born on a Mississippi plantation in 1889, having failed to gain admission into West Point, in 1910 Troy Houston Middleton enlisted in the US Army with the rank of Private. Two years later, having completed officer training, he attained the rank of Second Lieutenant, becoming a battalion, then regimental commander for the 4th Infantry Division during the Great War. Commanding his men during the Second Battle of the Marne and the Verdun offensive, by the end of the Great War, Middleton had forged a solid reputation as he became the youngest Colonel within the American Expeditionary Force. After the Great War, Middleton took various instructive positions within the US Army's War College and Command and General Staff School. Retiring from the military in 1937, Middleton became Dean, then Vice-President of Louisiana State University.

Recalled to service following America's entry into the Second World War, Middleton commanded the 45th Infantry Division during the 1943 invasions of Sicily and Salerno. Forced to relinquish command of the 45th Division due to an old knee injury, Middleton returned to America in late 1943 before being recalled to Europe in early 1944 having been personally selected by Eisenhower to command the US Army VIII Corps during the battle for Normandy, Eisenhower purportedly stating, *"I don't give a damn about his knees; I want his head and his heart... I'll take him into battle on a litter if we have to"*.

Commanding VIII Corps through Normandy and Brittany, the most celebrated moment of Middleton's military career arrived as, against the initial wishes of his Third Army superior, he oversaw the determined resistance of the town of Bastogne during the infamous Battle of the Bulge. Later leading his forces across the Rhine and then as far as the border with Czechoslovakia, in logging a total of 480 days of active command, Troy Middleton would become the most experienced American General during the Second World War. As one of Eisenhower's favourite Corps Commanders, and certainly as one of the most battle hardened American Generals of the Second World War, Middleton's steady if not spectacular record led to many accolades, one of which came from Eisenhower who cited Middleton not just as one of the best Corps Commanders of the Second World War, but a General worthy of command of a full army.

After the war, Middleton returned to Louisiana State University, serving 11 years as University President. Troy Houston Middleton died in 1976 aged 86 and is buried at the Baton Rouge National Cemetery.

was the Americans doing all the fighting and taking all the losses. Incredibly, this opinion was seemingly shared by the Supreme Commander, who in a letter to Montgomery dated 21 July stated...

While we have equality in size we must go forward shoulder to shoulder, with honours and sacrifices equally shared.[65]

Although at face value such words may seem rather innocuous, it became clear within the central circle of the Allied Command's highest echelons that Eisenhower shared the sentiment that the British were not pulling their weight, a suspicion endorsed by a letter sent to Montgomery from Alanbrooke on 28 July...

Ike lunched with the PM again this week and as a result I was sent for by PM and told that Ike was worried at the outlook taken by the American Press that the British were not taking their share of the fighting and of the casualties... It is quite clear that Ike considers that Dempsey should be doing more than he does - it is equally clear that Ike has the very vaguest conception of war![66]

Such news clearly irritated Montgomery who in his response to Alanbrooke, temporarily abandoned his usual respect for the American soldier and retaliated...

The C.I.G.S. told me that there was talk in certain circles that the Americans were doing all the fighting and having all the casualties, and the British were not doing their fair share. This is amazing. The bigger American casualties are due to their lack of skill in fighting.[67]

Tensions amongst the Allies continued to escalate. Frustrations mounted as it became palpable that British efforts were becoming increasingly degraded while the American effort was being exaggerated beyond all recognition of the reality of the actual battle, as the British Secretary of State for War wrote to Montgomery on 1 August, 1944...

The Americans at the best of times would do their damnedest to write down our effort and write up their own, to laud others and diminish you.[68]

Of course the claims of the British not going forward *'shoulder to shoulder, with honours and sacrifices equally shared'* were quite absurd. In suffering an average 2,354 casualties per day, the British Army was in fact losing more men in Normandy than were lost during the infamous Third Battle of Ypres during the Great War (casualties here are recorded at an average of 2,324 per day).[69] Seven weeks after D-Day, of the 591,000 Commonwealth troops who had joined the fray, 49,000 (8.2 per cent) had become casualties. Of the 770,000 Americans deployed, 73,000 (9.5 per cent) casualties had been suffered - hardly a disparity worthy of scandal and even more remarkable that Eisenhower himself should therefore feel inclined to directly approach Montgomery and suggest that the British Army should maybe try a little harder in losing more casualties in order to pacify the baying hacks of the American media.

Such comments must have stuck in the throat of many and were particularly galling coming as they did for the British and Canadians during the fifty-seventh month of their war, yet also in the very first month of the entire war that American forces had outnumbered their Commonwealth brethren in the fight against Nazi Germany.

As Generals Collins and Middleton were labouring their way up the Cotentin Peninsula, the American forces that had landed on Omaha were slogging their way through the hedgerows on the road to St Lo. This city, a medieval county capital at the centre of the local road network, represented an objective that would have to be secured before the Americans could manoeuvre in anticipation of breakout. The cruel irony of the enduring perception of the battle for Normandy is of the apparent slowness on the British front holding up proceedings to the west. In reality, the most detrimental delays were in fact being suffered within the American sector.

Given the recent launch of the Soviet summer offensive on the Eastern Front, by the end of June Montgomery realised that the deployment in the Commonwealth Sector of the 9th and 10th SS Divisions from the Russian front meant that pretty much all the troops the Germans had to commit were already now in Normandy and that from this point on the German Army facing the Western Allies would only ever become weaker, while at the same time the Allied strength would only increase. Although such intelligence could never be disclosed to the Press, at this point it seems remarkable that for those commentators who had been informed that the battle for Normandy would be anticipated to last for a duration of three months, that they should now be pronouncing stalemate after only three weeks!

More remarkable than the stinging criticism originating from the media, is the fact that Montgomery found himself having to justify his strategy to his own Supreme Commander, a man who was evidently becoming influenced more by public opinion and the Press than reports from his own generals in the field. At this time Montgomery, not a man usually renowned for his tact, remained calm and dignified, as he wrote to Eisenhower on 8 July…

I think the battle is going very well. The enemy is being heavily attacked all along the line; and we are killing a lot of Germans… Of one thing you can be quite sure – there will be no stalemate… If the enemy decides to concentrate very great and overwhelming strength against us, that will take a considerable time; and during that time we will relentlessly get on with ***our*** *business; we are very strong now and need not delay any longer for build up purposes… I shall always ensure that I am well balanced; at present I have no fears of any offensive move the enemy might make; I am concentrating on making the battle swing our way.*[70]

With hindsight, with the enemy having committed to battle all they had to muster, it could indeed be argued that victory in Normandy was inevitable. However, with Hitler insisting that his forces yield not a square yard of ground, a long bitter struggle would still lay ahead for the Allies before they could inflict a conclusive defeat on the Germans in Normandy.

Below: *British 5.5 inch gun – with great accuracy this gun could fire a 45kg shell to a maximum range of exceeding 9 miles.*

Chapter 10

Colossal Cracks

Above: *The fiercest resistance faced by American troops would be provided by the elite 3rd* Fallschirmjager *Division.*

A vital precursor to the manoeuvre that would lead American forces into position for breakout was the capture of the city of St Lo. In the first round of post D-Day operations, as the US Army V Corps made their inland advance from Omaha, opposition varied in intensity from one location to the next. In terms of the number of casualties suffered, the heaviest resistance was encountered by V Corps' 1st Infantry Division which was advancing adjacent to the British forces within the Gold Beach sector to the east. However, in contrast to the neighbouring British forces who were engaged against the might of either the 12th SS or the *Panzer Lehr* Division, the American advance in this sector was predominantly opposed by the Wehrmacht's 30th Mobile Brigade - a bicycle infantry reserve of administrative personnel fighting alongside a small detachment of troops drawn from the 17th SS who had themselves been drafted in to reinforce the shattered remnants of the 352nd Infantry Division, a formation already catergorised by their own Commanding Officer as *'annihilated to the point of almost non-existence.'*

Having consolidated their D-Day objectives, V Corps' advance on the road to St Lo, via Caumont, commenced in earnest on 9 June. Twenty-three-year-old Sergeant Walter Ehlers from Junction City, Kansas, takes up the story of the advance when closing in on the village of Goville...

We were hitting the German positions right on the nose... I told my men we've got to rush up to the hedgerow immediately, otherwise we will get caught in the middle of the field and they'll just pick us off. So we did... I went down to where a machine gun was firing and I ran into the enemy patrol and knocked them out. They were about four or five feet from me; I shot all four of them and kept going. It didn't draw the attention of the machine gunner that his own men were getting shot by somebody in the hedgerow. I guess he thought his men were shot by guys coming across the field; he got his targets all mixed up. I got close to the machine gun and knocked it out and killed the three men who were on it with my rifle.

There was another machine gun in the corner of the next field and I snuck up on it and knocked it out. I had my squad following me all the time. I went up on a mound and saw two mortar positions and about ten men in there. They saw me with my bayonet and got frightened and starting running. I tried to halt them but they wouldn't halt so I shot them, because we didn't want to have to fight them again later. Of course my squad helped me knock them all off. We went on further and got another machine gun that day.

Next day, we were going along up the side of a hedgerow instead of out in the middle... They started firing on us and the Company Commander ordered us to withdraw. I knew that if we turned and withdrew we'd probably all get knocked off. So we started firing in a semi-circle; my automatic rifleman knew what his job was, so he came up to help me - he fired to the right and I fired straight ahead and around to the left. As soon as our squad got back to the hedgerow behind us, we started back. As I was coming down the hedgerow, I saw [Germans] putting another machine gun in the corner with a three-man crew. So I sent three men down there and about the time I sent the last one, I got hit in the back and it spun me around. I saw a German in the hedgerow and shot him. Then I noticed my automatic rifleman was lying out in the field and I went out and got him. I got his arm around my shoulder and picked him up and carried him over to the hedgerow behind us.[71]

On first impression it had looked that Ehlers had been shot clean through his torso, however, in his own words, '*the bullet had hit my rib and went into my pack and hit my Mother's picture and a bar of soap, then turned and hit my shovel, so it looked like I had been shot clear through*".[72] Ehlers refused to be evacuated and would be wounded on a further two occasions in Normandy. Months later he would read about the battle for Goville in Stars and Stripes magazine; only then did he learn that he had been awarded the Medal of Honor. Although offered a ticket home and the role of promoting war bonds, maybe as a consequence of learning that his brother Roland had been killed on D-Day, Walt Ehlers decided to stay in Europe and continue the fight against Nazi Germany. He

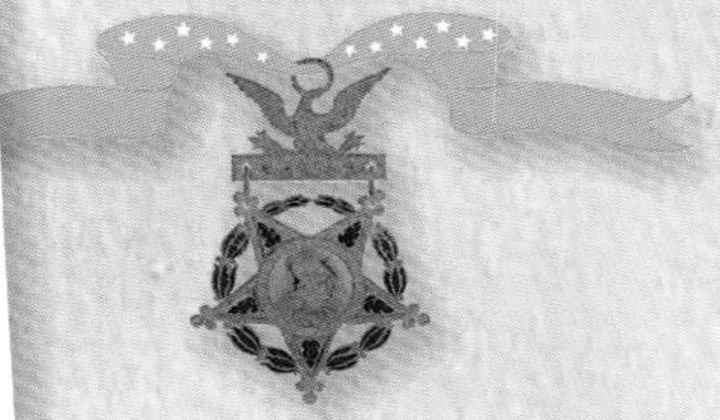

Staff-Sergeant

WALTER D. EHLERS

1st Infantry Division

For conspicuous gallantry and intrepidity at the risk of his life above and beyond the call of duty on 9-10 June 1944, near Goville, France. S/Sgt. Ehlers, always acting as the spearhead of the attack, repeatedly led his men against heavily defended enemy strong points exposing himself to deadly hostile fire whenever the situation required heroic and courageous leadership. Without waiting for an order, S/Sgt. Ehlers, far ahead of his men, led his squad against a strongly defended enemy strong point, personally killing 4 of an enemy patrol who attacked him en route. Then crawling forward under withering machine gun fire, he pounced upon the gun crew and put it out of action. Turning his attention to 2 mortars protected by the crossfire of 2 machine guns, S/Sgt. Ehlers led his men through this hail of bullets to kill or put to flight the enemy of the mortar section, killing 3 men himself. After mopping up the mortar positions, he again advanced on a machine gun, his progress effectively covered by his squad. When he was almost on top of the gun he leaped to his feet and, although greatly outnumbered, he knocked out the position single-handed. The next day, having advanced deep into enemy territory, the platoon of which S/Sgt. Ehlers was a member, finding itself in an untenable position as the enemy brought increased mortar, machine gun, and small arms fire to bear on it, was ordered to withdraw. S/Sgt. Ehlers, after his squad had covered the withdrawal of the remainder of the platoon, stood up and by continuous fire at the semicircle of enemy placements, diverted the bulk of the heavy hostile fire on himself, thus permitting the members of his own squad to withdraw. At this point, though wounded himself, he carried his wounded automatic rifleman to safety and then returned fearlessly over the shell-swept field to retrieve the automatic rifle which he was unable to carry previously. After having his wound treated, he refused to be evacuated, and returned to lead his squad. The intrepid leadership, indomitable courage, and fearless aggressiveness displayed by S/Sgt. Ehlers in the face of overwhelming enemy forces serve as an inspiration to others.

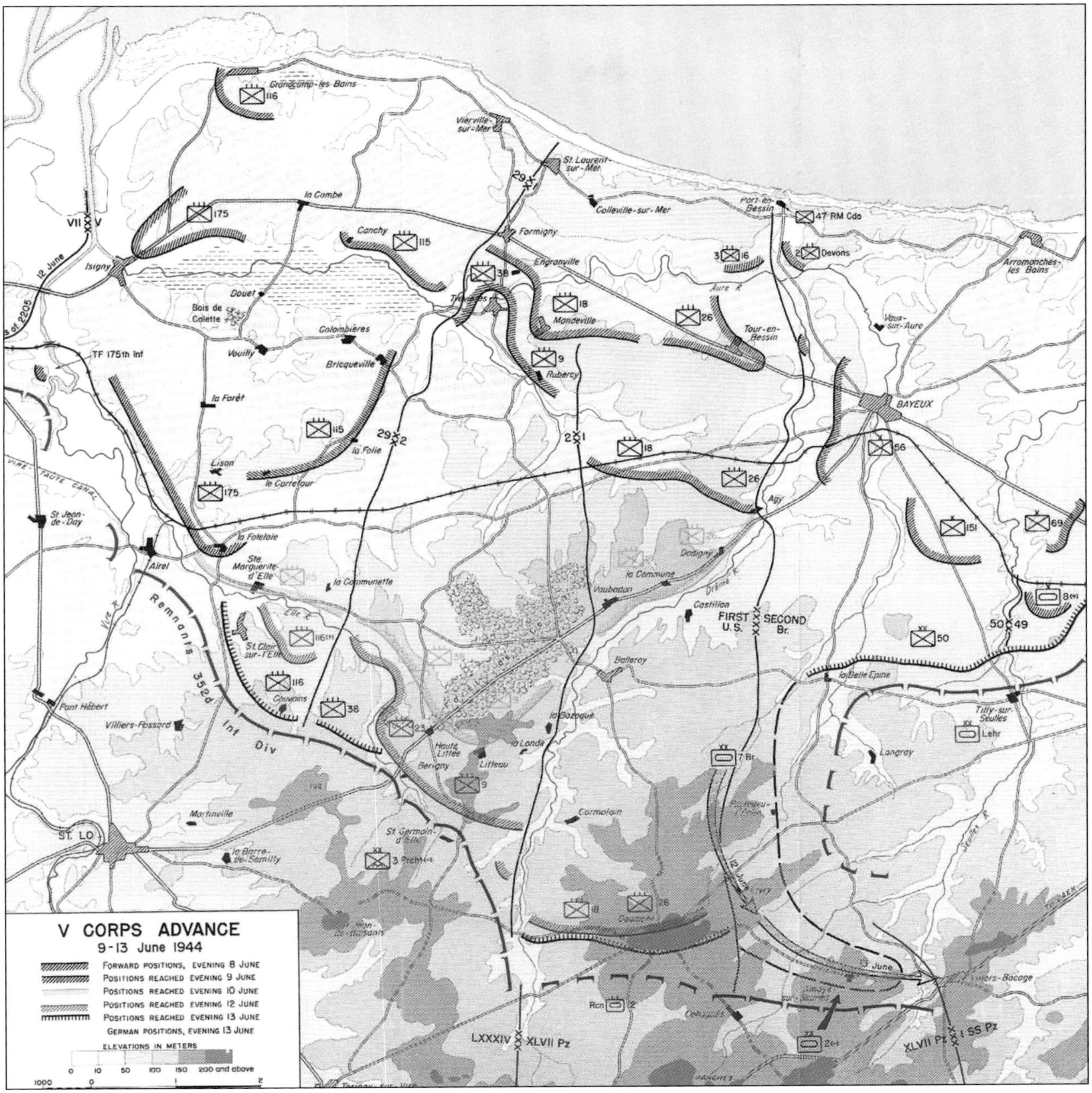

would survive the war and return to America. Moving to California, Walt Ehlers became a representative for American Veteran's Affairs and worked as a security guard at Disneyland in California. He died in 2014, aged 92 and is buried at Riverside National Cemetery, Riverside, California.

Located just a few miles from where Sergeant Ehlers led his men into battle, another Sergeant from the 1st Infantry Division was taking the battle to the enemy close to the small village of Vaubadon. Although already wounded, 25-year-old Sergeant Arthur

DeFranzo from Massachusetts, having previously been awarded the Silver Star for actions on 7 June, dragged a comrade to safety, only to be wounded for a second time as he overwhelmed an enemy machine-gun nest. Continuing the struggle in an attack on a second machine-gun position, DeFranzo would be wounded for a third time, this time fatally. Killed on 10 June 1944, he is today buried at the Riverside Cemetery in Saugus, Massachusetts.

Although the pockets of resistance encountered by Sergeants Ehlers and DeFranzo were exceptional, the majority of the American advance met only token resistance from an already crippled enemy. The official US History records that *'Virtually the whole of V Corps, during the week of 8 - 14 June, was pushing south through the bocage country, making rapid progress against a disintegrating German defence.'*[73] The American advance continued *'spearheaded by the 1st Infantry Division on a 3,000 yard front and made good progress against light opposition that soon gave way.'*[74] By 12 June, with the American advance now just a few miles short of the crucial objective of St Lo, V Corps encountered determined resistance for the first time since D-Day. Such a change in opposition led to another adjustment of the objectives assigned to American forces. The role of V Corps was now switched from the quick capture of St Lo, to orders which required *'V Corps to hold its present position while the First Army devoted its main effort to the capture of Cherbourg'.*[75] The ensuing hiatus came as a welcome respite for a German force al-

Above: *The city of St Lo will remain ingrained within American history for generations to come –but could it have been taken weeks earlier with far fewer casualties?*

Below: *Toward St Lo, 14-18 June 1944.*

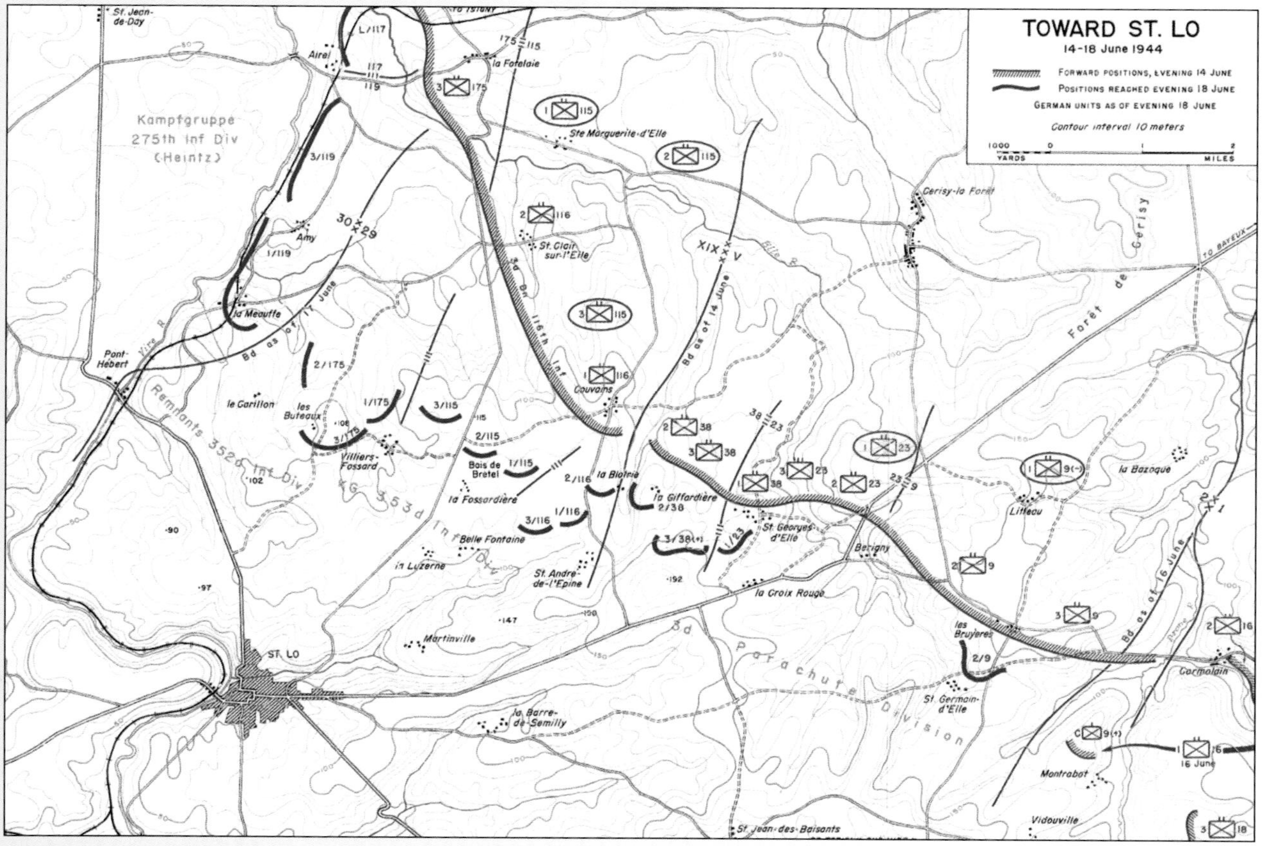

ready at breaking point, as an officer from 3 *Fallschirmjager* Division states, on 10 June... 'If the Americans... had launched an energetic attack from the forest of Cerisy, St Lo would have fallen'... The Americans *'...only decided on extremely limited objectives and failed to exploit achieved successes by continuing their thrusts in depth'.*[76]

Once again, being able to choose which sector received priority over another was a luxury afforded to the Americans only as a consequence of the bitter struggle faced by the British and Canadians. Instead of holding the might of the German war machine while the Americans moved against Cherbourg and St Lo, the British and Canadians would now have to wait for Cherbourg to be secured, only then would the Americans move against St Lo and into position for breakout! Such concessions justifiably irritated Montgomery, but he would not let his frustrations threaten his relationship with those in his immediate subordinate command. In his own words...

I tried very hard to get First US Army to develop its thrust southwards, towards Coutances, at the same time as it was completing the capture of Cherbourg. And I have no doubt myself that it could have been started in a small way, and gradually developed. But Bradley didn't want to take the risk; there was no risk really; quick and skilful regrouping was all that was wanted... I have to take the Americans along quietly and give them time to get ready.[77]

Whilst such comments have by some been interpreted as yet another example of Monty's arrogance, his words were certainly not interpreted this way by the American commander of ground forces...

We had long ago concluded that the best point for breakout lay somewhere along the sixteen-mile line between St Lo and Coutances... During those operations in the lodgment where Montgomery bossed the US First Army as part of his 21st Army Group, he exercised his authority with wisdom, forbearance, and restraint while coordinating

Staff-Sergeant
ARTHUR F. DEFRANZO
1st Infantry Division

For conspicuous gallantry and intrepidity at the risk of his life, above and beyond the call of duty, on 10 June 1944, near Vaubadon, France. As scouts were advancing across an open field, the enemy suddenly opened fire with several machine guns and hit one of the men. S/Sgt. DeFranzo courageously moved out in the open to the aid of the wounded scout and was himself wounded but brought the man to safety. Refusing aid, S/Sgt. DeFranzo re-entered the open field and led the advance upon the enemy. There were always at least two machine guns bringing unrelenting fire upon him, but S/Sgt. DeFranzo kept going forward, firing into the enemy and one by one the enemy emplacements became silent. While advancing he was again wounded, but continued on until he was within 100 yards of the enemy position and even as he fell, he kept firing his rifle and waving his men forward. When his company came up behind him, S/Sgt. DeFranzo, despite his many severe wounds, suddenly raised himself and once more moved forward in the lead of his men until he was again hit by enemy fire. In a final gesture of indomitable courage, he threw several grenades at the enemy machine gun position and completely destroyed the gun. In this action, S/Sgt. DeFranzo lost his life, but by bearing the brunt of the enemy fire in leading the attack, he prevented a delay in the assault which would have been of considerable benefit to the foe, and he made possible his company's advance with a minimum of casualties. The extraordinary heroism and magnificent devotion to duty displayed by S/Sgt. DeFranzo was a great inspiration to all about him, and is in keeping with the highest traditions of the armed forces.

our movements with those of Dempsey's. Monty carefully avoided getting mixed up in US command decisions, but instead granted us the latitude to operate as freely and as independently as we chose. At no time did he probe into First Army with the indulgent manner he sometimes displayed among those subordinates who were also his countrymen. I could not have wanted a more tolerant or judicious commander.[78]

In front of St Lo two weeks of self-imposed inactivity would follow Bradley's decision for his forces to dig in until Cherbourg had fallen. With the arrival of General Corlett's US Army XIV Corps, with V Corp's 29th and 2nd Infantry Divisions attached, the advance on St Lo would not resume until the end of June and not until the town's defences had been substantially reinforced by the elite 3 *Fallschirmjager* Division, a unit whose command was clearly astonished at the unexpected respite they had been gifted by the American hiatus, a fact emphasised by *Oberst* Ziegellmann…

It is noteworthy that the cautious American infantry, with very little daring, stopped when they came up against determined resistance... Had tanks supported the American infantry on 16 June, St Lo would not have been in German hands any longer that evening.[79]

A crucial objective that could have been taken cheaply would now be reinforced to the extent that the Americans would lose tens of thousands of casualties before the city finally fell on 18 July. The pause imposed before the advance on St Lo resumed

Below and right: *The delay in advancing against St Lo would allow the Germans time to reinforce the city and lead to huge loss of both American and civilian lives.*

was undoubtedly a blunder, possibly the greatest blunder to be made throughout the entire Normandy campaign. Such a situation, created as it was exclusively by the Americans, held dire consequences for the British and Canadians, as confirmed by General Bradley...

For another four weeks it fell to the British to pin down superior enemy forces in that sector while we manoeuvred into position for the US breakout... the British endured their passive role with patience and forbearing.[80]

Patience and forbearing despite the barbs of the critic's tongues, at the time and long since after, and not to mention, as a direct consequence, thousands of casualties.

If the criticism aimed against the British front suggested a crisis was in the making, for the Germans in Normandy, there was absolutely no denying that their crisis had well and truly arrived. On 3 July, their Commander in Chief in the West, the much respected (by everyone but Hitler), *Generalfeldmarschall* Gerd von Rundstedt, was relieved of his command and replaced by *Generalfeldmarschall* Gunther von Kluge. The day after, Generalmajor Léo Geyr von Schweppenburg was replaced as commander of Panzer Group West by *Generalmajor* Heinrich Eberbach.

Against the enemy's new guard, Monty's grand strategy continued with British and Canadian forces finally securing Caen on 9 July, some five weeks after the King's Shropshire Light Infantry had advanced to within two miles of the city during the afternoon of D-Day. There is no dispute that in the first weeks and months of operations in Normandy the Allies had suffered numerous tactical failures. As a consequence *both* the American and Commonwealth fronts were at times well behind the progress

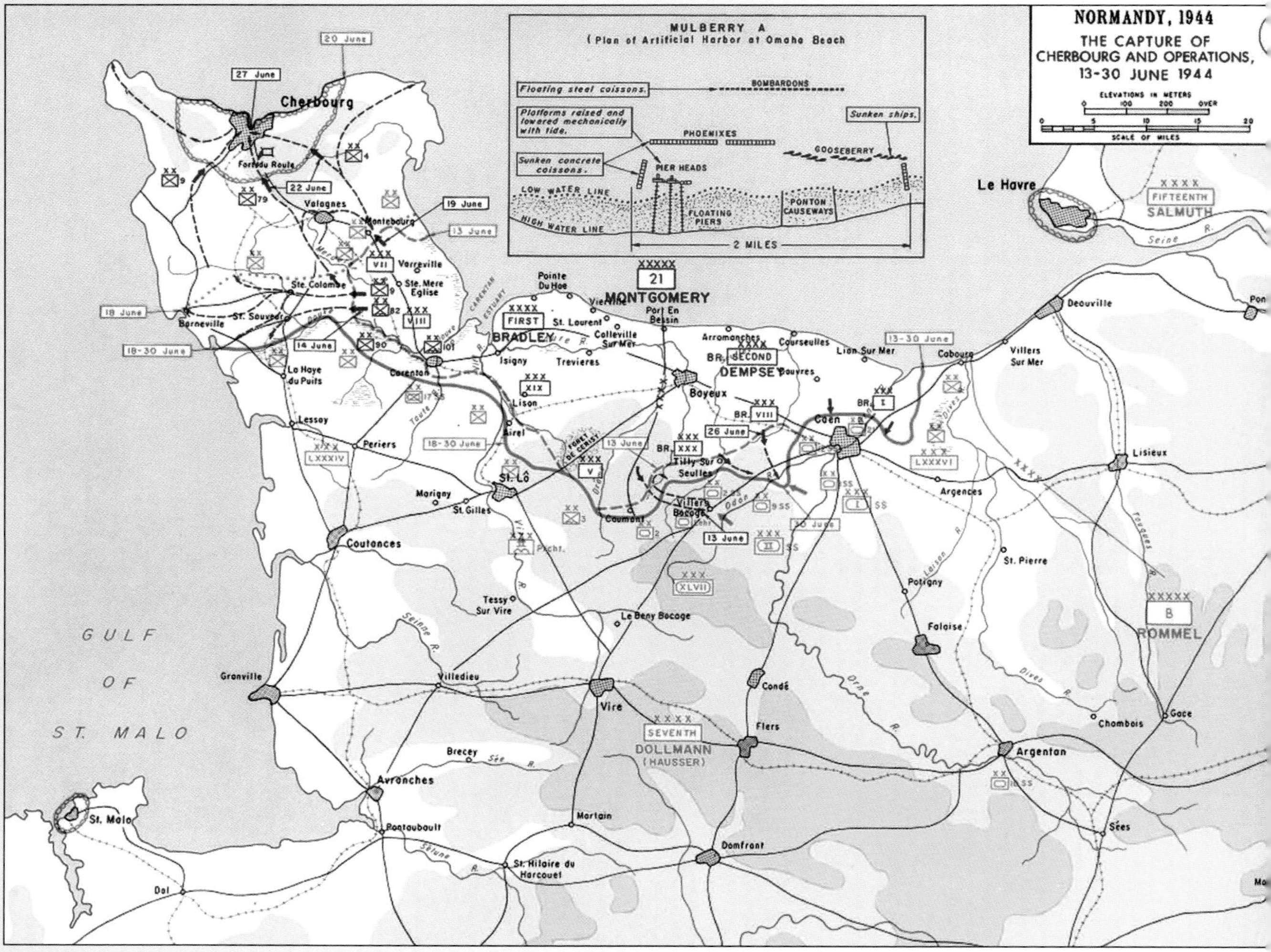

of pre-invasion expectations. However, the broad strategy of Montgomery's masterplan remained intact, and this strategy had indeed succeeded in drawing the enemy exactly where Montgomery had wanted them, setting the stage for the eventual breakout from within the confines of the American sector. Montgomery had anticipated the Allies reaching the banks of the River Seine after ninety days, so far less than half of this timeframe had elapsed.

Above: *Operations 13-30 June 1944*

It is accurate to state that whilst this strategy was developing to Montgomery's satisfaction, his doctrine had been contrived as a means, not only to defeat the enemy, but also to preserve what limited manpower Great Britain, a nation in its fifth year of war, and very much the one nation of all the Western Allies that had carried the main weight of the war up to this point, still had in the fight. As Montgomery himself declared…

My military doctrine was based on unbalancing the enemy while keeping well balanced myself. I had learned it in battle fighting since 1940 and I knew from experience how it helped to save men's lives.[81]

Generalfeldmarschall Gerd von Rundstedt 1875-1953

Commander of *Oberbefehlshaber West* (from 15 March 1942 to 2 July 1944)

Karl Rudolf Gerd von Rundstedt was born in 1875 into a military family possessing a long history of service within the Prussian Army. Graduating from the Berlin War Academy in 1892, at the outbreak of the Great War, von Rundstedt held the rank of Hauptmann (Captain). Promoted to Major by April 1915, this would remain his rank throughout the duration of the Great War. Avoiding the post-war cull of the German military imposed through the Treaty of Versailles, von Rundstedt remained within the German Army. Promoted to *Generalleutnant* (Lieutenant General) in 1927, then *General der Artillerie* (full General) in 1932, von Rundstedt was employed in several staff positions during this time. In November 1938, now aged 63, he retired from the military only to be recalled by Hitler four months later to be given command of *Heeresgruppe Sud* (Army Group South) - the force that would capture Warsaw during the invasion of Poland.

Impressing Hitler during these early campaigns, and in anticipation of the upcoming offensive aimed at the Netherlands, Belgium and France, von Rundstedt was appointed commander of *Heeresgruppe A* (Army Group A). In July 1940, amidst the euphoria of Germany's emphatic and rapid victory in the west, von Rundstedt would be promoted to *Generalfeldmarschal* (Field Marshal). In June 1941 von Rundstedt returned to take command of *Heeresgruppe Sud* (Army Group South) for the launch of Operation Barbarossa, Germany's attack against the Soviet Union. As Hitler's interference with military matters intensified, von Rundstedt grew increasingly tired of not being able to fight battles his own way. Frustrations mounted to the extent that in December 1941, von Rundstedt tendered his resignation from the German Army.

Summoned back to service in March 1942, von Rundstedt would be appointed *Oberbefehlshaber West* (Commander in Chief of all Western Forces). From this point, many working within his inner circle of command would detect a distinct lack of zeal within their commander. Whilst carrying out what was expected of him, it seemed that he no longer possessed any of his former vigour or enthusiasm. Charged with strengthening the defences of the Atlantic coastline that faced Great Britain, this role was delegated away completely to the Todt Organisation (the paramilitary construction branch of the German armed forces). With continuing unrelenting interference from the Fuhrer, with his authority demeaned as Hitler offered favour to subordinate officers such as Rommel, von Rundstedt's influence, like his enthusiasm, was clearly on the wane. Having failed to defeat the Allied invasion of Normandy,

von Rundstedt was relieved of his command on 2 July 1944, only for Hitler to reappoint him two months later after von Kluge and Model had likewise failed to stem the tide of the Allies, who were by now firmly established in France.

Sacked again by Hitler on 9 March 1945, von Rundstedt ended the war without a command and was taken prisoner in May 1945. In the aftermath of the war, there were many who called for von Rundstedt to be put on trial for war crimes. Accusations included the shooting of both prisoners and civilians during the occupation of Poland, the condoning of the death groups that commenced the genocide of the Jews in the east, the implementation of Hitler's 'Commando' order of 1942 (which enforced the policy of the shooting of Allied forces captured behind German lines) and also the disregarding of the massacre of civilians at Oradour sur Glane in 1944. Persistently maintaining the defence that he and others were simply following Hitler's orders, a combination of political interference and ill health meant von Rundstedt was never brought to trial and was released from captivity in May 1949. He died four years later aged 78, and is buried at the Friedhof Stocken Cemetery in Hannover.

Monty's deliberate strategy, a technique known as Colossal Cracks has been defined by the pre-eminent Stephen Hart...

Operationally, Montgomery would seek to maintain the initiative and remain balanced: respectively, to force the enemy merely to react to his moves, and to have his forces

so deployed that any sudden enemy move could be countered rapidly. 'Colossal Cracks' was an attritional method based on materiel which eschewed operational manoeuvre.[82]

Above: *St Lo - the day of liberation arrives although there are no cheering crowds to welcome the victors.*

So many commentators, both during the battle or ever since, have failed to realise, either intentionally due to ulterior motive, or because of simply not being able to comprehend the concept, that there is an enormous difference between attrition and stalemate. The fact remains that the objective of the Allies was to destroy the enemy, and this was successfully achieved through the persistence and sacrifice of the British and Canadian forces in engaging and destroying the bulk of the enemy's strength during the battle for Normandy. Whilst this battle at times was undeniably one of attrition, it nonetheless paved the way for the mobility of the breakout of American forces. Once again, in the words of Stephen Hart…

Despite its appearances, *'Colossal Cracks' was not merely an attritional technique, but rather an essential precursor to achieving fluid operations, where superior mobility would decisively defeat the Germans: attrition and manoeuvre were not necessarily diametrically opposed.*[83]

Throughout the entire battle for Normandy, the enemy was dancing to Monty's tune. However, it would not be until the third week of July, more than a month later than anticipated, that Bradley's First US Army at last manoeuvred into a favorable position to attempt the long-awaited breakout from the confines of the Normandy bridgehead. The road to St Lo had been a long hard slog, characterised to a certain extent by a series of lost opportunities. There would still be much work to do before Bradley's Americans were finally in position for breakout. Until that time it would remain down to the British Second Army to continue in holding the weight of the enemy's strength.

General der Panzertruppen
Leo Freiherr Geyr von Schweppenburg 1886-1974
Commander of Panzergruppe West (from 18 November 1943 to 2 July 1944)

Leo Freiherr Geyr von Schweppenburg was born in Potsdam in 1886 into a family which, having already produced two Generalfeldmarschalle, was regarded within military circles as Prussian aristocracy. Joining the German Army in 1904, and serving under the rank of *Hauptmann* (Captain) during the Great War, 'Geyr' remained in Germany's post-war army and between the years of 1933 to 1937 served as the military attaché to the German Embassy in London. It would be during this posting that he would be promoted to *Generalmajor*.

At the outbreak of war, von Schweppenburg commanded the 3rd Panzer Division, a formation he led with distinction during the invasion of Poland. Promoted to *General der Kavallerie* (full General) and then given command of the German XXIV Panzer Corps, Geyr's forces were at the forefront of the *Blitzkreig* charge during the battle for France in 1940. Heading east during Operation Barbarossa, Geyr's forces were again at the vanguard, this time spearheading the *Heeresgruppe Mitte* (Army Group Centre) advance against Moscow. With German fortunes subsequently waning, in September 1942, Geyr was relieved of his command and would spend more than a year without an active posting.

In 1943, he was appointed commander of *Panzergruppe West* (commander of all armoured forces in the west), tasked with coordinating the initial counterattack against the Allied invasion of Normandy. Despite gathering one of the greatest concentrations of armour in the history of warfare, *Panzergruppe West* failed to dislodge the British and Canadians who had landed to the east of the Allied beachhead. Geyr's plight was certainly not aided by the fact that on 10 June his headquarters at La Caine was attacked by the Royal Air Force, with Geyr himself being wounded and many of his staff killed or injured. Relieved of his command on 4 July 1944, Geyr would spend the rest of the war in a staff role.

Taken prisoner in 1945, Geyr spent just two years in captivity, part of this time spent in the paid employment of the US Army assisting the Americans in operational studies and histories for the US Army Historical Division. On returning to Germany he would publish his memoirs whilst working within the Bundeswehr (post-war West German Army).

Leo Freiherr Geyr von Schweppenburg died in 1974, aged 84. He is buried in Irschenhausen near Munich.

PART FOUR
Chapter 11
Breakout for Victory

By the third week of July, as the US Army V Corps secured the capture of St Lo, amongst the continued accusations of a supposed stalemate to the east, the American forces to the south of the Cotentin Peninsula were themselves advancing in a manner which could be best described as anything but rapid, a fact emphasised by their own most senior commander in the field…

At 5:30 on the morning of July 3, Middleton started his VII Corps down the west road (Le Hayes du Puits – Coutances) *on the offensive we hoped would secure a line of departure for the breakout. Six days later Middleton had budged only a few miles south… On July 14, I ordered Middleton to discontinue his Coutances attack. In twelve days, he had advanced only 12,000 yards.*[84]

On 10 July, Monty issued a directive to all his immediate subordinate commanders, emphasising the urgency for the Americans to get into position for breakout…

It is important to speed up our advance on the western flank; the operations of the [British] *Second Army must therefore be so staged that they will have a direct influence on the operations of the [US] First Army, as well as holding enemy forces on the eastern flank.*[85]

To assist the Americans, once more a diversionary attack was launched by the British Second Army. This operation, codenamed Goodwood, would deploy a mass of armour, forming up on the eastern bank of the River Orne, in an attempt to drive hundreds of tanks from their start line to the high ground of the Bourguebus Ridge, and if the opportunity arose, to the main road heading south toward the city of Falaise. This operation, again so misrepresented and misunderstood in the annals of popular history, held the intention of keeping in place the Germans already present on the front of British Second Army, whilst concurrently attracting any new arrivals to this front, away from the Americans in the west.

Goodwood itself was undeniably unconventional in its composition. Deploying a preponderance of armour, with little in the way of infantry support, such a steel heavy blend was a direct consequence of Dempsey's Second Army possessing an abundance of armoured formations, whilst holding very little in the way of surplus infantry that could be afforded the luxury of being disengaged away from the role which they had already been set. Goodwood was indeed a flawed operation from the start. Such flaws however were as a direct consequence of the lack of resources available. These resources, in this case infantry, had already been spent as a consequence of Dempsey's forces having to hold the line for a much longer duration than had ever

General Sir Miles Dempsey 1896-1969

Commander of the British 2nd Army

Graduating from Sandhurst in 1915, Miles Christopher Dempsey subsequently joined the Royal Berkshire Regiment as a Second Lieutenant. He served on the front line for three years during the Great War, being awarded a Military Cross. During the interwar period his main celebrity would arrive due to his prowess on the cricket field, playing in both first class and minor County Championship matches.

Dempsey's inter-war advancement through the ranks was steady if not remarkable and at the outbreak of the Second World War, as a Brigade Commander, he sailed for France as part of the British Expeditionary Force. As the German Blitzkrieg raced across Northern France and the British Army retreated towards Dunkirk, Dempsey's brigade would fight determinedly as a rearguard, for his command of which Dempsey would be awarded the Distinguished Service Order.

Posted to North Africa as a Lieutenant General, he would command XIII Corps as part of General Montgomery's Eighth Army. Monty liked and respected Dempsey and would select him to command forces during the invasions of both Sicily and Italy. It was before and during these campaigns that Dempsey's skills as a planner and commander of combined operations came to the attention of the higher echelons of British Command. At the beginning of 1944 Monty gave Dempsey command of the British Second Army, a force comprising all British and Canadian land forces that would invade the Gold, Juno and Sword sectors on D-Day.

Once hostilities ceased in Europe, Dempsey became Land Forces Commander of South East Asia. As the war in the Pacific came to an end he would be promoted to General and Commander in Chief of Middle East Land Forces before retiring in 1947.

Not one to seek attention, Miles Dempsey was a man of great ability who quietly went about his work and got results. He was certainly not just Montgomery's 'yes man' as he is often portrayed; his opinion often greatly differed to that of his superiors and he was not afraid to voice his point of view.

Miles Dempsey retired from the British Army in August 1947 and died at the age of seventy- two, on 5 June 1969 - the eve of the 25th anniversary of the D-Day landings. He is buried in the churchyard at Yattendon, Berkshire.

been predicted prior to the battle, a delay which was of no fault of their own. On 15 July, Montgomery wrote to General O'Connor to outline the objectives of Operation Goodwood, for which O'Connor's British VIII Corps would be the designated spearhead. Monty wrote…

Object of this Operation. To engage the German armour in battle and write it down to such an extent that it is of no further value to the Germans as a basis of the battle. To gain a good bridgehead over the Orne through Caen and thus to improve our positions on the eastern flank. Generally to destroy German equipment and personnel, as a preliminary to a possible wider exploitation of success.

Effect of this operation on the Allied policy. We require the whole of the Cherbourg and Brittany peninsulas. A victory on the eastern flank will help us to gain what we want on the western flank. But the eastern flank is a bastion on which the whole future of the campaign in North West Europe depends; it must remain a firm bastion; if it were to become unstable, the operations on the western flank would cease.[86]

At the same time that Montgomery outlined the strategy of Operation Goodwood to General O'Connor, he also despatched a representative (Colonel *Kit* Dawnay) to brief the War Cabinet in London. Dawnay reported…

The real object is to muck up and write off enemy troops. On the eastern flank he [Montgomery] *is aiming at doing the greatest damage to enemy armour... On the security and firmness of the eastern flank depends the security of the whole lodgement area. Therefore, having broken out in the country south east of Caen he has no intention of rushing madly eastwards and getting Second Army on the eastern flank so extended that that flank might cease to be secure... All the activities on the eastern flank are designed to help the* [American] *forces in the west while ensuring that a firm bastion is kept in the east.*[87]

Launched on 18 July, Goodwood failed in reaching its geographical objectives but undoubtedly succeeded in tying down the enemy forces which, decrypts of the German codes had informed the Allies, would otherwise have been transferred to the American front in advance of the US First Army's imminent attempt at breakout. Despite the clear and concise briefings made long before, during, and after the battle, despite the memoirs of all Montgomery's subordinate commanders testifying to these aims, many have stated that Montgomery had intended Goodwood, not to just pin down the bulk of the enemy's strength, but to instead produce an armoured thrust out of the confines of the Normandy beachhead in the east, creating a breakout in the direction of Paris. Again, incredibly, even the Supreme Commander seemed ignorant, not just of the aims of Goodwood, but arguably the whole Allied grand strategy. In the words of Montgomery…

Above: *Although weeks later than anticipated, finally Operation Cobra launches the Allied breakout in the west.*

Many people thought that when Operation Goodwood was staged, it was the beginning of the plan to break out from the eastern flank towards Paris, and that, because I did not do so, the battle had been a failure. But let me make the point again at the risk of being wearisome. There was never at any time any intention of making the breakout from the bridgehead on the eastern flank. Misunderstandings about this simple and basic conception were responsible for much trouble between British and American personalities. Here, for example, is an extract from page 32 of Eisenhower's report on the campaign, dated the 13 July 1945, to the Combined Chiefs of Staff:

> *Nevertheless, in the east we had been unable to break out towards the Seine, and the enemy's concentration of his main power in the Caen sector had prevented us from securing the ground in that area we so badly needed. Our plans were sufficiently flexible that we could take advantage of this enemy reaction by directing that the American forces smash out of the lodgment area in the west while the British and Canadians kept the Germans occupied in the east. Incessant pressure by the Second Army to contain the enemy was therefore continued by Field Marshal Montgomery during July.*

The impression is left that the British and Canadians had failed in the east (in the Caen sector) and that, therefore, the Americans had to take on the job of breaking out in the west. This reflection on Dempsey and the Second Army is a clear indication that Eisenhower failed to comprehend the basic plan to which he had himself cheerfully agreed. [88]

The inescapable conclusion is that the Supreme Commander was at this point simply so far detached from the battle that he held not even the most basic grasp of the reality on the ground. Eisenhower made only infrequent and even then fleeting visits to Normandy, preferring instead not to immerse himself within his subordinate command in the field but leave himself open to the inevitable disconnection from the battle. He had neither the knowledge, experience nor ability to choose which of his commanders to place his confidence in during this crucial period of battle. It is indeed remarkable that Eisenhower's permanent headquarters was, in 1944, never in the same country as the Allied front line. As the Allies battled through Normandy, Eisenhower remained detached from the battle, preferring to stay in England, away from the front and safely within the administrative tail of his headquarters, surrounded by many who thought that they had been overlooked and denied by Montgomery the positions they believed were due to them. Combined with interference from the Press, such a situation ensured that there was no shortage of bitterness within Eisenhower's HQ which quickly developed into a veritable nest of vipers, with so many possessing axes to grind against Montgomery and all too eager to poison the chalice against Montgomery whenever the opportunity arose.

Maybe a passage from what is arguably the very finest history of the campaign in North-West Europe can enlighten us, in the words of Chester Wilmot's 'The Struggle for Europe'…

Eisenhower presumed that the plan had gone astray. He had not Montgomery's long and intimate experience in the daily conduct of operations, and he was not close enough to the current battle to see the steady unfolding of the basic strategy which

Montgomery had proclaimed in April... Montgomery on the other hand, drew encouragement from the very facts which alarmed Eisenhower. He knew that the tenacity of the defence was no yardstick of the enemy's continued power of resistance, for the German divisions were being steadily consumed in the fire of battle. He knew that the concentration of German armoured reserves against Second Army was ensuring the opportunity for 1st Army.[89]

Once again, as the British and Canadians took the strain of the main enemy strength placed against Second Army, the media did nothing but criticise them for their apparent ineffectiveness, a fact not missed by General Miles Dempsey...

The Press interpreted the battle as a deliberate attempt to break out, and one that had failed... Maurice Chilton, my Chief of Staff, was very upset about it and urged me to take steps to check such a 'slander'. I told him; 'Don't worry – it will aid our purpose and act as the best possible cover plan.' For I could see that such criticism would tend to convince the enemy that we were trying to break out in the Caen area, and would help to keep him fixed there while Bradley was mounting his fresh breakout attack.[90]

Meanwhile, the Press was portraying the situation in Normandy as one of crisis, of an Allied plan lying in ruins, in danger of descending to the kind of stalemate resembling those disasters so abundant within the Great War. The great irony of course is that the continued operations to the east, so maligned by so many, were only necessary because of the delays to the west. Weeks behind schedule, Goodwood was only necessary in the first place as Bradley had still to rally his troops into position for breakout. Further adjournments only added to the misrepresentation of the whole campaign. In the words of the acclaimed historian, Henry Maule...

The only facet that had gone exactly according to plan was the drawing in of the bulk of the enemy armour against the British and Canadians. But if the Americans did not soon take advantage of this bloody self-sacrifice, then the invasion might well be doomed.[91]

Whilst it is understandable that such misinformation was being disseminated by a media which was purposely kept from the facts, less the Allies give away their strategy, what is truly astonishing is how such a myth can endure within publications such as the official American history of the Normandy campaign, published in 1966 (15 years after Bradley's memoirs), which states...

The (British) *Second Army launched a strong attack (Goodwood) that promised the Allies an excellent chance of achieving a breakthrough. Had it succeeded Cobra would probably have been unnecessary.*[92]

Below: *Men of the US 9th Infantry Division advance through the hedgerows during Operation Cobra.*

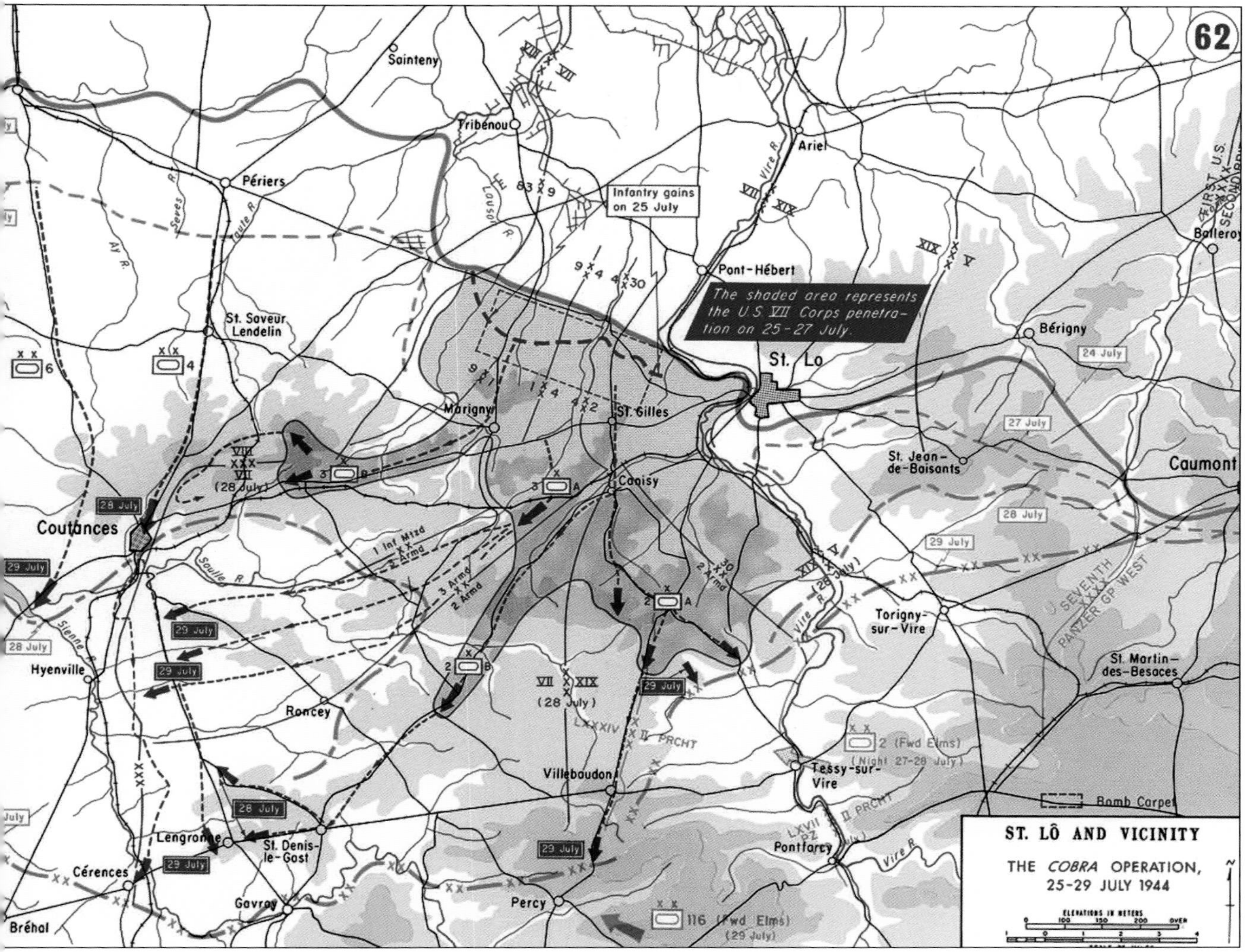

Above: *The Cobra Operation.*

Surely the US Army's official historian would have been aware of the communiques between the Allied commanders in the lead up to the assault? It seems that Mr Blumenson not only missed this particular source, but also neglected to consult the operational orders issued in the run up to Goodwood. So how can a historian holding such office make such a misjudgement? Was it simply a case of exceptionally poor tradecraft from a historian who really should know better, or could it be a deliberate attempt to distort the true history in order to detract from the selfless sacrifice of one army, to continue the innate self-aggrandisement of another?

Goodwood did not achieve the amount of ground intended to be taken, and in this regard, and in this regard only, can Goodwood be classed as a defeat or failed operation. Once again, to repeat the words of General Bradley…

In the minds of most people, success in battle is measured in the rate and length of advance. They found it difficult to realise that the more successful Monty was in stirring up German resistance, the less likely he was to advance.[93]

Goodwood's main objectives, clearly and categorically defined by Montgomery before, during and after Goodwood were multi-faceted and predominantly designed to 'write-down' German armour and once more keep the enemy strength pinned against Commonwealth forces and away from the American front. These aims were again more than successful, not just in keeping the present enemy strength in place, but once more attracting new arrivals to the battlefield. It does seem very strange that the only Allied general who did not understand the finer detail was the Supreme Commander himself.

It is incredible that to this day the grand strategy is so greatly misunderstood. This is despite it having been laid bare beyond doubt during the pre-invasion briefings and the operational directives being available within the National Archives. In addition, the strategy is fully defined in Montgomery's memoirs, as well as those of General Bradley, himself no fan of Montgomery and therefore surely a figure who would have been disinclined to extol the virtues of any self-serving boasts peddled by Monty either during or after the battle. However, as Bradley's memoirs state, on 30 June…

Monty published the plan as part of his 21st Group directive. In that directive he carefully reviewed Overlord strategy for the advance to the Seine, emphasising again for the record that [US] *First Army was to deliver the main thrust whilst Dempsey's Army pinned down the enemy's armour at Caen.*[94]

Despite the allegations of the slow nature of the British campaign, it was by now appreciated by Eisenhower that the situation on the American front was not all as it had been portrayed. In Eisenhower's own words, *'Bradley's advance to the southward has been disappointingly slow'.*[95] Indeed, in the month since the Americans had taken Cherbourg, Bradley's forces had lumbered just twenty-four miles in twenty-eight days.[96] In the words of the American's own official historian, *'fumbling and ineptitude had marked the opening days of the July offensive'.*[98] This had led to *'hesitation, inertia, and disorganization'.*[98]

Finally, by the last week of July, Bradley was happy that his American forces were now occupying a position of strength, both geographically and strategically, from which he could launch the long-awaited breakout from the confines of the lodgment area. Codenamed Cobra, Bradley's offensive would accumulate a huge force that would attack a line held by an already shattered enemy, many of whom were already exhausted after seven weeks of continuous fighting.

Confidence was high as General Barton of the 4th Infantry Division proclaimed, *'We outnumber them 10:1 in infantry, 50:1 in artillery, and an infinite number in the air.'*[99] At last the time of reckoning had arrived; everything was in place and no risk would be taken. On the eve of the assault, Bradley met General *'Lightning Joe'* Collins, (commander of the US Army VII Corps designated as the spearhead of the Cobra assault) to put in place the final touches to the much anticipated breakout. Concluding the meeting, Bradley left Collins with the words, *'Anything else we can give you? You've got everything now but my pistol.'*[100]

Opposing Cobra would be the shattered remnants of various formations, only two of which could be considered as being anything like first rate. Even now, as the Americans postured for breakout, eight weeks after D-Day, and five weeks later than Bradley had first anticipated, the bulk of the German forces were still irrepressibly glued to the British front, a fact emphasised by *Generalmajor* von Gersdoff (Chief of Staff of the German 7th Army) when commentating on the eve of Cobra. *'The point of*

Above: *Men of the US 4th Infantry Division advance on Coutances on the 29 July during Operation Cobra.*

the main effort... was concentrated, as before, in the centre of the sector of Panzer Group West in the Caen area.' [101] Again, Bradley acknowledged such in his memoirs. *'Cobra had caught the enemy dangerously off balance with six of his eight panzer divisions concentrated on Montgomery's front.'* [102] Even the two panzer divisions now facing the American front, the 2nd SS *Das Reich* and the *Panzer Lehr* were long since broken beyond any resemblance of their former incarnation. In essence, these formations were now divisions in name only. For example, by the time the *Panzer Lehr* was moved west from the British front to the American sector, it had lost over 5,000 of its original 8,000 combat troops and its initial pre-invasion strength of 237 tanks and assault guns,[103] was down to a strength of only twenty tanks.[104]

D-Day for Operation Cobra was set for Monday 24 July. In anticipation of the assault, Bradley massed his forces one mile to the north of the main Periers to St Lo highway. This dead straight road would be a crucial point of reference that could be used by the 8th US Army Air Force to orientate a preliminary bombardment, intended to destroy any will the shattered enemy defenders might still possess in resisting General Collins' assault against their thinly spread line.

As dawn broke, it became apparent that the weather that day was less than acceptable with regard to the air force being able to achieve any kind of precision in their bombing. Reluctantly, Bradley passed word for the operation to be postponed for twenty-four hours. However, these orders were issued too late. Having already left their airfields in the south of England, one of the three waves of bombers failed to receive the order to abort. Worse still, because of the fear of heavy anti-aircraft fire, the bombers had veered, against Bradley's orders, and changed the direction of their approach. Instead of flying along the line of the main road, from east heading west, they flew from the north heading south and directly above the American front line positions. With little or no margin for error, many bombs were dropped on friendly positions, most notably upon the forward elements of the US Army's 30th Infantry Division. With little time for reassessment or reproach, and with the element of surprise now lost, Bradley deferred any recriminations and hastily rescheduled the assault for the following day.

Brightly shone the dawn of 25 July as over 2,000 American bombers of the US Army Air Force once again departed airfields in southern England to support the rescheduled American offensive. Bradley had located his headquarters a few miles to the rear of the front line. As H-Hour approached, he eagerly awaited news of Cobra. As the first reports filtered through, an adjutant broke the tense silence in declaring *"They've done it again."* Absurdly, the preliminary bombardment had once more fallen short. In these two episodes of friendly fire, referred to as 'blue on blue', almost 750 American troops fell as casualties before first contact had been made with the enemy. Amongst the dead was General Leslie McNair, Commander of the General Staff College and the highest-ranking American to be killed in action during the Second World War. Ironically, McNair was only present as an observer, killed during a mission to identify how combined operations could be made more efficient.

Although part of the preliminary bombardment had fallen short, at least two-thirds of the ordnance had hit the German lines with devastating effect, a fact recorded within the communiqués between the headquarters of Field Marshal von Kluge[105] and the Panzer Lehr's General Bayerlein. As Cobra was launched, von Kluge urged Bayerlein to hold the line at all costs, a request to which Bayerlein replied…

Out in front everyone is holding out. Everyone. My grenadiers and my engineers and my tank crews – they're all holding their ground. Not a single man is leaving his post… They are lying silent in their foxholes for they are dead. You may report to the Field Marshal that the Panzer Lehr Division is annihilated.[106]

Despite the might of American superiority in numbers, within the first hours of Cobra, the operations' success remained unclear. However, with Joe Collins' VII Corps as spearhead, and Middleton's VIII Corps in support, the sheer weight of American strength eventually told, and within five days the American advance had progressed an impressive twenty-five miles.

Finally, Monty's masterplan was in full effect. After seven weeks of bitter combat, the enemy had been emasculated through the combined efforts of the Anglo-Canadian coalition. By the time the majority of American forces were committed to battle, the enemy held neither the will, nor the resources, to offer anything other than token resistance in the face of irresistible numerical supremacy. At last the shackles had been broken, the Allies were on the move.

Four days into Cobra, the tanks of the US Army's 2nd Armored Division were negotiating the narrow lanes which ran through the dense hedgerow country at the bottom of the Cotentin Peninsula. Amongst the ranks of the Hell on Wheels Division was Hulon

B. 'Rocky' Whittington, a 23-year-old sergeant from Bogalusa, Louisiana. Approaching midnight on 29 July, fifteen miles south of the start line of the American breakout, a strong enemy attack advanced upon the village of Grimesnil. With the attack infiltrating American positions, Sergeant Whittington calmly organised his section's defence and, whilst under fire, courageously crawled from one foxhole to another in order to check the situation at the front line.

With the advancing enemy now overwhelming an American road block, Sergeant Whittington mounted a tank, and communicating with the crew by shouting through the turret, directed it into position to fire at the enemy's lead tank at almost point blank range. The tank was destroyed, bringing all the enemy's mechanised units behind it to a standstill. The column of blocked vehicles was then methodically destroyed before Whittington himself commanded a bayonet charge against the enemy's infantry. When the unit's medic became a casualty, Sergeant Whittington personally administered first aid to the wounded. For his actions that day he would receive the Medal of Honor.

Remaining in the military after the war, Whittington was promoted to the rank of Major in September 1960 and served during the Vietnam War. Retiring from the Army in March 1963, he then lived and worked in Toledo, Ohio. Major Hulon Whittington died on 17 January 1969, at the age of 47. He is buried at Arlington National Cemetery.

Huge columns of men and material were now surging through the broken German line, out of the Cotentin peninsula and into relatively open country. The British and Canadian forces may be forgiven in thinking it was now time for some well-earned rest and relaxation. There would be no such luck!

As the American breakout once again dominated the newspaper headlines, it was left to Commonwealth forces to take the strain and hold the bulk of the enemy to their front, so that the Americans, in facing the minimum opposition, could continue to exploit their advantage. To this effect, on 30 July, Montgomery launched the Normandy campaign's largest sub-operation to date. Operation Bluecoat, involving 200,000 British and Canadian troops, held the tactical goal of making an advance up to the line of the main Vire to Vassy road, the main strategy of such an advance being the creation of an immediate buffer to shield the left flank of the adjacent American advance.

Intelligence gained through decrypting German codes had informed Montgomery that elements of the SS forces intended to disengage from the battle of Caen, to counter against the American forces now streaming through the frail German line. Bluecoat would block this movement and write down any German attempt to move to the west.

Sergeant
HULON B. WHITTINGTON
2nd Armoured Division

For conspicuous gallantry and intrepidity at the risk of life above and beyond the call of duty. On the night of 29 July 1944, near Grimesnil, France, during an enemy armoured attack, Sgt. Whittington, a squad leader, assumed command of his platoon when the platoon leader and platoon sergeant became missing in action. He reorganized the defence and, under fire, courageously crawled between gun positions to check the actions of his men. When the advancing enemy attempted to penetrate a roadblock, Sgt. Whittington, completely disregarding intense enemy action, mounted a tank and by shouting through the turret, directed it into position to fire point-blank at the leading Mark V German tank. The destruction of this vehicle blocked all movement of the remaining enemy column consisting of over 100 vehicles of a Panzer unit. The blocked vehicles were then destroyed by hand grenades, bazooka, tank, and artillery fire and large numbers of enemy personnel were wiped out by a bold and resolute bayonet charge inspired by Sgt. Whittington. When the medical aid man had become a casualty, Sgt. Whittington personally administered first aid to his wounded men. The dynamic leadership, the inspiring example, and the dauntless courage of Sgt. Whittington, above and beyond the call of duty, are in keeping with the highest traditions of the military service.

Operation Bluecoat would be launched with VIII British Army Corps in the lead, alongside the British XXX Corps to their left. General *Pip* Roberts' 11th Armoured Division was assigned as the British spearhead of the VIII Corps' advance. From the off, the 11th Armoured made light work in progressing through some of the worst of Normandy's bocage country. Seemingly at will, Roberts' *Black Bull* Division charged its way through the area known to the locals as the Suisse Normand (an area supposedly reminiscent of the Swiss Alps).

All opposition the enemy could muster was swept aside as the *Black Bull* drove deep into bocage country, to the extent that the British vanguard was now, not only supporting the US forces, but in fact outrunning the Americans to their right. Nonetheless, Montgomery ordered VIII Corps to maintain the momentum, and using the Amer-

Below: *British infantry and armour advance through the Normandy bocage during Operation Bluecoat.*

ican colloquialism *'Step on the gas'*, Montgomery ordered the British advance to proceed upon the town of Vire, known locally as the capital of the bocage country and a key hub of the region's road network. By coincidence, Vire was the perimeter of operations of the German 7th Army and Panzer Group West. Incredibly, neither party had deemed it their responsibility to defend such a crucial position, and with the prized objective wide open, Roberts' 11th Armoured continued their night march with the dexterity and skill that would have had the world basking in awe if executed by the likes of General Patton.

Above: *The ruins of the ancient town of Vire after its liberation in August 1944.*

Within seventy-two hours of the operation's start, reconnaissance patrols of the 2nd Household Cavalry entered the town and reported it undefended and ripe for the taking. With such a prized possession laying wide open, and available for what Roberts described as *'what would have been nothing more than a skirmish'*, the prize was cruelly wrestled from the jaws of the *Black Bull* - not by the enemy, but by the actions of their own high command.

Maybe because of growing sensitivity from the Americans, having now witnessed British troops advance through the kind of terrain which had previously caused virtual paralysis on their front, General Gerow, commander of the US Army V Corps insisted

Left: *Infantry of the 2nd Glasgow Highlanders, 15th Scottish Division, advance during Operation Bluecoat.*

that Vire, an objective originally allocated to American troops, should indeed be taken exclusively by American, and not British forces. With the British and American commands bickering, and Gerow petitioning the highest echelons of American command, Montgomery backed down in the interest of Allied harmony and allowed the Americans their desire of claiming yet more headlines.

Above: *British infantry advance upon Mont Pincon – the highest ground in Normandy.*

Once more, like at St Lo six weeks previously, an advance which would have led to an objective being taken quickly and relatively cheaply, was once again needlessly left open for the enemy to reinforce. As a consequence, it would not be for another four days and an additional 3,000 American casualties had been suffered, that Vire was taken and Gerow got his name in lights in taking the town that British forces could have secured virtually unopposed four days earlier.

If the armoured charge of the *Black Bull* was impressive, the advance of the British XXX Corps to the east did not match the same pace. Bogged down by a combination of the thick bocage and the presence of the remnants of the Nazi's most committed fighting men, by 6 August, the eastern flank of Operation Bluecoat had descended into a brutal slogging match fought between SS and British troops, a struggle centred upon Mont Pincon, the highest ground in Normandy.

Pitted not only against the 1st SS *Liebstandarte*, but also elements of both the 2nd SS *Das Reich* and the 12th SS *Hitler Jugend*, XXX Corps' Bluecoat advance had stalled. By 5 August the 3rd Battalion of the Monmouthshire Regiment had been holding the northern slopes of Perriers Ridge, close to the hamlet of Pavee, for three long days against intense attacks from the grenadiers and armour of three SS Panzer

Divisions supported by the Tiger tanks of the *Schwere SS-Panzer-Abteilung.*

Around midnight on 5 August, the 1st Norfolk Battalion was instructed to relieve the shattered remnants of the Monmouths, as Major Wilson of the Norfolks explained...

At around midnight I made contact with Brigadier Jack Churchill who pointed out a burning ridge in the distance and said "There are the Monmouths, or what is left of them. Be careful how you go as we are only in wireless touch with them. Be prepared to take over from them at first light".[107]

It was under the most horrific mortar and artillery fire that this transition took place. As the Norfolks moved forward, before the Monmouths could disengage, the combined force of fewer than 550 men encountered the full wrath of the heaviest attack to be made by the enemy during the whole three-day engagement. With the counter-attack about to overwhelm the British line, 23-year-old Londoner Sidney Bates, having just witnessed an 18-year-old from his section die in his arms, entered the fray. As Captain Ian Dye recalled...

The most enormous barrage came down on us which made any movement out impossible... This barrage was a prelude to a major German armoured assault... Because the German attack was preceded by two or three Tiger tanks, the Germans came forward in column, the Panzer Grenadiers riding on the backs of tanks. And when they got to within, say, 200 yards, the tanks in echelon came out behind them so you had a solid row of a dozen or fourteen tanks with Panzer Grenadiers between them running with their rifles... the tanks were firing an 88... The Panzer Grenadiers got to within a hundred and fifty yards... Bates said to his section, "You stay here. I'm going to sort this lot out"... He left the trench, carrying a Bren Gun... He ran forward about thirty yards firing at these Grenadiers... Then he was hit and he went down, and he actually

Corporal

SIDNEY BATES

1st Battalion of the Royal Norfolk Regiment, 185th Brigade of the 3rd Infantry Division

In North-West West Europe on 6 August, 1944, the position held by a battalion of the Royal Norfolk Regiment near Sourdeval was attacked in strength by 10th SS Panzer Division. The attack started with a heavy and accurate artillery and mortar programmed on the position which the enemy had, by this time, pin-pointed. Half an hour later the main attack developed and heavy machine-gun and mortar fire was concentrated on the point of junction of the two forward companies. Corporal Bates was commanding the right forward section of the left forward company which suffered some casualties, so he decided to move the remnants of his section to an alternative position whence he appreciated he could better counter the enemy thrust. However, the enemy wedge grew still deeper, until there were about 50 to 60 Germans, supported by machine guns and mortars, in the area occupied by the section.

Seeing that the situation was becoming desperate, Corporal Bates then seized a light machine-gun and charged the enemy, moving forward through a hail of bullets and splinters and firing the gun from his hip. He was almost immediately wounded by machine-gun fire and fell to the ground, but recovered himself quickly, got up and continued advancing towards the enemy, spraying bullets from his gun as he went. His action by now was having an effect on the enemy riflemen and machine gunners but mortar bombs continued to fall all around him.

He was then hit for the second time and much more seriously and painfully wounded. However, undaunted, he staggered once more to his feet and continued towards the enemy who were now seemingly nonplussed by their inability to check him. His constant firing continued until the enemy started to withdraw before him. At this moment, he was hit for the third time by mortar bomb splinters - a wound that was to prove mortal. He again fell to the ground but continued to fire his weapon until his strength failed him. This was not, however, until the enemy had withdrawn and the situation in this locality had been restored.

Corporal Bates died shortly afterwards of the wounds he had received, but, by his supreme gallantry and self-sacrifice he had personally restored what had been a critical situation.

changed the magazine, got up and went forward again another forty yards and he was hit again. He stayed down, a minute possibly, and then he got up, still firing, and staggered another fifteen yards and then he went down and he didn't move again. And the Company seeing this – you could hear them shouting "Go on Basher"! – They got their heads up and they started firing in spite of all the amount of firing coming at them. And you could see the German Grenadiers falter and stop and then they went to ground… We kept firing at them and they got up and started to fall back… We brought anti-tank weapons in and we called our own artillery down on top of ourselves because it was so close… All of us who witnessed this had no doubt at all that, if Bates had not done what he did, within a short time the Panzer Grenadiers would have been amongst us'.[108]

Right: *Fighting street by street, Caen is finally liberated during the second week of July.*

Stretcher-bearer Ernie Seaman was part of the team that evacuated Sidney Bates from the battlefield; *'Basher killed at least seventeen Germans firing a Bren Gun from the hip… I was involved picking him up. He had a bullet hole through the throat and through his legs but he was still alive'.*[109] Sidney Bates succumbed to his wounds two days after he was evacuated. For his actions on 6 August 1944, Sidney Bates would receive the Victoria Cross. He is buried at the Bayeux Commonwealth War Graves Cemetery.

Mont Pincon fell to the British on the same day that Sidney Bates was mortally wounded. With the loss of the highest ground in Normandy, here ended the last hope of the Germans being able to switch a significant force from the Caen sector to oppose Operation Cobra. However, with battlegroups formed from the shattered remnants of the II SS Panzer Corps surviving the battle to fight another day, a fraction of this force was then switched against US Forces. Critics of Montgomery, and there are plenty, have contrived to cite Operation Bluecoat as a strategic defeat and whilst it is true that elements of the II SS Panzer Corps did indeed survive Bluecoat, the mere fact that the II SS Panzer Corps' records indicate that post-Bluecoat, the combined strength of the 9th SS and 10th SS Panzer Divisions numbered no more than 30 armoured vehicles (less than ten per cent of the strength with which it first engaged), it seems a little disingenuous for those who benefited so much from the neo-destruction of this formation to make complaints that such a diminutive fraction survived before being moved against the American forces further west.

Below: *Men of the 15th Scottish Infantry Division advance during Operation Bluecoat.*

With the American breakout in full flow, and with Mont Pincon now lost, *Generalfeldmarschall* von Kluge was under no illusion that he was facing anything but a hopeless cause. Having already had his requests for a withdrawal to the banks of the River Seine dismissed out of hand by Hitler, on 7 August, having received orders pub-

lished directly by the Fuhrer himself, helpless in voicing opposition, lest he face inevitable replacement, von Kluge was instructed to detach what was left of his armour from the Caen front, and attempt to drive through to Avranches and stem the flow of the American breakout.

Codenamed *Luttich*, von Kluge's operation attempted to detach elements of the 1st SS and 2nd SS Panzer Divisions to face the Americans at the bottom of the Cherbourg Peninsula. Doomed to failure before *Luttich* even commenced, the German spearhead was unable to extract enough strength from the Commonwealth sector to rally a force anywhere near capable of achieving such ambitious aims. The German situation was made increasingly untenable given that, through decrypts of their codes, General Bradley had learned of the enemy's intent on the eve of their offensive. Aware that any major redeployment of the American forces may make the Germans aware that the German codes had been broken, although Bradley primed the better part of two Army Corps toward the threat, General Hobbs, commanding the 30th Infantry Division, the forces most likely to make first contact, was not informed of the impending attack which was soon to arrive against his troops, an attack launched not in a huge concentration of strength, but an attack made by the enemy's elite, a level above what the American forces had so far encountered, a fact remarked upon by the official American historian…

Below: *Operations 25-31 July 1944.*

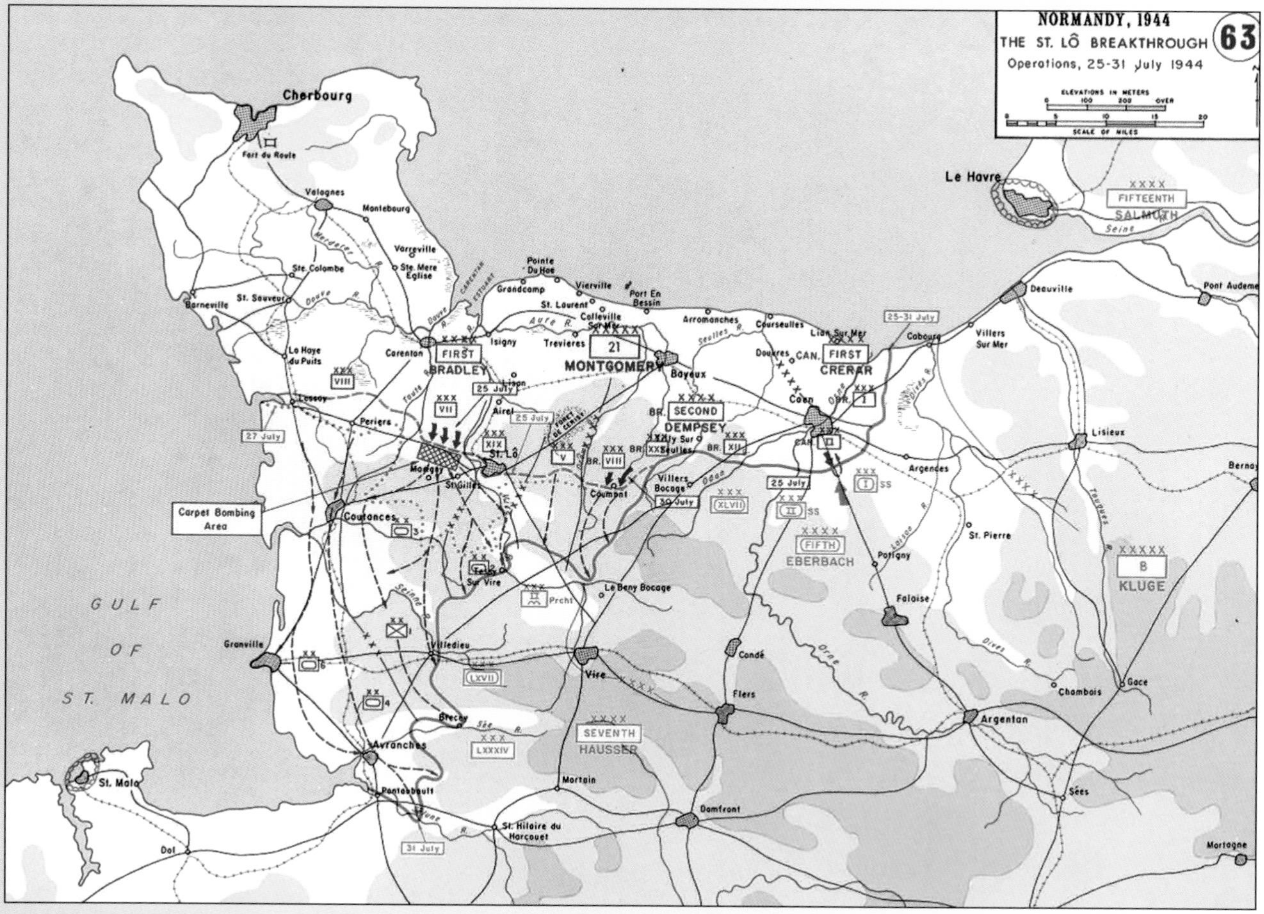

Left: *For two months British and Canadian troops fended off all of Rommel's attempts to throw the Allies back into the sea.*

The German troops were good. Not invincible, but the regular Wehrmacht units nevertheless had "staying power," while SS forces and paratroopers were a breed apart: Elite troops, with an unshakable morale, they asked no quarter and made certain that they gave none.[110]

Such a revelation was a detail long since appreciated by the British and Canadians.

At Mortain, although heavily outnumbered and suffering crippling losses, with the assistance of the rocket firing Typhoons of the Royal Air Force hammering the enemy's advancing armour, the American line held. The 30th Division's stand at Mortain has become legendary, but the German portrayal of the battle offers two different explanations as to why the attack ultimately failed. Whilst in no way belittling such an achievement, it is now generally accepted amongst most historians, that von Kluge, in committing only a nominal force against the American line, had offered just enough of a threat to save face, whilst at the same time, not destabilising his whole front to an immediately fatal extent. Secondly, in the words of Geyr von Sweppenburg (commanding Panzer Group West), *'Whether you realise it or not, it was British rocket-carrying planes that halted our counter-attack at Avranches, not your 30th Infantry Division'.*[111]

Luttich never had a realistic chance of presenting a serious danger to Bradley's breakout. Instead, a force was mustered which was just strong enough to appease the suspicions of those sent to von Kluge's headquarters to ensure that the Fuhrer's orders were adhered to. Nonetheless, dispersed across the entire line, von Kluge's force was becoming so far unhinged that the opportunity finally arrived for the Allies to encircle and then annihilate the German Army in Normandy.

Despite the hopeless cause, von Kluge remained under pressure from Hitler to maintain contact on the Mortain front, as General Eberbach (at the time Commanding Panzer Group West) later stated...

Above: *American troops tentatively advance through Mortain after the German counter attack of 7 August 1944.*

General der Panzertruppen Heinrich Eberbach 1895-1992

Commander of Panzergruppe West (from 4 July 1944 – 9 August 1944), subsequently designated _Panzergruppe Eberbach_ (from 10 August 1944 to 21 August 1944)

Heinrich Alfons Willy Eberbach was born in Stuttgart in 1895. The son of a merchant and one of five siblings, Eberbach's father died when he was six years old, leaving his mother to raise the family alone. Graduating from high-school on 30 June 1914, and joining the Wurttemberg Regiment as a *Gefreiter* (Corporal) the day after, he would be wounded twice before being taken prisoner by the French during the Great War. Eberbach would work as a policeman during the inter-war years before enlisting into a resurgent Wehrmacht in 1935.

Fast establishing himself as a naturally talented leader, Eberbach would be given a regimental command within the 4th Panzer Division in 1938. His ever-growing reputation would be further enhanced during the invasion of Poland in 1939 and the battle for France in 1940. In June 1941, he would be assigned command of the 5th Panzer Brigade within Geyr von Schweppenburg's XXIV Panzer Corps.

Arguably the pinnacle of Eberbach's career arrived in September 1941 as he commanded his own *Kampfgruppe* (battlegroup) during the German advance in the east. Suffering minimal losses to his own force, in just two days Eberbach drove over 70 miles into enemy territory, leaving the Soviet forces in a state of disarray, taking over 1,500 prisoners, capturing the city of Orel and placing the vanguard of the German advance just 200 miles from Moscow. Given command of the 4th Panzer Division in March 1942, then appointed commander of XLVIII Panzer Corps in November of that year, Eberbach's epic journey from *Gefreiter* to *General der Panzertruppen* would have to be put on hold as a kidney complaint forced his hospitalisation until the spring of 1943. His rehabilitation would be almost half a year in the making, albeit during this time he did hold various staff roles within Germany before rejoining the fight against Soviet forces in November 1943.

With the tide turning against the Germans on the Eastern Front, Eberbach would be sent west to face a potential invasion by the Western Allies. On 2 July 1944, after Geyr von Schweppenburg was wounded, Eberbach would take command of Panzergruppe West which, eight days later, would be redesignated as *Panzergruppe Eberbach*. With the Germans facing an increasingly incurable situation, Eberbach would escape the chaos of the Falaise Pocket, only to be taken prisoner by British forces a few days later. Held in captivity until 1948, during which time Eberbach would gain paid employment through the US Army Historical Division – with his most noted work being entitled *'Panzer Group Eberbach and the Falaise Encirclement'*.

Eberbach died aged 96 in 1992, he is buried at the municipal cemetery at Notzingen, near Stuttgart.

This would have been the right time for Field Marshal von Kluge to act against Hitler's orders to save the two armies. But after [the failed assassination attempt of] *July 20, he was watched in such a sharp way that it would have been especially difficult for him. The result would have simply been his substitution by a more manageable tool.*[112]

By 11 August, with the Americans now having secured Le Mans and now moving toward Alencon, with Mont Pincon now in British hands, the Allies were threatening to envelop the remnants of the Germans in Normandy. With the Americans closing in on the Germans from the west and south, with the British presence acting as the mainstay to the north, the scene was set for the Canadians to tighten the noose from the east.

Chapter 12
Setting the Trap

Launched on 7 August, Operation Totalize would amass three infantry and two armoured divisions, with an additional two armoured brigades attached, a combined force exceeding 100,000 men and more than 350 tanks, to drive down the dead straight Caen to Falaise road, deep into the enemy and to a position upon the high ground to the north of the ancient town of Falaise. Such a manoeuvre would not just once more tie down enemy forces, in this instance the remnants of the 1st SS Panzer Corps and the German 15th Army's newly arrived 89th Infantry Division, but also, and most importantly, initiate an eastern pincer, which in combination with the operations to the west, would now initiate the encirclement of the remnants of the German Army in Normandy.

Primarily a Canadian affair, Operation Totalize was commanded by 41-year-old Guy Simonds, Canada's youngest Corps Commander. For Totalize to succeed, Simonds would have to overcome the very same problems which had blighted the previous campaigns launched upon the Caen plains. Operation Goodwood had achieved its strategic goal of tying down German armour, but failed in its tactical goal of advancing through the same terrain that Simonds would have to conquer if Totalize was to succeed. The level plains, stretching in places as far as the eye can see, and

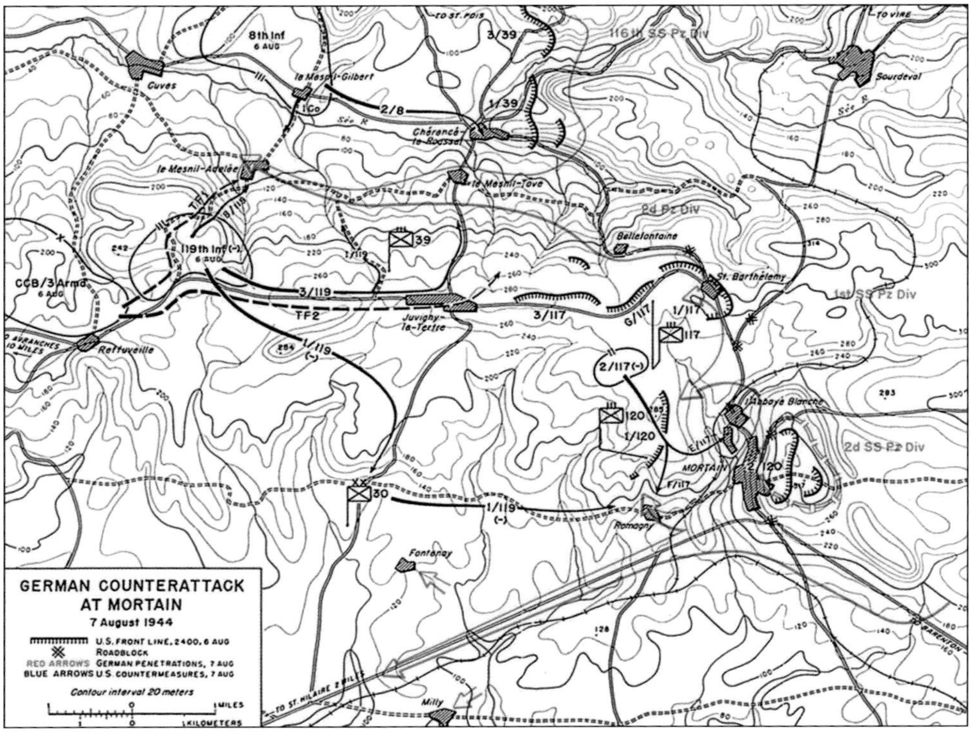

Left: *German Counterattack at Mortain, 7 August 1944.*

largely devoid of any feature, bar a defender's dream of a combination of copses of woods and ancient fortified villages, represented what one Canadian historian has described as *'the worst possible country for armour'.*[113] Operation Totalize would face, not just the remnants of the 1st SS Panzer Corps, but also a layered defensive line of over 100 anti-tank guns. Just the assembly of such a force, let alone the launch of such a huge combined attack of both tanks and infantry, under the very nose of a watching enemy, would need much consideration.

Thankfully, in Guy Simonds, the Allies possessed a man already nurturing a growing reputation for innovation, a skill that would lead him to become one of the highest regarded Generals of the whole North West European campaign. Through the implementation of several pioneering techniques, Simonds plotted to overcome the same problems that had hindered previous endeavors such as Goodwood. Knowing that it would be impossible to position his force at its start line in daylight hours, he chose to use a system first developed by the British Army during the North African campaign. Nicknamed *Monty's Moonlight,* Simonds guided his forces to their start line at night using the glow generated by bouncing rays from searchlights off low-lying cloud. Armour was manoeuvred into position through the darkness in columns following the immediate path of the tank in front of them. Each tank would position itself according to a system of radio waves, which would remain constant if those following stayed directly in formation. If a tank strayed, the transmission became intermittent and the crew would correct its position accordingly.

Instead of laying solely a conventional artillery barrage on the enemy's front line in preperation of the assault, the air force would pave the way in pounding the enemy's forward positions before artillery laid a rolling barrage in the immediate path of the advancing armour. Realising the necessity, but appreciating the difficulty of integrating infantry within an armoured assault; aware that since D-Day a huge number of Commonwealth gunners had swapped their self-propelled guns (Sextons) for the conventional 25lb artillery piece, at breakneck speed, Simonds ordered over 2,000 British and Canadian engineers to *de-frock* the guns from the chassis of their tracked carriers. Seventy-two armoured infantry carriers were promptly improvised. Nicknamed *Kangaroos*, each could carry a dozen infantrymen, providing mobility and protection to the foot soldiers who otherwise could so easily be mowed down when moving through such open ground.

Above: *General Simonds' Kangaroos roll during Operation Totalize.*

Just before midnight on the evening of 7 August, over 1,000 RAF bombers delivered almost 3,500 tons of high explosives upon the enemy's front line, located four miles to the south of Caen, the subsequent rolling artillery barrage paving the way for Simonds' armoured juggernaut. Although stiff resistance in towns and villages such as May sur Orne, St Andre sur Orne and Tilly la Campagne cost elements of the

Lieutenant General Guy Granville Simonds 1903-1974

Commander of Canadian Army II Corps.

Guy Granville Simonds was born in 1903 into a military family from Suffolk, England. With his Great-Grandfather, Grandfather and Father all having served within the British Army, Guy would become the fourth generation of his family to reach at minimum the rank of Colonel. At the age of 9, Simonds' family would emigrate to Canada. Upon graduation from the Royal Military Academy of Canada in 1926, Simonds was awarded the Sword of Honour, the award for the year group's best all round graduate. Commissioned into the Royal Canadian Artillery, by the commencement of the Second World War, Simonds had gained the rank of Major within the staff of the 1st Canadian Infantry Division.

Arriving in Great Britain three months after the outbreak of war, and subsequently gaining commands at regiment and then brigade level, it was at this time, whilst serving under the command of Generals Harry Crerar (Commanding I Canadian Army Corps) and Andrew McNaughton (General Officer Commanding First Canadian Army), that Simonds first endured what became increasingly fractious relationships with his immediate superiors. Whilst tensions mounted within the Canadian command, at the same time, Simonds became recognised in a very positive light to the British General, Bernard Montgomery.

In January 1943 Simonds became Chief of Staff to the First Canadian Army. However, eager to have rid of Simonds, Mc-Naughton placed him on detachment to Montgomery's Eighth Army which was at the time vanquishing Rommel's forces from Tunisia. Three days before his 40th birthday, on 20 April 1943, Simonds was again promoted meaning that in less than three and a half years, Guy Simonds had now advanced from the rank of Major to Major General – this journey made in a shorter timeframe than any other Canadian before him.

Given command of the 1st Canadian Infantry Division for the invasion of Sicily, Simonds was now Canada's youngest ever officer to lead a division in combat. Losing that command due to illness, following his recovery, Simonds would be recalled as commander of the Canadian 5th Armoured Division, a command at the equivalent level he held prior to illness, and an appointment which led to the rekindling of Simonds' ever deteriorating association with Harry Crerar (now commanding Canadian I Corps). Recalled to Britain in January 1944, Simonds' meteoric rise to the top continued as he was given command of Canadian II Corps, a formation he led through the battle for Normandy until September 1944 when he temporarily took command of the Canadian First Army as Crerar recovered from a bout of dysentery. Many would state that this was a defining moment in the history of the Canadian First Army; *'Simonds' assumption of command reinvigorated the Army HQ; where Crerar managed, Simonds commanded'.** Although thoroughly successful, his time as commander of First Canadian Army was short lived and Simonds would move back to command II Corps upon Crerar's return to duty. After the war, Guy Simonds would become Chief Instructor at the Imperial Defence College in London. In 1949, he returned to Canada as Commandant of the Royal Military College of Canada. In 1951 he was appointed Chief of the Canadian General Staff.

Remembered as one, if not the very best Canadian General of the Second World War, Guy Simonds died of lung cancer aged 71 in 1974. He is buried at Mount Pleasant Cemetery in Toronto.

* P Dickson – *The Limits of Professionalism: General H.D.G. Crerar and the Canadian Army, 1914-1944.* PhD Thesis, University of Guelph, 1993.

Canadian infantry valuable time, and in some instances substantial casualties, the first hours of the operation witnessed Totalize driving 60,000 Commonwealth troops eight miles into enemy held ground.

Having reached the initial objective line, the vanguard of the advance temporarily paused to let the second assault wave pass in anticipation of the final push to the ultimate objective of the high ground north of the city of Falaise. This transition would be supported by a second aerial bombardment, this time courtesy of the US Army Air Force. With chilling parallels to the events preceding the launch of Bradley's Operation Cobra, as the 4th Canadian and 1st Polish Armoured Divisions moved forward to resume the assault, they were hit by their own bombs. Stunned into a state of inertia, their line was then immediately hit by a counterattack from the 12th SS *Hitler Jugend*. With American bombers obliging the fanatical SS Grenadiers with the kind of supporting bombardment they could only dream of being provided by their own *Luftwaffe*, SS infantry and tanks took the initiative. Within just a few minutes, forty of the fifty-two Sherman tanks of the Polish 24th Lancers were in flames.

With momentum lost, the second phase of Totalize would persist for another three days, whilst no ground was conceded, the second phase yielded only limited gains. Having claimed eight miles in the first twelve hours, stunned by the shortfall of the second phase aerial bombardment, combined with the counterattacks of the fanatical 12th SS, reinforced by the 89th Infantry Division, themselves subsequently joined by the newly arrived 85th Infantry Division (initially intended to be placed against the American breakout), Totalize concluded after four days, seven miles short of the objective of Falaise.

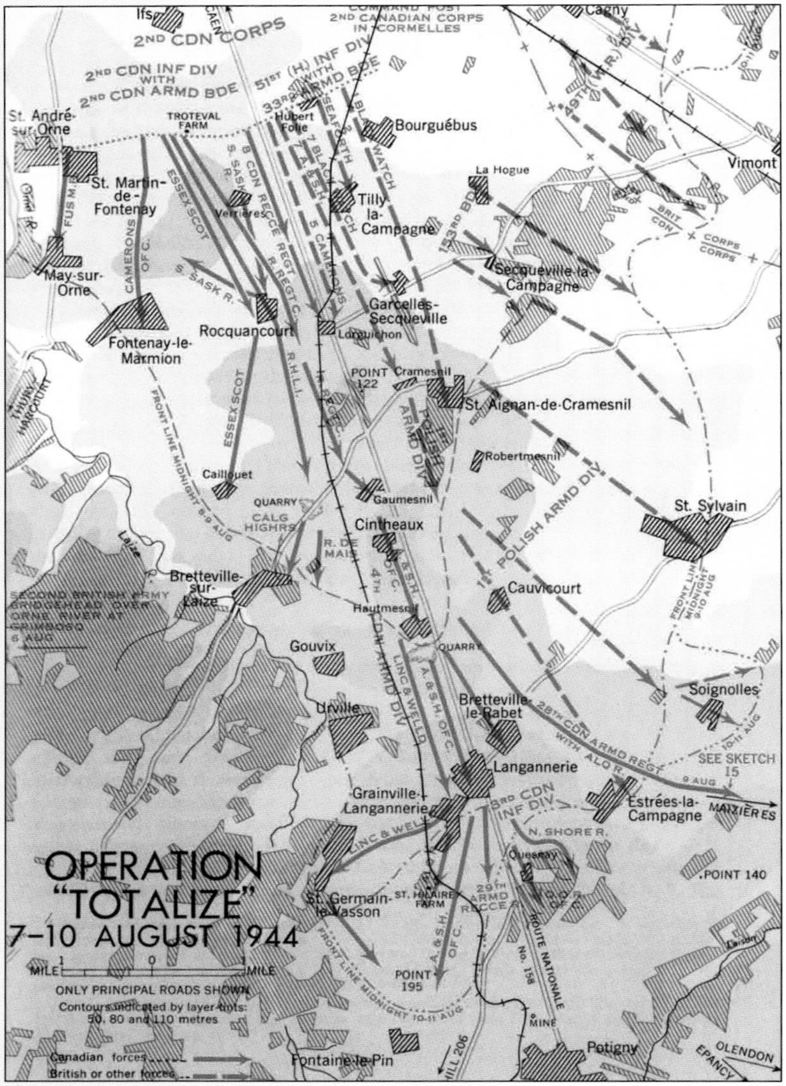

Above: *Operation Totalize.*

As Guy Simonds' Canadian II Corps took the thrust deep into enemy held ground, their right flank was being held by the British XII Corps. On 8 August, close to the village of Grimbosq, the British 59th Infantry Division was facing a bitter struggle to cross the River Orne. It was here that an engagement took place which led to only the third Victoria Cross being awarded for actions during the Battle of Normandy.

An Old Etonian, 23-year-old David Jamieson was the eldest son of Sir Archibald Jamieson, Chairman of Vickers Armstrong, a British arms manufacturer that designed and built anything from machine guns to Spitfires. At the forefront of the British war effort, such a corporation was undoubtedly one of the most important manufacturers of war material during the Second World War. Having volunteered to join the Territorial Army three months before the outbreak of war, at the age of just 18, Jamieson was deemed too young for overseas service and was therefore left out of the strength of the 7th Battalion of the Royal Norfolk Regiment as it set sail for France in 1939.

Captain

DAVID A. JAMIESON

7th Battalion of the Royal Norfolk Regiment, 176th Brigade of the 59th Infantry Division

Captain Jamieson was in command of a Company of The Royal Norfolk Regiment which established a bridgehead over the River Orne, south of Grimbosq in Normandy. On 7 August 1944 the enemy made three counter-attacks which were repulsed with heavy losses. The last of these took place at 1830 hrs when a German Battle Group with Tiger and Panther tanks attacked and the brunt of the fighting fell on Captain Jamieson's Company. Continuous heavy fighting ensued for more than four hours until the enemy were driven off, after suffering severe casualties and the loss of three tanks and an armoured car accounted for by this Company. Throughout these actions, Captain Jamieson displayed outstanding courage and leadership, which had a decisive influence on the course of the battle and resulted in the defeat of these determined enemy attacks.

On the morning of 8 August the enemy attacked with a fresh Battle Group and succeeded in penetrating the defences surrounding the Company on three sides. During this attack two of the three tanks in support of the Company were destroyed and Captain Jamieson left his trench under close range fire from enemy arms of all kinds and went over to direct the fire of the remaining tank, but as he could not get in touch with the commander of the tank by the outside telephone, he climbed upon it in full view of the enemy. During this period Captain Jamieson was wounded in the right eye and left forearm but when his wounds were dressed he refused to be evacuated. By this time all the other officers had become casualties so Captain Jamieson reorganised his Company, regardless of personal safety, walking amongst his men in full view of the enemy, as there was no cover. After several hours of bitter and confused fighting the Germans were driven from the company position.

The enemy counter-attacked the Company three more times during that day with infantry and tanks. Captain Jamieson continued in command, arranging for artillery support over his wireless and going out into the open on each occasion to encourage his men. By the evening the Germans had withdrawn, leaving a ring of dead and burnt out tanks round his position.

Throughout this thirty-six hours of bitter and close fighting, and despite the pain of his wounds, Captain Jamieson showed superb qualities of leadership and great personal bravery. There were times when the position appeared hopeless, but on each occasion it was restored by his coolness and determination. He personally was largely responsible for the holding of this important bridgehead over the River Orne and the repulse of seven German counter-attacks with great loss to the enemy.

Although bitterly disappointed, this did mean that Jamieson was spared the fate of the rest of the battalion, which as part of the British Expeditionary Force's 51st Highland Division, during the battle for France in 1940, had the majority of its strength killed or taken prisoner as it became cut off behind enemy lines near Rouen. The battalion reformed in 1941 and then, at the age of 20, Jamieson was given command of 'D' Company of the resurrected 7th Battalion, a post he held on 8 August 1944, when, in his own words…

We arrived on the bank of the River Orne… and the colonel said that I and Jim Walcott, another company commander, were to take down a reconnaissance patrol to see whether it was possible to get over the river… I was told to lead the battalion at

Left: *Guy Simonds, Churchill, Montgomery and Miles Dempsey.*

night through a wood down to the new crossing place that had been found… I was in charge of seven hundred men, all carrying enormous loads… I found a way through but of course we were getting mortared… By dawn we'd dug in… I don't know how many times we were attacked… We saw the German tanks… Out they came, out of the wood straight across our front, and Sergeant Courtman knocked out all three just like that. Next thing that happened they attacked a bit further over… They came round behind and they shot two of my Churchills, so I only had one Churchill left… The next day, another attack came in. And I tried to signal to the final tank to keep back because we were under great fire and the German tanks were coming in to our position… I leapt out of my little hole and I rushed up… I climbed up the back of the tank and lent over and banged and said 'get the hell out of here!' At that moment the tank was blown up… I was covered in blood and god knows what and of course the tank brewed up and that of course was my last tank gone. I returned to my hole, feeling very sorry for myself… All I'd got was one eye completely gone and my arm was bleeding a lot, but not seriously, mostly from little bits of tank. Well, I didn't feel so bad so we went on.[114]

Jamieson's personal testimony, with typical stoic understatement, belies the intensity of the struggle he faced, a struggle which may be better understood through the narrative of the citation for his Victoria Cross.

After the war, Jamieson moved to Australia where he worked managing several sheep ranches. On his return to the UK, and back home in Norfolk, he would become a director of numerous businesses, including the National Westminster Bank. In 1969, Jamieson, quite aptly due to his height of 6 feet 5 inches, was made High Sheriff of Norfolk. Again, quite appropriately, he would also become, the occasional official umbrella bearer for Queen Elizabeth, the Queen Mother.

Major David Jamieson VC CVO died aged 80 in May 2001. He is buried in the churchyard at Burnham Norton, Norfolk and his Victoria Cross is displayed at the Royal Norfolk Regimental Museum at Norwich Castle.

The battles fought between the cities of Caen and Falaise bore witness to some of the fiercest struggles endured during the entire war. This fact, if not appreciated by him at the time, was certainly acknowledged after the war by the Allies' Supreme Commander who in 1946 wrote in his official report of operations in North-West Europe...

From our landings in June until that day, the enemy resistance in this sector had exacted more Allied bloodshed for the ground yielded than in any other part of the campaign. Without the great sacrifices made here by the Anglo-Canadian armies in the series of brutal, slugging battles, first for Caen and then for Falaise, the spectacular advances made elsewhere by the Allied forces could never have come about.[115]

Below: *A column of Polish armour leads the charge of Operation Totalise.*

Within two weeks, through Operation Totalize, then Tractable, General Guy Simonds had engaged the 12th SS *Hitler Jugend* and the 85th and 89th Infantry Divisions to the point of near annihilation. In facing the 88mm guns of the *Luftwaffe's III Flak Corps*, through twenty miles of terrain which offered barely any cover for advancing troops, Simonds' reputation continued to grow, but not without a price. Having been in the field for less than three weeks, the infantry of the 1st Canadian Army were now at a little over half of their original strength. Despite such losses the Canadians were now at the edge of the city of Falaise, and with General Patton's American forces approaching Argentan, by 15 August, the gap between the Commonwealth and American forces was now less than fifteen miles. The Germans in Normandy were by now in complete disarray, the noose was tightening but there remained a narrow corridor for the German forces to attempt to slip the net.

Above: *With its gun removed, this former 'Sexton' becomes a 'Kangaroo' armoured personnel carrier.*

To prevent the surviving enemy forces fleeing the setting trap, it was crucial that British forces maintained the pressure from the north. As part of this objective, the 53rd Welsh Infantry Division were to cut the main road into the city from the west. However, as their attack was launched, it immediately faltered. With elements of the 12th SS offering far fiercer than anticipated resistance, new orders were issued, changing the operational objective to advancing to a position upon, but not now beyond, the main road. However, one company, with their radios destroyed, and therefore unaware of the new directive, advanced beyond the line held by the rest of their brigade.

Unaware of their plight, elements of the 1/5th Battalion of the Royal Welch Regiment crossed the main road, oblivious that they were now occupying a salient in which they were surrounded on three sides. Now fighting a desperate struggle through the hamlet of Bafour (misspelled Balfour in official accounts), they were isolated, surrounded and facing unrelenting murderous fire when a miner's son from the Welsh valleys took the initiative in an action which surely saved his company from what otherwise would have been total obliteration.

Growing up in a small Welsh mining town during the Great Depression, fighting the odds and showing naturally outstanding ability at practically every task he set himself to, the award of a Grammar School scholarship would be just the first of many occasions when Tasker Watkins' natural talents were acknowledged and rewarded. Not just academically talented, Watkins was an accomplished athlete who captained his school's first team at football, cricket and rugby. At the outbreak of war, at the age of just 21, having qualified as a teacher, and now living in London, Tasker Watkins joined the British Army as a Private soldier in October 1939. In May 1941 he was selected for officer training before being commissioned as a Second Lieutenant within the 53rd Welsh Division. Serving with the Division from 1941 to July 1944, garrisoned solely on home defence duties during this time, the 53rd Welsh Division would face their baptism of fire in Normandy. From the very start they would be pitted against some of the most fanatical enemy forces to fight in the whole of the European Theatre.

Three weeks after arriving in Normandy, located three miles to the west of Falaise, on 16 August Tasker Watkins would find himself as the only surviving officer from his company engaged in a bitter fight against the *Hitler Jugend*. Unaware that his unit was now surrounded by the SS on three sides, he attempted to cross a railway line close to Bafour. Advancing through fields riddled with booby traps, Watkins' men, held a line which they should never have had to reach for five hours. In an action that is said to have accounted for fifty-five of the enemy's dead, Watkins himself led his ever-dwindling force in two attacks against the enemy's line, one of these being a desperate charge with fixed bayonets. Only when it became fully apparent that no other friendly unit was in proximity did Tasker Watkins give up his position and attempt to head back to British lines, taking just twenty-seven survivors from a starting strength of sixty men with him. For his actions at Bafour, Watkins would receive the Victoria Cross.

After the war, Watkins attended law school, once again excelling as he became a barrister, then a judge. A knighthood would follow in 1971 as Watkins became a leading figure of the British legal system, serving as Lord Justice of Appeal and deputy Lord Chief Justice. Back home in his native Wales, Watkins' passion for sport, particularly rugby, would lead him to become the longest serving President of the Welsh Rugby Union (1993 to 2004). Despite his humble beginnings, a lowly miner's son, Tasker Watkins is frequently cited as the greatest Welshman of the 20th Century.

The Right Honorable Sir Tasker Watkins VC GBE DL died aged 88 in September 2007. He was cremated at Thornhill Crematorium, Cardiff and his Victoria Cross is today displayed at the Lord Ashcroft Gallery at the Imperial War Museum in London. After his death, a statue of his likeness was erected at the Welsh National Stadium in Cardiff.

Lieutenant
TASKER WATKINS
1/5th Battalion, The Welch Regiment, 158th Brigade of the 53rd Infantry Division

In North-West Europe on the evening, of 16 August 1944, Lieutenant Watkins was commanding a company of the Welch Regiment. The battalion was ordered to attack objectives near the railway at Bafour. Lieutenant Watkin's company had to cross open cornfields in which booby-traps had been set. It was not yet dusk and the company soon came under heavy machine-gun-fire from posts in the corn and farther back, and also fire from an 88mm gun: many casualties were caused and the advance was slowed up.

Lieutenant Watkins, the only officer left, placed himself at the head of his men and under short range fire charged two posts in succession, personally killing or wounding the occupants with his Sten gun. On reaching his objective he found an anti-tank gun manned by a German soldier: his Sten gun jammed, so he threw it in the German's face and shot him with his pistol before he had time to recover. Lieutenant Watkin's company now had only some 30 men left and was counterattacked by 50 enemy infantry. Lieutenant Watkins directed the fire of his men and then led a bayonet charge, which resulted in the almost complete destruction of the enemy. It was now dusk and orders were given for the battalion to withdraw. These orders were not received by Lieutenant Watkin's company as the wireless set had been destroyed.

They now found themselves alone and surrounded in depleted numbers and in failing light. Lieutenant Watkins decided to rejoin his battalion by passing round the flank of the enemy position through which he had advanced but while passing through the cornfields once more, he was challenged by an enemy post at close range. He ordered his men to scatter and himself charged the post with a Bren gun and silenced it. He then led the remnants of his company back to battalion headquarters.

His superb gallantry and total disregard for his own safety during an extremely difficult period were responsible for saving the lives of his men, and had a decisive influence on the course of the battle.

Chapter 13

Tying the Noose

By the second week of August, von Kluge's much beleaguered forces were facing a seemingly terminal situation. To both the west and the north, the condition was beyond critical. The Americans had now taken Vire and were advancing on Argentan. The British, in securing Mont Pincon, were in full control holding the central ground, whilst the Canadians, on the edge of Falaise, were threatening to close the right pincer. For von Kluge, now surrounded on three sides, the only way to avoid total destruction would be to execute a mass withdrawal to the east, toward the River Seine. However, the dilemma remained as to how he could disengage and send his troops in the opposite direction to which Hitler was still insisting he placed his main effort. The whole German Seventh Army, now joined by elements of the Fifteenth Army, were in great peril of being encircled, and if this came to be, up to half a million German troops would be facing inevitable annihilation.

As von Kluge's crisis peaked, a great opportunity presented itself to the Allies. It had always been Montgomery's intent, having glued the bulk of the enemy's forces to the east, that the Americans would encircle from the rear. Whilst adhering to this core principle, with the German forces still committed to the long since hopeless mission of stemming the flow of the American breakout, it now became apparent that an encircling manoeuvre could be implemented, and with it the enemy could be trapped, not against the banks of the River Seine as was first anticipated, but instead within the valley of the River Dives, to the south of Falaise. However, for the Western Allies to succeed they would have to execute the kind of operation which they, even Montgomery himself, held no previous experience. Unlike the Russians on the Eastern Front who had implemented several operations which had enveloped and destroyed huge numbers of German troops, this was a new phenomenon for the Western Allies. Such a manoeuvre would take great planning, and involve intricate co-ordination amongst all parties to complete an effective outcome.

As the realisation of such an opportunity became fully appreciated by the high command, it was clear that the crucial questions were which troops would be allocated as the spearhead of the two pincers, and at what location should they meet. With a gap of only fifteen miles now separating them, it seemed only logical that Patton's Third Army and General Crerar's Canadian First Army should liaise directly and arrange to convene at a mutually agreed location. With Montgomery outlining such intent to General Crerar, and having conferred with General Bradley, the scene was set as the Allies now attempted a once in a lifetime opportunity representing every General's dream - to implement a full envelopment of the enemy. If successful, this would leave von Kluge's forces with just two options; capitulate or face total annihilation.

Patton's Third Army had been activated on 1 August in the immediate aftermath of Operation Cobra. Having waited so long to be finally let off the leash, Patton's relief threatened to spill over as he released the frustration that had been simmering away during the previous two months which he had spent as an unwilling spectator. In his own words, *'It is hell to be on the sidelines and see all the glory eluding me'.*[116] Not

Generalfeldmarschall Hans von Kluge 1882-1944

Commander of *Oberbefehlshaber West* (from 5 July 1944 to 17 August 1944) and combined commander of *Oberbefehlshaber West* and *Heeresgruppe B* (from 19 July 1944 to 17 August 1944)

Hans Gunther von Kluge was born in 1882 into an aristocratic family from Posen in Prussia (now Poznan, Poland). Joining the German Army in 1901, he served during the Great War as a staff officer with the rank of *Hauptmann* (Captain). Escaping the post-war purge of the German military, von Kluge remained within the restricted strength of the German Army during the inter-war years, and by the outbreak of the Second World War, had advanced to the rank of *General der Artillerie* (full General).

Commanding his 4th Army through Poland, Belgium, Holland and France, at the conclusion of these victorious campaigns von Kluge was promoted to *Generalfeldmarschal* (Field Marshal). Leading his 4th Army into the Soviet Union at the commencement of Operation Barbarossa, von Kluge would later take command of *Heeresgruppe Mitte* (Army Group Centre) in late 1941. Two years later, he was forced from command as he was seriously injured when his staff car overturned on the Minsk-Smolensk road. After almost a year of recuperation, von Kluge returned to active service when he replaced Gerd von Rundstedt as *Oberbefehlshaber West* (commander in chief of all western forces). Two weeks later, after Rommel was wounded, von Kluge combined the command of both *Oberbefehlshaber West* and *Heeresgruppe B* (Army Group B).

After just six-and-a-half weeks as Commander-in-Chief in the west, a combination of the continued failure of what was already an ever detoriating situation for the Germans in Normandy, combined with Hitler's suspicion that he had been involved in the failed July 20 assassination attempt, von Kluge was relieved of his command and recalled to Berlin for questioning. Believing he already faced an inevitable fate, on the way to Berlin, von Kluge committed suicide by taking poison. It is doubtful that von Kluge could be classed as a true conspirator in the assassination plot, but there is credible evidence to suggest that he at least knew of it but refused to play an active role and would only have cooperated with the conspirators, to allegedly quote the words of von Kluge himself, *"if the pig was already dead"*.* Taking his own life at the age of 61, Hans Gunther von Kluge is buried in an unmarked grave in the town of Bohne.

* Although this quote is largely attributed to von Kluge, the author has been unable to verify its source.

that such exile had subdued his characteristic bluster; '*Brad says he will put me in as soon as he can... He could do it now with much benefit to himself, if he had any backbone. Of course, Monty does not want me as he fears I will steal the show, which I will.*[117]

Within two weeks, in sweeping southeast at breakneck speed, Patton had advanced an astonishing distance exceeding 100 miles. On face value such a feat was impressive, that is until it is realised that Patton had failed to obtain a single objective. Montgomery's Directive (M512), issued to Bradley, Dempsey, Patton and Crerar on 21 July defines Patton's Third Army's objectives as being, *'to clear the whole of the Brittany Peninsula'*.[118] The importance of this objective was clearly appreciated and reiterated by Eisenhower who wrote to Montgomery on 21 July, *'We must get the Brittany Peninsula... this is essential... Time is vital. We must not only have the Brittany peninsula – we must have it quickly. So we must hit with everything.*[119]

Despite these calls, Bradley explains in his memoirs that *'Patton blazed through Brittany with armoured divisions and motorized infantry. He conquered a lot of real estate and made big headlines, but the Brittany campaign failed to achieve its primary objectives'.*[120] Indeed, the objectives of the Brittany ports of Lorient and St Nazaire, despite being declared as secured by Patton by the end of the first week of August, would not be in Allied hands until 10 and 11 of May, 1945 – three days after Victory in Europe Day. Once more, just like the previous campaign in Sicily, Patton was proving himself to be nothing short of a liability. Although revered amongst the majority of today's American historians, such admiration for Patton was not shared amongst those who had to command him, including General Bradley…

My own feelings on George were mixed. He had not been my choice for Army Commander and I was still weary of the grace with which he would accept our reversal in roles… I was apprehensive in having George join my command, for I feared that too much of my time would probably be spent in curbing his impetuous habits.[121]

With both previous and present campaigns demonstrating that Patton was seemingly incapable of seeing the battle through to the necessary conclusion, there is much evidence to suggest that Patton was more concerned in the claiming of headlines than inflicting a conclusive defeat upon the enemy. Bradley explains his frustration at Patton's ineptitude to apply himself fully to the task in hand…

As Middleton's VIII Corps carried Patton's colours around the corner at Avranches to head for the Brittany ports, I ordered George to post a strong force on guard in the centre of the Brittany neck. There he could stave off any threat from the east while Middleton's columns raced toward St Malo, first fortress on the Breton north shore… While visiting Middleton in his CP in the neck on August 2nd, I found him worried over an exposed left flank and rear. Patton had ignored the group order to establish a strong force in the Brittany neck and instead had ordered Middleton to race on toward Rennes and Brest. As a result Middleton was left with nothing between his extended columns and the main force of the German 7th Army to his rear… "Dammit", I said angrily to Middleton, "George seems more interested in making headlines with the capture of Brest than in using his head on tactics".[122]

Bradley resumes the story four days later…

On August 6 Patton called me at the Army Group CP to report that Brest had been taken. I found the report difficult to believe for the enemy did not customarily relinquish so important a prize without a struggle. Patton however stood his ground… Two days later, while seeking confirmation on the report from the column at Brest, we learned that George's call had been premature, for instead of surrendering, the enemy had burrowed into Brest for a siege… Not until 19 September, forty-four days after Patton had reported it taken, did the garrison at Brest surrender its 20,000 troops. By then the siege had taken its toll. Enemy demolitions together with artillery and air had totally destroyed the port… At Lorient and St Nazaire the enemy held out until the end of the war… Why then did we spend three divisions at Brest at a cost of almost 10,000 in American dead and wounded?[123]

Despite failing to achieve a single objective assigned to him within the Breton peninsula, Patton drove his Third Army on, and with the taking of Le Mans the Americans were now a full fifty miles closer to Paris than von Kluge's Germans. Consequently, as the

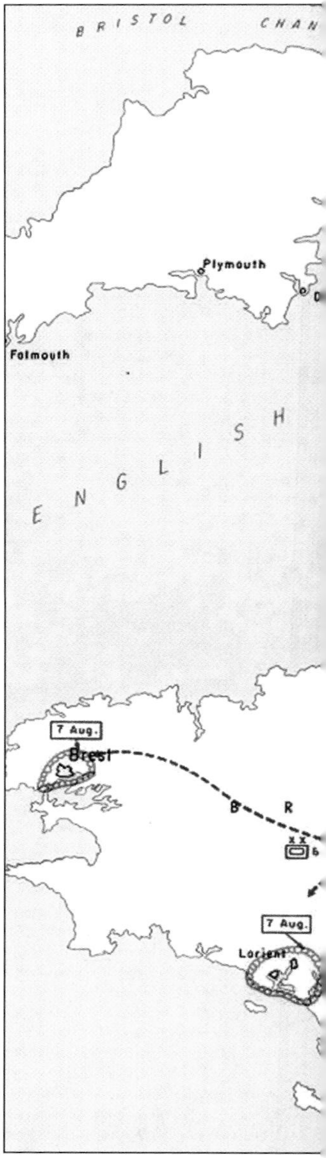

Above: *The Breakout in to Brittany : August 1944.*

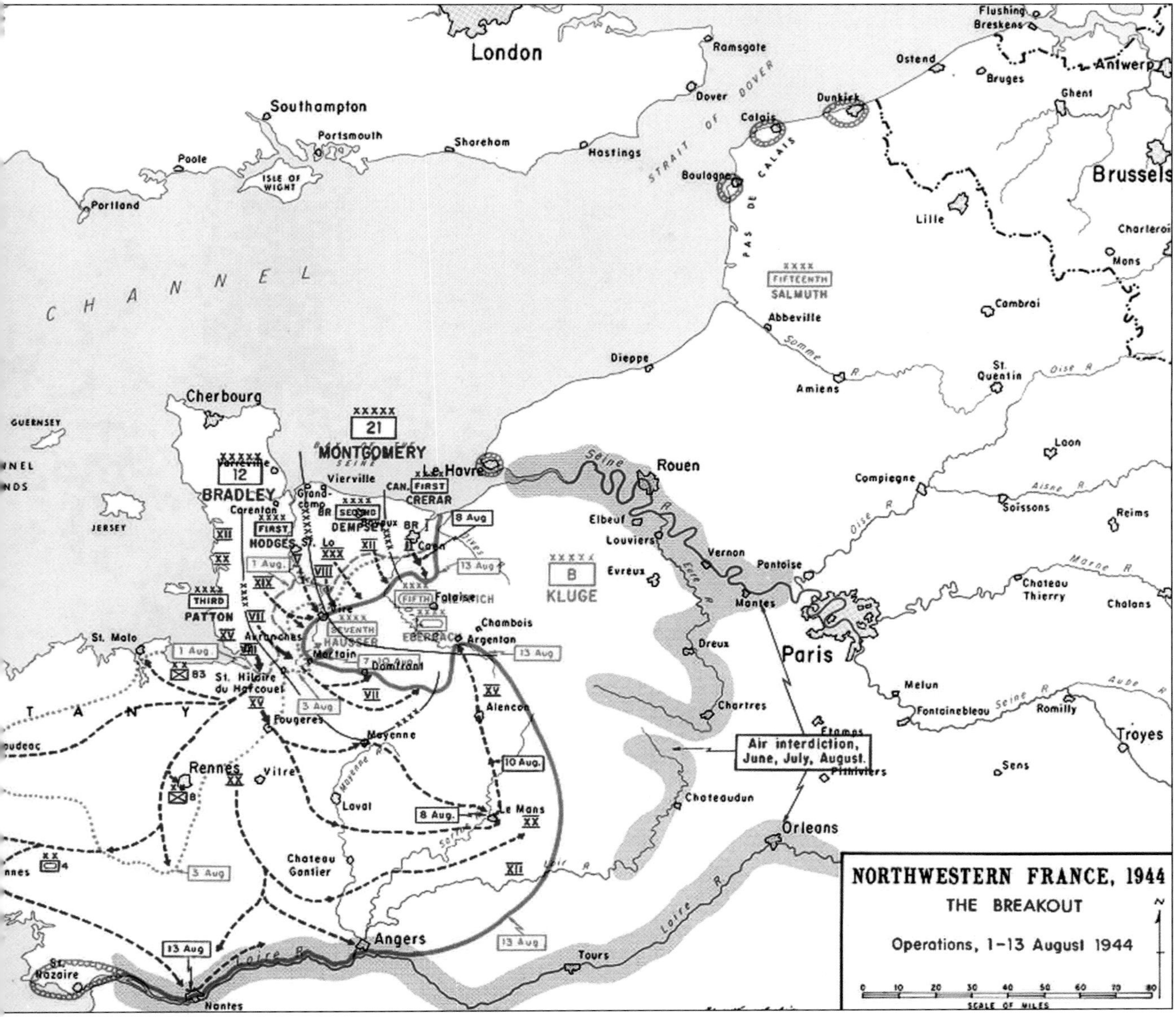

enemy divisions were still committed to attacking toward Mortain, they found themselves surrounded on three sides and occupying a salient running eighty miles into held ground. Having been in the field for less than two weeks, and despite facing anything but minimal resistance, Patton, was in no mood to take anything but full credit for the incurable scenario the Germans now faced. Courting the baying hacks of a fervent media, many of whom were clearly in awe of the blaspheming, ivory handled pistol-packing American Hero, Patton declared that his *'Third Army has advanced further and faster than any army in history'.*[124] Cultivating further his own legend, Patton held the correspondents firmly in his spell. Rather than relay the story of the hard-won victories fought elsewhere, the American newspapers lapped up every word from their idol before crying out for more.

Patton's advance over such a distance was undeniably an impressive logistical feat, but surely any objective appraisal must consider that it was only possible as a direct consequence of a distinct lack of opposition, in huge contrast to the scenario being faced elsewhere. In the words of General Eisenhower...

The opposition encountered by General Patton's flying columns in the course of this sweep was negligible, for the enemy's flank had collapsed so completely that there was hardly any resistance offered by organised units above company strength'.[125]

In addition to this lack of resistance, the opportunities presented to Patton were only conceivable because of his deviation from the original objectives assigned to him within Brittany. On pretty much first contact with any substantial enemy presence, he delegated this task away in preference of a more mobile role. Even then, the favourable situation Patton faced had only been made possible through the bitter struggles undertaken by forces deployed within fierce battles, weeks, sometimes months, before Patton's Third Army had even arrived on the continent.

Throughout his career, Patton's reputation, and no little fame, was forged through operations where the groundwork had already been completed by others or through those manoeuvres which encountered the least of opposition, a fact emphasised by the celebrated historian, Max Hastings...

When Patton's army later met serious German resistance, the American divisions under his command fought no better and no worse with his leadership than under that of any other commander... it would be absurd to suppose that he had discovered a key to the downfall of the German armies which had escaped his peers. It was they who had made possible the glory that he now reaped with such relish.[126]

With the news dominated by headlines of the American advance, resentment grew amongst those engaged at what was very much the sharp end of the campaign, again a situation recognised by Bradley within his memoirs...

British prestige had suffered by mid-August as a result of our glittering advance. For while we sped around the rim of enemy resistance toward Paris, 21st Group fought in its assigned corner near Caen, accomplishing the task that had been allotted it in the Overlord scheme of manoeuvre.[127]

Patton's forces were now sweeping irrepressibly through Le Mans, Alencon and Sees. Only as General Haislip's XV Corps approached Argentan did the resistance stiffen. As the going got tough, the first cracks started to appear in what had to this point been a fairly harmonious coalition between the American and Free French forces which formed Patton's Third Army. During the first days these forces had been brought together on the Normandy front, the Americans had quickly developed a sense of bewilderment, if not a little exasperation, when observing a very distinctive brand of liberation which was becoming increasingly typical of General Leclerc's French 2nd Armoured Division. Since coming ashore on Utah Beach in a blaze of glory on 1 August (D+56), the Free French tended to become somewhat independently-minded as to how their forces be best deployed. As one of Patton's liaison team recorded...

General Philippe François Marie Leclerc de Hauteclocque 1902-1947

Commander of the French 2eme Division Blindee

Phillipe Francois Marie de Hauteclocque was born in 1902 into an aristocratic family from the Somme region of northern France. Home-schooled for the majority of his formative years, at the age of 17 he was sent to a preparatory school in Versailles. Joining the French Military Academy at Saint-Cyr, graduating in 1924, he went on to attend the French Cavalry School at Saumur, finishing top of the class of 1925. De Hauteclocque spent the next thirteen years serving either in the occupation forces of the Ruhr, fighting against insurgents in the French colonies in Africa or teaching at the French Military Academy in Morocco before returning to the French Army Staff College in 1938.

During the battle for France in 1940, de Hauteclocque, now the commander of three infantry battalions, became encircled by the enemy in close proximity to the city of Lille. With the battle lost, on two occasions he would escape captivity by feigning the identity of a French refugee. Rejoining the fight before the armistice, de Hauteclocque would be wounded during a German air attack. It was whilst laying in his hospital bed that German forces overran the area and de Hauteclocque was once more taken prisoner, only to escape captivity for a third time as he absconded through an unguarded hospital window. With the signing of the French surrender came increased freedom of movement which enabled de Hauteclocque to return to his family in the north of France. Making the decision to re-join the fight, under false identity papers in the name of Leclerc, he made his way through France and Spain before crossing the border with Portugal and presenting himself at the British Embassy in Lisbon. With the British arranging his passage, de Hauteclocque made his way to London where he met with de Gaulle who made him a Major within his newly-formed Free French forces.

Joining de Gaulle in Africa, often taking the fight against his own countrymen of the Vichy French, from now on de Hauteclocque would take on his *nom de guerre* of Phillipe Leclerc in order to hide his true identity and protect his family back in occupied France. At the conclusion of the campaign in North Africa, *Leclerc*, now commanding the 2e Division Francais Libre, reorganised his force as an armoured division. Before leaving North Africa and setting sail to Britain in anticipation of the invasion of Normandy, Leclerc's division transferred out its non- white troops and reorganised on the model of American formations.

Disembarking at Utah Beach eight weeks after D-Day, Leclerc's forces would make their way through Normandy before being given the honour of leading the Allied forces into Paris. After Paris, the Leclerc Division would partake in Patton's ill-fated Lorraine Campaign before crossing the Rhine at the end of April 1945 and ending their war at the Nazi bastion of Berchtesgaden in Bavaria.

Having received word of the German surrender, on 8 May 1945 (Victory in Europe Day), Leclerc was presented with a group of French volunteers from the SS Charlemagne Division. Having asked one of these men why he was wearing a German uniform, Leclerc was himself asked why he was wearing an American one. Instructing his men to get rid of them, accurately or not, Leclerc's instruction was interpreted as a death sentence; the SS soldiers were executed without trial.

At the end of the war in Europe, Leclerc became France's representative during the Japanese surrender in September 1945. Two months later, he permanently adopted his nom de guerre in officially changing his name to Jacques-Phillipe Leclerc de Hauteclocque. In March 1946, Leclerc commanded a contingent of French Forces tasked with retaking control of French- Indochina. Realising the situation there to be far too complex and virtually an impossible task for the French military to retake control, Leclerc advocated a policy of political diplomacy rather than forced intervention. His counsel created a huge controversy back in France and Leclerc himself would only last four months in that role before being summoned back to France to be subsequently made inspector of French Forces within the French colonies in North Africa. Leclerc died in 1947, killed during an air crash in Algeria. His funeral was held at Notre Dame Cathedral before his body was interred within a crypt at Les Invalides, Paris.

General Leclerc always adapted the Corps plan to suit his own type of fighting of "liberating and celebrating." He set a pattern of action for his division; he would have a meeting of his officers to set out his own battle plan. Invariably he would say, "Our objective is there but we will go on to here because I will contact my friend the Mayor, or a friend in the underground, who will order a feast to be prepared for us." After taking an objective there would be a splendid meal with wine and champagne.[128]

So far, with little opposition, there had been no need to curtail Leclerc and clip the wings of the French contingent. In the interests of diplomacy, and not wishing to upset the notoriously highly strung French command, as long as Leclerc's forces were not hindering the overall effort, they were allowed free rein as to how they carried out their own business in their own distinctive manner. All this changed on 12 August, as Haislip's XV Corps advanced through the Foret d'Ecouvres, a large forest located on the approach to Argentan. Against direct orders published with the intention of keeping open the main N158 road, after facing resistance offered by an enemy force consisting of what one historian has quoted as being no more than a company of bakers, Leclerc ordered his division into the town of Sees, a manoeuvre perceived by the Americans as being nothing more than a ploy for the French to take the adulation of the newly liberated villagers. With the French 2nd Armoured now blocking the main road to Argentan, Haislip fumed as almost a full day was wasted as the glorious liberators partied long into the night.

At dawn on 13 August, with the debacle of Sees behind him, Haislip reported back to Patton that he was ready to resume his advance on Argentan. There seemed no reason to doubt that the objective would not be anything other than taken quickly and without major resistance, and so Haislip probed Patton as to what direction his Corps should take after the town had been secured.[129] Patton responded that Haislip should continue the advance beyond Argentan and press on toward Falaise. This

Below: *Allied armour rolls through the Normandy countryside.*

General Wade Hampton Haislip 1889-1971

Commander of US Army XV Corps.

Born in Virginia in 1889, Wade Hampton Haislip was commissioned as a Second Lieutenant after graduating from West Point in the class of 1912. As America entered the Great War, Haislip would join the American Expeditionary Force, participating in the Battle of Saint-Mihiel and the Meuse-Argonne offensive before serving in the post-war occupation force.

On his return from Europe, between 1921 and 1923, Haislip served as an instructor at West Point before attending the US Army School of Infantry (1923-1924), the Command and General Staff School (1924-1925) before heading back to France to attend the French Military Academy at Saint-Cyr (1925-1927). Haislip spent the remaining inter-war years serving in various staff roles including a two years working in the office of the War Department and a four-year spell working as a senior instructor at the General Staff School.

Haislip's first command of the Second World War would involve the raising and training of the 85th Infantry Division, a unit the US Army activated under Haislips leadership in April 1942. Although never seeing combat under his command, the 85th would be commanded by Haislip until February of 1943 at which point he took command of the US Army XV Corps, a formation he would lead through Normandy and up to the conclusion of the war in Europe.

After the war, Haislip served in numerous advisory roles both within the American government and military. Retiring in 1951, eighteen years later he served as a pallbearer at the funeral of his lifelong friend and former President, Dwight D. Eisenhower.

Haislip died at the age of 82 in 1971, and is buried at the Arlington National Cemetery.

order was neither issued nor permitted by Bradley, who unlike Patton, fully appreciated that the narrower the gap between forces became, the resistance would inevitably intensify. To Patton's fury, Bradley countermanded the order and instead instructed that Haislip's XV Corps, Third Army, consolidate at the edge of Argentan, awaiting reinforcement. Not taking no for an answer, Patton, with his own typical brand of absurdity, pleaded to Bradley, *'Let me go on to Falaise and we'll drive the British back into the sea for another Dunkirk'.*[130]

Realising Patton had neither the strength, ability, nor it could be argued, the aptitude to execute the drive on to Falaise, Bradley reigned in his hotheaded subordinate. Incredibly, many commentators at the time and ever since, have pointed the finger at Montgomery for not allowing Patton an attempt to close the gap. Again such critics may be wise to heed Bradley's own words…

Monty had never prohibited and I never proposed that US forces close the gap from Argentan to Falaise. I was quite content with our original objective and reluctant to take on another… Although Patton may have spun a line across that narrow neck, I doubted his ability to hold it… The enemy could not have only broken through, but he might have trampled Patton's position in the onrush. I much preferred a solid shoulder at Argentan to the possibility of a broken neck at Falaise… In halting Patton at Argentan… I did not consult Montgomery. The decision to stop Patton was mine alone, it never went beyond my CP.[131]

If Patton fumed in the immediate aftershock of Bradley's decision, his indignation did not last long. The very next day he petitioned Bradley to release him from the current task in hand, to carry out yet another new venture. Realising the road to Paris was wide open, Patton formulated a plan which would deploy two thirds of his Third Army in carrying out a second, wider envelopment, which would include the liberation of the French capital.

Incredibly, having stopped Patton before Argentan, citing a lack of strength in the face of mounting resistance, Bradley considerably weakened his position and allowed Patton to disengage one half of his Third Army to concentrate, not on the defeat of the German Army in Normandy, but to ensure Patton would be the first into Paris. This would be a decision Bradley would long regret, and one which he found difficult to justify when reporting his decision to Montgomery …

While Monty caught his breath on the other end of the line, I struggled to fight off the doubts that now assailed my earlier decision. For had we not rushed on to the Seine, we might have closed the Falaise trap at Chambois and bettered our PW [prisoner of war] catch within that pocket… For the first and only time during the war, I went to bed that evening worrying over a decision I had already made. To this day I am not yet certain that we should not have postponed our advance to the Seine and gone on to Chambois instead. For although the bridgehead accelerated our advance, Chambois would have yielded more prisoners.[132]

Once again, just like the objective of the Brittany ports, as soon as the potential of persistent opposition arose, Patton detached the majority of his forces from the job in hand in what a cynic could perceive as the will, not to commit whatever it takes to defeat the enemy, but rather to claim yet more headlines. As quickly as he had arrived, Patton departed the battle for Normandy. With half of his Third Army now heading for Paris, with one of his four corps continuing to fail in making headway in Brittany, Patton left within Normandy just one of his four corps – even this consisted of the much maligned French 2nd Armoured Division, the 90th Infantry Division (once dubbed the single worst formation in the European Theatre), and the untested 80th Infantry Division - hardly the most substantial, nor the most dependable of forces to be entrusted with the American responsibility of closing the gap around what was now becoming known as *the Falaise Pocket*.

Finally, on 14 August Hitler finally gave up on the fantasy of stemming the tide of the American breakout at Avranches. Whilst this news may have been welcomed weeks earlier, coming at the time it did, this was of no consolation to von Kluge who had long since realised he was facing an impossible task. In the eyes of Hitler, von Kluge had failed him, but was this failure intentional? Was von Kluge just another conspirator against him? As Hitler's paranoia escalated, von Kluge was relieved of his command on 17 August and summoned back to Berlin to account for his perceived incompetence. En-route he was allowed the courtesy of making a detour to a location between Verdun and Metz, scene of a battle fought in the Great War during which von Kluge served as a staff officer. Under virtual guard, having just been informed that he was under suspicion of involvement in the 20 July assassination plot on Hitler's life, von Kluge stepped into a field and took cyanide.

Chapter 14
Dante's Inferno

As *Generalfeldmarschall* Walter Model filled the void left by von Kluge, in taking command of the shattered remains of the German forces in Normandy, it must have been clear that nothing could save the defence of France, surely the only hope was to salvage what forces he could to fight another day. In Model, the Germans undoubtedly possessed the best man for the job. Having made his name during the first half of the war, by August 1944, Model had become renowned as Germany's best general with regard to commanding defensive operations. Nicknamed the Lion of Defence, Model had already masterminded several escapes of German troops from what appeared to be overwhelming Russian offensives on the Eastern Front. Such a feat would have to be repeated in Normandy, but on a previously unprecedented scale, way beyond any situation previously encountered.

Model quickly gave orders for an improvised battlegroup from the II SS Panzer Corps to halt the advance of the Polish 1st Armoured Division, which as part of Crerar's Canadian First Army, was setting the trap from the east. In the meantime,

Below: *The horrific aftermath of battle within the 'Corridor of Death'.*

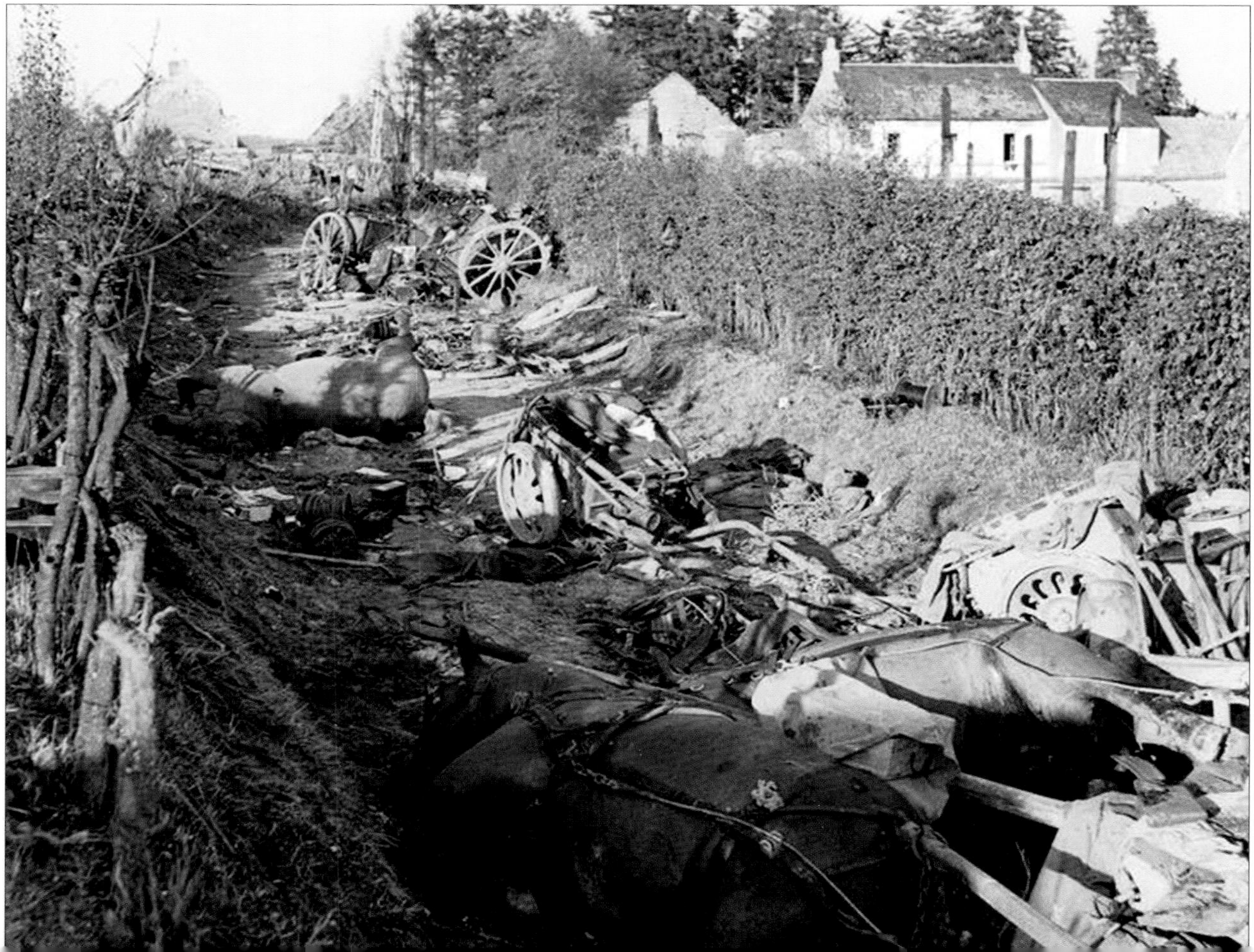

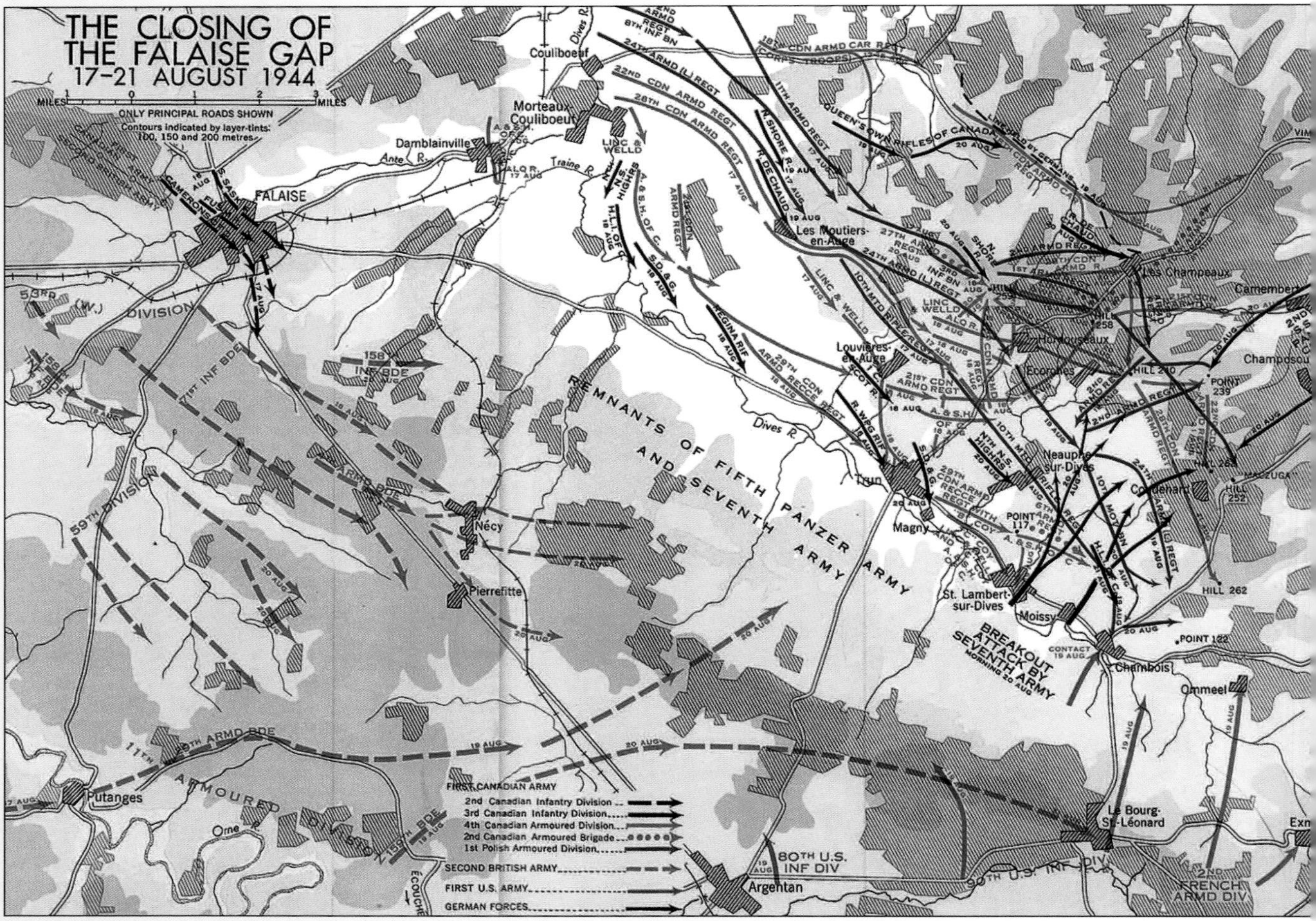

Above: *The Closing of the Falaise Pocket.*

remnants of the Wehrmacht's 116th and 2nd Panzer Divisions were instructed to fight like the devil to keep the gap open from the American snare approaching from the southwest. The only available route of escape for the remnants of the German 7th Army and Panzer Gruppe West (now renamed Panzer Gruppe Eberbach) would be through an ever-narrowing corridor, centred upon a short strip of land, bisected by the River Dives and located between the small towns of Trun and Bourg St Leonard. Within an area no more than twenty miles wide and ten miles deep, over 100,000 Germans - the shattered remnants of what was just two months before, over thirty divisions of the German war machine - were now under relentless fire from the ground and from the air, enduring a neo-apocalyptical fight for survival.

Model's second day in command coincided with the battle of the Falaise Pocket's most desperate phase. Despite all that the German Army in Normandy had endured throughout the last seventy-two days, there were no signs of them waning in their attempts to escape this most catastrophic of struggles.

With the noose tightening, the need for Montgomery to co-ordinate Allied movement reached an intricate crescendo. At such a critical moment, coming as it did for the first time within the final stages of a ten-week battle, it could be argued that this was maybe not the best time for Eisenhower to assume a more proactive role in man-

Generalfeldmarschall Walter Model 1891-1945

Commander of Oberbefehlshaber West and Heeresgruppe B (from 16 August 1944 to 3 September 1944)

Otto Moritz Walter Model was born in Genthin, Saxony in 1891. The son of a music teacher, Model enlisted at the Neisse Military College in 1910, graduating in 1912 before being commissioned as a *leutnant* (Lieutenant) in the 52nd Infantry Regiment. Serving in the Great War, Model came to the attention of his superiors and although quickly developing the reputation as a rather tactless and blunt character, he nonetheless showed great potential which earned him a posting within the German General Staff. Having received the Iron Cross, First Class and the House Order of Hohenzollern with Swords for valour during the Great War, at the end of the conflict, now a *Hauptmann* (Captain), Model remained in the German military as a lecturer. By 1939, Model, having been promoted to *Generalmajor* (Brigadier General) was serving as chief of staff to the German IV Corps.

As part of von Rundstedt's *Heeresgruppe Sud* (Army Group South), IV Corps invaded Poland in 1939. Promoted to *Generalleutnant* (Major General) in April 1940, Model would serve as the Chief of Staff of the Wehrmarcht's 16th Army during the invasion of the low countries and France in the spring of 1940. Heading east during the German invasion of the Soviet Union, Model would earn yet more accolades as his 3rd Panzer Division spearheaded the offensive against Kiev. Promoted to *General der Panzertruppe* (Lieutenant General) in October 1941, in November Model would take command of XLI Panzer Corps, leading his force to within 20 miles of Moscow.

As the Russian winter forced a halt to the advance on Moscow, with the subsequent Soviet counterattack forcing the Germans into retreat, there would be no solution to the downturn of German fortunes. Promoted to *Generaloberst* (full General) and given command of the German Ninth Army, Model now became known by the nicknames of either *Hitler's Fireman* or the *Lion of Defence* as he skilfully consolidated what was ever becoming an increasingly desperate situation. Even managing the occasional successful counter of his own, despite the overall terminal situation, Model excelled, and as his reputation grew in January of 1944 he was awarded command of *Heeresgruppe Nord* (Army Group North) before being promoted to *Generalfeldmarschall* (Field Marshal) two months later.

Temporarily stemming the tide of Zhukov's advances in the east, Model, now considered as Hitler's trouble-shooter in chief, was summoned west to face the Allies in Normandy in his new office as commander of both *Oberbefehlshaber West* and *Heeresgruppe B.* Failing to subdue the might of the Allies in Normandy, unable to meet the demands of both offices, at the end of September 1944, Model relinquished control of *Oberbefehlshaber West* but retained his command of *Heeresgruppe B.* Like his previous achievements in the east, Model did realise brief moments of glory as he commanded the defeat of Operation Market Garden in September 1944 and in late December 1944 it may have even seemed to the most optimistic of Germans that their fortunes were changing as Model masterminded both the defeat of the American offensive in the Hurtgen Forest and the counterattack of *Unternehmen Herbstnebel* (known in the west as the Battle of the Bulge). Such actions would ultimately only delay the inevitable and as the Allied pressure increased, leading to the Rhine Crossing in the spring of 1945, the writing was on the wall for Model and the rest of Hitler's remaining forces.

As the noose tightened around the final remnants of Hitler's war machine, wishing neither to surrender nor to follow Hitler's absurd order for *Heeresgruppe B* to fight to the last man, Model disbanded what he could of his remaining forces whilst at the same time giving his remaining troops the choice of continuing the fight or laying down their arms, an action leading Model to be branded by Hitler as a traitor. With the realisation that the war was undoubtedly lost, with news that the Soviets were seeking his arrest for war crimes in the East, on 21 April 1945, Model took his own life, shooting himself in a forest close to Dusseldorf. Initially buried where he fell, in 1955 his body was taken for permanent burial at the German military cemetery in Vossenack.

aging the final stages of the battle for Normandy. Although unable to deny the Supreme Commander his legitimate right of command, again, without letting his frustrations show, it is obvious that by this stage Montgomery's patience with Eisenhower was wearing thin. He wrote to Alanbrooke on 14 August…

Ike is apt to get very excited and to talk wildly – at the top of his voice!!! He is now over here; which is a very great pity. His ignorance as to how to run a war is absolute and complete; he has all the popular cries but nothing else.[133]

As the gap between the American and Canadian forces narrowed, it became apparent that the two pincers would meet in proximity of the town of Chambois. On 17 August Montgomery gave the orders that he hoped would finally close the trap on the German Army in Normandy…

I rang up Crerar on the telephone at 0700hrs and impressed on him the vital need to get two armoured divisions to Trun-Chambois area today. If he can do so, the enemy is caught and we may capture over 100,000 Germans; if he does not do so, many Germans may escape.[134]

The Canadian First Army's attempt to close the snare centred upon the small village of St Lambert sur Dives. On 18 August, under the command of Major David Currie, a battlegroup of tanks from the South Alberta Regiment and infantry drawn from the

Below and right: *Shattered bodies and equipment litter the road to Chambois in the heart of the Falaise Pocket.*

Argyll and Sutherland Highlanders were given orders to take St Lambert, to move through the hamlet of Moissy, before linking up with the Americans at Chambois.

Unbeknown to Major Currie, it would be through his unit's positions that, on 20 August, the last elements of the enemy's 1st SS, 10th SS, 12th SS, 353rd Infantry and 2nd Panzer Divisions would combine their remaining strength in the attempt to escape the hangman's noose. Here follows Major Currie's own account of the struggle which would earn the only Canadian Victoria Cross in Normandy.

Friday 18 August 1944 - In the early hours, before first light... we arrived at our designated area, somewhere north of Trun, on the high ground overlooking the Dives valley... Our normal strength would be 19 tanks. On this particular day, we were 15 tanks strong, which means 75 men; 5 men per tank... As the sun rose... we found that we had a wonderful panoramic view of the Dives valley. In the distance, we could see rising clouds of dust... we were witnessing... the remnants of the German forces in France trying to escape the pocket. The columns were about three to four miles from our location and seemed to consist of every type and kind of vehicle, gun, tank and horse drawn equipment that the German Army possessed. The column stretched as far as we could see. It was an awe inspiring sight, and from the distance, it appeared to be a crushing force.

I was informed by the Colonel that he had a rather tough assignment that we were to take on. For this job, we were to have under command a company of the Argyle and Sutherland Highlanders whose depleted strength was about 55 all ranks... The assignment given us by the Colonel was to take the village of St Lambert sur Dives; and from a study of the plan, I could see this was placing us squarely in front of the vast array of the German forces that we had been watching for most of the day. The Colonel also stressed the importance of this task in relation to the whole campaign and indicated that the German withdrawal had to be stopped. I still remember my first reaction to this task. I remember saying to myself, "Well, Dave, up to now this has been a pretty good war, but this is it…"

We had decided that the tanks would lead the attack and, as and when we were able to penetrate the village, the infantry would come up and consolidate the position… The first tank had been hit by 88 mm fire… I then proceeded to St Lambert, on foot, to the tank that had been hit. The men from the tank were lying in the ditch beside the road. One was rather badly wounded and two others had minor wounds… By this time, it was getting pretty dark. I made a reconnaissance about half way into St Lambert to see if there was a possibility of getting to the main crossroads, where the 88 mm fire had come from, by another route other than up the main street. I could hear the voices of Germans in some of the buildings, but did not run into anyone during my reconnaissance on foot… I returned to the edge of St Lambert where I had left the three remaining tanks of Number 1 Troop and we pulled back about 200 yards, where we took up positions covering St Lambert.

Saturday 19 August - At the first sign of dawn, we once again put in an attack on the village. We lost our lead tank, but this time we located the opposition. We were up against a Tiger tank and a MkIV tank. We got about one quarter of the way down the main street. Shortly afterward, my own command tank was able to knock out the MkIV tank. The boys made sure that it was on fire before they stopped firing. The Tiger tank was put out of commission by the supporting infantry, who had worked their way down the street through the houses. They shot two of the crew and put a grenade into the turret, which finished off the rest of the crew. We were then in possession of about two thirds of the village… During the rest of Saturday, the fighting was bitter and at one point late in the afternoon, the tanks were running around in circles firing at one another, to keep the Germans from climbing on top of them. At this point, I was able to get some artillery support. They laid down a barrage on our own position… Pressure from the Germans mounted again near dark… I decided to draw the force in tighter for the night… During the night, there was considerable firing and no one got much sleep. In the morning we found that we had inflicted a considerable number of casualties on the Germans during the night.

Sunday 20 August - With the coming of daylight, the attacks started to intensify… In the early hours, two tank commanding officers were wounded in the head by small arms fire… A little later, one of my tank officers was on the ground and was wounded by shellfire. He later died from his wounds. Late in the morning… one of the crew from my tank called to me that the Colonel wished to speak to me on the radio. I had just climbed into the tank when in came an 88 mm high explosive shell… both of the officers had been killed... This meant that at this stage, all my officers were out of action – five wounded and two killed… In the early evening… we spotted an 88 mm ground gun and a MkIV tank moving into a position about 400 yards from our Headquarters. We immediately opened fire, using 8 tanks firing armour piercing and high explosive shells. One of the first shots fired hit the 88 mm gun. It must have hit the ammunition carrier as there was a tremendous explosion… There were a number of large buildings and apparently the Germans had massed behind them in preparation for this attack. We fired through these buildings using armour piercing shells. We fired about 100 rounds and stopped. We could hear the cries and hollering, but there was no attack.

Monday 21 August - The day dawned hot and clear... You could feel the change in the situation this day; we could tell that the end was in sight. There was some shelling but it was rather sporadic. Prisoners started rolling in, in a never-ending stream... The fight had apparently gone out of the enemy. When night came, I was able to get some sleep. This was my first sleep for three days.

Tuesday 22 August - Shortly after breakfast, we received orders to pull up stakes and move on. Within an hour we were heading for the Seine, on the heels of the fleeing Germans. So ended St Lambert. We had arrived early in the morning and three days later left in the morning. We had been sorely tried by the Germans and for many, this was their last fight. The men had been asked to take on incredible odds, and while at times I am sure that they were all afraid, I know I was, every last man did the job asked of him, without complaint, even though at times the situation seemed so hopeless and I know that they felt it. When we came to St Lambert, it was a neat small quiet French village, and when we left, it was a fantastic mess. The clutter of equipment, dead horses, wounded, dying and dead Germans, had turned it into a hellhole. It seems incredible that such devastation could be wrought in such a short space of time.[135]

Above: *Major David Currie VC takes the surrender of the last Germans trapped within the confines of the Falaise Pocket.*

Major Currie's testimony, although at times graphic in nature, maybe still falls short in explaining just exactly what damage his small force had inflicted upon the enemy. From the citation, which led to the award of his Victoria Cross, the substantial losses inflicted by Currie's improvised force may be better understood.

Meanwhile, the orphans of Patton's Third Army's XV Corps were left by their absent commander to continue the fight against the Germans in Normandy. Continuing

Above: *Huge columns of German prisoners surrender during the battle of the Falaise Pocket.*

the advance towards Chambois, and therefore effect a link up with the Canadian 1st Army, this effort would witness the baptism of fire for the US 80th Infantry Division. Straight away this green formation started to suffer the same kind of problems previously experienced by its Corps brethren of the 90th, as recalled by Colonel McHugh of the 80th Division…

This was our first real fight and I had difficulty in getting the men to move forward. I had to literally kick the men up from the ground in order to get the attack started, and to encourage the men I walked across the road without any cover... The commanding officer of my leading battalion panicked and the battalion took fright from him. It was necessary to replace his entire battalion to restore their nerve.[136]

With the French contingent seemingly content with celebrating the liberation of their homeland, and the 80th Division proving themselves less than effective in their opening struggles, the vanguard of the American advance in closing the gap would be entrusted to the much-maligned 90th Infantry Division. The tribulations of the Tough Ombres, first encountered in the Cotentin Peninsula hours after D-Day, continued well into July, with one regimental commander causing so much 'chaos and confusion' that

Major DAVID V. CURRIE
South Alberta Regiment, Canadian 4th Infantry Division

In Normandy on 18 August 1944, Major Currie was in command of a small mixed force of Canadian tanks, self-propelled anti- tank guns and infantry which was ordered to cut one of the main escape routes from the Falaise pocket.

This force was held up by strong enemy resistance in the village of St. Lambert-sur-Dives, and two tanks were knocked out by 88mm guns. Major Currie immediately entered the village alone on foot at last light through the enemy outposts to reconnoitre the German defences and extricate the crews of the disabled tanks, which he succeeded in doing in spite of heavy mortar fire.

Early the following morning, without any previous artillery bombardment, Major Currie personally led an attack on the village in the face of fierce opposition from enemy tanks, guns and infantry, and by noon had succeeded in seizing and consolidating a position half-way inside of the village.

During the next 36 hours the Germans hurled one counter-attack after another against the Canadian force, but so skilfully had Major Currie organized his defensive position that these attacks were repulsed with severe casualties to the enemy after heavy fighting.

At dusk on the 20 August the Germans attempted to mount a final assault on the Canadian positions, but the attacking force was routed before it could even be deployed. Seven enemy tanks, twelve 88 mm guns and forty vehicles were destroyed, 300 Germans were killed, 500 wounded and 2,100 captured. Major Currie then promptly ordered an attack and completed the capture of the village, thus denying the Chambois-Trun escape route to the remnants of two German armies cut off in the Falaise pocket.

Throughout three days and nights of fierce fighting, Major Currie's gallant conduct and contempt for danger set a magnificent example to all ranks of the force under his command.

On one occasion he personally directed the fire of his command tank on to a Tiger tank which had been harassing his position and succeeded in knocking it out. During another attack, while the guns of his command tank were taking on other targets at longer ranges, he used a rifle from the turret to deal with individual snipers who had infiltrated to within fifty yards of his headquarters. The only time reinforcements were able to get through to his force, he himself led the forty men forward to their positions and explained the importance of their task as part of the defence. When, during the next attack, these new reinforcements withdrew under the intense fire brought down by the enemy, he personally collected them and led them forward into position again, where, inspired by his leadership, they held for the remainder of the battle. His employment of the artillery support, which became available after his original attack went in, was typical of his cool calculation of the risks involved in every situation. At one time, despite the fact that short rounds were falling within fifteen yards of his own tank, he ordered fire from medium artillery to continue because of its devastating effect upon the attacking enemy in his immediate area.

Throughout the operations the casualties to Major Currie's force were heavy. However, he never considered the possibility of failure or allowed it to enter the minds of his men. In the words of one of his non-commissioned officers, "We knew at one stage that it was going to be a fight to the finish but he was so cool about it, it was impossible for us to get excited." Since all the officers under his command were either killed or wounded during the action, Major Currie virtually had no respite from his duties and in fact obtained only one hour's sleep during the entire period. Nevertheless he did not permit his fatigue to become apparent to his troops and throughout the action took every opportunity to visit weapon pits and other defensive posts to talk to his men, to advise them as to the best use of their weapons and to cheer them with words of encouragement. When his force was finally relieved and he was satisfied that the turnover was complete he fell asleep on his feet and collapsed.

There can be no doubt that the success of the attack on and stand against the enemy at St. Lambert-sur-Dives can largely be attributed to this officer's coolness, inspired leadership and skillful use of the limited weapons at his disposal.

The courage and devotion to duty shown by Major Currie during a prolonged period of heavy fighting were outstanding and had a far-reaching effect on the successful outcome of the battle.

his deputies were instructed to countermand every order he gave and in fact to *'shoot him'* if his outrageous behaviour continued.[137] Although the appointment of General McClain on 1 August seemed to many as a selection which would steady the ship somewhat, on 17 August the Division's worst traits resurfaced. As the 90th made their approach to the town of Bourg St Leonard, a minor wound to the little finger of a Lieutenant Dame sent a whole company into full flight, an event witnessed by a fellow officer...

The sudden opposition and the fact that he was wounded slightly must have rattled Dame for he grew excited... The patrol pulled back hastily in complete confusion. The rest... noting the little finger of Dame's left hand gashed and spouting blood as well as seeing him with blood all over his face – probably from rubbing it with his bloody hand – got excited, too, and withdrew in poor order. They fell back, badly shaken and out of control, men going in all directions.[138]

Although it would take three days to secure Bourg St Leonard, by 20 August, at last, the scene was set for the American forces to move into Chambois and to finally link up with the 1st Canadian Army, therefore securing their assigned role in closing the *Falaise Pocket.*

As the 90th Division advance crept closer toward Chambois, mounting resistance ensured that the *Tough Ombres* were now experiencing a situation akin to that being endured by Currie's Canadians just three miles distant. The entry into Chambois proved an erratic manoeuvre due to the chaotic and irregular traffic to the front. That traffic was, of course, the final remnants of Model's armies desperately trying to flee the setting trap through what was now the only escape route left open. One moment the line could be judged as being held in relative strength, then only moments later it would be overrun by fanatical hordes, masses of ravaged forces, fighting for their very lives, a situation recalled by the official historian of the 359th Regiment of the 90th Division...

At 0700 [on 20 August], Germans in considerable numbers, estimated to be remnants of two panzer divisions, attacked from the west. Their attack was in such strength that, when it hit the K Company positions, the latter broke and folded back into F Company, leaving a gap between the two companies. Before the gap could be filled six German tanks piled on through this gap, followed by several-hundred infantrymen. Three of the tanks were knocked out almost immediately but the others (with infantry) succeeded in getting into the town and occupying several buildings.[139]

It was during this struggle that a 20-year-old sergeant from San Francisco took the fight to the enemy during an action which would lead to the final award of the US Army's sixteen Medals of Honor bestowed for actions during the Battle of Normandy.

As the 90th Division moved in on Chambois, the magnitude of the desperation of the German attempts to flee the setting trap dawned upon Sergeant John Hawk...

My God, the sky was falling down, the earth was blowing up, and if ever there was a hell on earth, this was it. I thought, honest to God, I won't survive. My philosophy was, they may get me, but I aint gonna make it easy. It was absolute carnage: animals, people, equipment, an incomprehensible slaughterhouse.[140]

Realising that the fleeing Germans were beyond the view of the advancing American armour, Hawk, completely devoid of cover, exposed himself to enemy fire by moving into the middle of an open orchard, a position elevated enough so that Hawk could direct the American guns against the fleeing Germans.

Identifying the location of German tanks, he first shouted directions. Then, as the noise of battle became too loud for him to be heard, he made hand signals as he became a *human aiming stake* as the tank destroyers zeroed in to destroy two German tanks, leading to a mass surrender.

Hawk, shot twice that afternoon, recovered from the wounds which he sustained in Normandy and, although wounded on a further three occasions before the end of the war, would return home in 1945. Graduating from the University of Washington, Sergeant Hawk became a high school teacher. In 2008 he was presented with the *Medal of Honor Flag* at a ceremony held in Olympia, Washington during which he made a speech...

What I did was not such a big thing. I never did anything more than the people I served with. The [medal] is a symbol and it stands for service, everybody's service. I did it for the people who were there and they were doing the same thing for me.[141]

John Hawk died on 4 November 2013 at the age of 89. After his death, Jackson Park Elementary School in his home town of Bremerton was renamed in his honour. He is buried at Bremerton's Miller-Woodlawn Memorial Park.

Despite the heroics of both David Currie and John Hawk, Model's forces continued their attempts to flee the trap. Such efforts were especially brutal in the area between the hamlets of Moissy and Mont Ormel, a sector whose control had been delegated to a battlegroup of approximately 1,500 men and 80 tanks drawn from General Stanislaw Maczek's 1st Polish Armoured Division. On 17 August, Maczek received orders to advance on Chambois and effect a link up with the Americans. The subsequent advance of Polish armour would send Maczek's men along a line running parallel to the north of Major Currie's Canadians and would inevitably involve the

Sergeant
JOHN D. HAWK
90th Infantry Division

On 20 August 1944, near Chambois, France, a key point in the encirclement which created the Falaise Pocket. During an enemy counterattack, his position was menaced by a strong force of tanks and infantry. His fire forced the infantry to withdraw, but an artillery shell knocked out his gun and wounded him in the right thigh. Securing a bazooka, he and another man stalked the tanks and forced them to retire to a wooded section. In the lull which followed, Sgt. Hawk reorganized 2 machine gun squads and, in the face of intense enemy fire, directed the assembly of 1 workable weapon from 2 damaged guns. When another enemy assault developed, he was forced to pull back from the pressure of spearheading armour. Two of our tank destroyers were brought up. Their shots were ineffective because of the terrain until Sgt. Hawk, despite his wound, boldly climbed to an exposed position on a knoll where, unmoved by fusillades from the enemy, he became a human aiming stake for the destroyers. Realizing that his shouted fire directions could not be heard above the noise of battle, he ran back to the destroyers through a concentration of bullets and shrapnel to correct the range. He returned to his exposed position, repeating this performance until 2 of the tanks were knocked out and a third driven off. Still at great risk, he continued to direct the destroyers' fire into the Germans' wooded position until the enemy came out and surrendered. Sgt. Hawk's fearless initiative and heroic conduct, even while suffering from a painful wound, was in large measure responsible for crushing 2 desperate attempts of the enemy to escape from the Falaise Pocket and for taking more than 500 prisoners.

occupation of two strategically dominant hills. Labelled on maps as Hill 262 (North and South) and Hill 263, the contour lines of these features reminded General Maczek of the shape of the medieval mace weapon, a title which Maczek would adopt as the name to the desperate struggle which lay ahead for the high ground which dominated the Falaise Gap.

As Polish tanks manoeuvred into position on the Mace, with very little in the way of infantry support, Maczek's men became separated from their Canadian brethren and found themselves in the middle of some of Model's forces most brutal efforts to force a way out of the trap. Ill-equipped, with a shortage of fuel, rations and ammunition, with no reinforcement or resupply, a bitter close quarter battle raged for seventy-two hours between Maczek's tankers and an enemy force consisting of the very last surviving grenadiers of the SS, fixated on escape and prepared to fight to the last man, and to the last bullet.

Above: *Stopping for tea – German prisoners guarded after their capture in the Falaise Pocket.*

With the Canadians in St Lambert and the Americans in Chambois, there remained one escape route for the Germans, a shallow ford crossing the River Dives within the hamlet of Moissy. As thousands of men, vehicles, horses and military equipment of every kind approached the ford, artillery zeroed in on potential escapees, leaving the majority of the enemy no option but to dismount and abandon all that they could not physically carry in a desperate attempt to cross the Dives upon a road which would become known as the Corridor of Death. One of those who successfully crossed the Dives was General von Luttwitz, commander of the 2nd Panzer Division…

On the evening of 19 August, large numbers of our troops were crowded together… Some of them had already made repeated attempts to escape to the north-west with vehicles and horse-drawn columns. Quite apart from attacks from the air, the entire terrain was being swept by enemy artillery fire and our casualties increased from hour to hour. On the route leading into St Lambert sur Dive from Bailleul, where my division was collected, a colossal number of shot up horses and vehicles lay mixed together with dead soldiers in large heaps which hourly grew higher and higher. That evening the order was given to force a breakthrough near St Lambert. I ordered all my remaining tanks (there were 15 left out of the 120 with which I had arrived in Normandy) and other armoured vehicles to form a vanguard behind which we intended to breakthrough.

For some unknown reason enemy artillery fire had practically ceased on the evening of 19 August and remained quiet until the next morning. In this lull we began to move in the early morning mist of 20 August. As a narrow lane near St Lambert was known still to provide an escape route across the Dives river, columns of all the encircled units were streaming towards it, some of them driving in rows of eight vehicles abreast. Suddenly, at 7 o'clock in the morning, the artillery fire which had been so silent now broke out into a storm such as I had never before experienced. Alongside the Dives the numerous trains of vehicles ran into direct enemy fire of every description, turned back and in some cases drove round in a circle until they were shot up and blocked roads. Towering pillars of smoke rose incessantly from petrol tanks as they were hit, ammunition exploded, riderless horses stampeded, some of them badly wounded. Organised direction was no longer possible, and only a few of my tanks and infantry got through to St Lambert.[142]

Despite having to abandon the majority of their armour, the fleeing Germans immersed Hills 262 and 263 as the Polish-held positions became two islands engulfed by a tsunami of retreating enemy. For Maczek's men the crisis peaked in the evening of 20 August as the relentless pressure, combined with an ever-decreasing supply of ammunition, collectively threatened to end the heroic and what must have appeared at the time, ultimately futile defence of *The Mace*. The German pressure was unyielding and came from every direction…

A German company which, for some unknown reason, chose to climb the steepest slope of the "Mace", and which, scattering grenades, went forward shouting madly, only to break down in the terrible fire of the tracers of the anti-aircraft tanks. Within a few minutes the company ceased to exist, and the shouts, which were meant to buoy up their spirits in the assault changed into the horrible cries of men dying in the midst of burning grass.[143]

SS grenadiers, fighting alongside the paratroopers of the 3 Fallschirmjager Division now infiltrated the Polish lines from the rear. Incredibly these troops had already successfully fled the pocket only to be sent back into the fray in an attempt to force an escape route for those still trapped within the snare. As fierce hand-to-hand fighting broke out, and with all order of command long since broken, the Poles fought their fanatical foe face-to-face. With the situation growing ever more desperate, SS grenadiers, now fully within the Polish positions, mounted the Polish armour in an attempt to place grenades within the turrets of Maczek's Shermans. Only one option remained as Maczek's men turned machine guns upon their own tanks.

As the battle met its chaotic end, the fury of the SS grenadiers was not reserved exclusively for the Polish troops. Any German force being witnessed attempting a surrender could also become targets, as one of Maczek's men recalls…

Above: *The charred remains of a German tank crew who failed to escape the Falaise Pocket.*

White handkerchiefs were waved and a whole crowd of Germans appeared, walking towards the tanks with their hands up. There were quite a lot of them, probably over a hundred. Karp (a Pole) ceased firing and leaned out of the turret. He had never before taken so many prisoners all at once. But there seemed to be something the matter with the crowd of Germans, some of them fell down wounded or killed. Who was firing at them? German tanks! Germans must not surrender, rather should they die, if necessary by German shells.[144]

Finally, by midday on 21 August, reinforcements in the guise of the tanks, and crucially, infantry of the Canadian 4th Armoured Division arrived. Here ended seventy-two hours of hell for Maczek's Poles. Battered, bruised and having lost around half their initial strength, Maczeks depleted forces were unbroken in making one of the most heroic stands endured throughout the whole of the Normandy campaign.

Popular history, although acknowledging the heroism shown by those commanded by the likes of General Mascek and Major Currie, has, on the face of it, been more concerned in concentrating upon the apparent shortfalls of the greater struggle faced in closing the Falaise Pocket. Questions do remain unanswered as to why a greater force from both the Canadian 4th Armoured Division and Patton's Third Army were not deployed in closing the gap. Although such criticisms endure to this day, a much more curious and unmerited myth has been cultivated in which blame for any potential fault be laid at the feet of the British forces who once more supposedly blundered their way through a campaign dominated by the Americans. As the British historian Robin Neillands explains…

The myth holds that the battle at the Falaise pocket was another missed opportunity and adds that the fault lay – again – with the slowness and timidity of the British and Canadians. The arguments on the last point have gone on almost since the battle ended but if national chauvinism is taken out of the frame the picture is fairly clear.[145]

Whilst there are many who would not think twice in doing so, to make such slurs against British forces, the only Ally within the whole coalition that effectively let zero enemy forces slip through their lines during the whole affair, simply confirms that those who make such claims are completely ignorant of the complexities of the overall battle.

Despite persistent claims that the Falaise Pocket was a majorly flawed operation, and that far too many Germans escaped to fight another day, there is no disputing, that from a German perspective, this battle represented anything but a conclusive defeat. Figures still vary as to just how many Germans were taken out of the battle and how many were able to extricate themselves from the snare. Bradley claims in his memoirs that 70,000 Germans were either killed or taken captive during the battle. The official US Historian states that, whilst 50,000 were taken prisoner and 10,000 were killed in the pocket itself, some 20,000 to 40,000 of the enemy escaped. In isolation, these figures do not mean much due to a striking omission that has plagued the historiography of the battle for the Falaise Pocket – this being the almost complete lack of context through examination of similar operations occurring elsewhere during the Second World War. Whilst such operations are relatively rare, and very much vary in scale and therefore difficult to compare, there is context to be found if observers care to look to the Eastern Front. Indeed, when the Falaise Pocket is compared with

Below: *The Polish 1st Armoured Division bury their dead at Mont Ormel.*

battles such as that fought at Demyansk (a failed attempt by the Soviets to encircle German troops in the aftermath of the battle for Leningrad) or Korsun (a battle fought in the Ukraine in February 1944, a battle almost universally adjudicated as a momentous Soviet victory, despite the case that some say up to two thirds of the German forces escaped that particular envelopment), then the outcome at Falaise may seem rather more effective than some pundits have previously claimed. Once more it is important to emphasise that there is no doubt the Germans were under no illusion that they had endured anything but a catastrophic disaster, a defeat which left the previously lush valley of the River Dives, a pyre of apocalyptical wasteland, a scene described within the memoirs of General Eisenhower...

Left: *Battered, bruised and utterly exhausted. Shell-shocked Polish troops rest after the battle for 'the Mace'.*

The battlefield at Falaise was unquestionably one of the greatest killing grounds of any of the war areas. Roads, highways, and fields were so choked with destroyed equipment and with dead men and animals that passage through the area was extremely difficult. Forty-eight hours after the closing of the gap I was conducted through it on foot, to encounter scenes that be described only by Dante. It was literally possible to walk for hundreds of yards at a time, stepping on nothing but dead and decaying flesh.[146]

It is often forgotten that the Allies were attempting to inflict absolute defeat on the remnants of a force which had held some of the most fanatical fighting men of the Second World War. Commanded by *Generalfeldmarschall* Model (the *Lion of Defence*), although the Allies had repeatedly politely requested that the Germans be so kind as to lay down their arms and come along quietly, the enemy was in fact fighting like the devil to live to fight another day. To inflict, as the Allies did, a devastating blow to such a formidable foe, and then to have this achievement dissected to the extent that the battle is depicted as a neo-defeat, seems rather extreme. A retrospective appraisal, gained only through the context of hindsight, may indeed suggest that aspects of the operation could have been realised in a more efficient manner, but cannot this be said of any other battle within history?

Questions do remain unanswered which include why Bradley, having already gone on record in doubting that he possessed the necessary punching power needed to close the gap, allowed Patton, without even consulting, let alone gaining permission from Montgomery, to take half of his Third Army away from the immediate task in hand on the whim of a relative sideshow. Even then, why did Bradley tolerate a unit which he himself had previously classed as a *'problem division'*, a unit assessed by many as the single worst formation in the European Campaign, to be allocated as the American vanguard and be allocated pretty much full responsibility for the American share of closing the gap? It also has to be asked why such a small proportion of the Canadian 4th Armoured Division's infantry deployed with either Major Currie to St Lambert sur Dives, or as support to Maczek's Polish Armoured Division at Mont Ormel. Whilst these issues undoubtedly delayed the linkup between the two pincers, and the closing of the gap, subsequently allowing the escape of thousands of enemy soldiers, all these faults were initiated by commanders at a level subordinate to that of Montgomery. It is therefore somewhat fantastical that, when Bradley acknowledged his error in his memoirs, and while General Simonds sacked the commander of the Canadian 4th Armoured Division in the immediate aftermath of the Falaise Pocket, those with an axe to grind consistently blame Montgomery, and indeed the British, for missing the opportunity of executing a more decisive victory.

Chapter 15
Conclusion

On 21 August, the surviving Germans remaining within the confines of the Falaise Pocket laid down their arms and surrendered. Although there would still be weeks of struggle ahead for the Allies in Normandy, particularly for the British and Canadian troops tasked, not only with the pursuit of the German retreat across the River Seine toward Rouen and Vernon, but also in clearing the fortress ports upon the channel coastline of stubborn rearguard resistance, the main battle in Normandy had concluded with an emphatic Allied victory.

This victory had of course come at a great cost. Almost 20,000 civilians had been killed and hundreds of thousands more were wounded or homeless. Twenty-four thousand British and Canadian troops had been killed, as had 28,000 Americans. As for the enemy, a final figure in terms of loss of life has never been definitively calculated. Some say 90,000, while others say that between D-Day and the completion of the encirclement of the Falaise Pocket, well over 100,000 Germans were killed.

During this time, the lush orchards and pastures, alongside many of the ancient medieval towns of Normandy, had been transformed into a killing ground. It would take decades for the region to recover and those who survived would bear psychological scars for the rest of their lives. But through this great struggle, much of France was free from the tyranny which had blighted its shores for four years and the Allies now held a lodgement area from which future operations could be launched at the heartland of Nazi Germany.

In the subsequent exorcism of the Nazi occupation of France, the Allies achieved a victory which would eventually shape the Free World as we know it today. This victory was achieved by a great coalition of Allied nations, fighting together, committed to a common cause against a common enemy. However, as time goes by, the reality of this struggle has been distorted through what can only be branded as nationalistic chauvinism, creating a common myth that bears absolutely no reality to the actual history. The British historian Robin Neillands defines that myth…

The strategy developed, and plan prepared for Operation Overlord by the Allied Ground Force Commander, the British General Sir Bernard Law Montgomery, was flawed in concept and failed to work in practice. Eventually, frustrated by the failure of Montgomery's strategy and the caution and timidity of the British and Canadian troops, American forces under General Eisenhower, Bradley and Patton seized the initiative, revised the plan, broke out in the west, drove back the German forces in disarray, to win the Normandy Battle – and then the war.

All this they would have done much sooner if the British and Canadians had not sat in their trenches drinking tea – American historians never fail to mention tea – while the US forces did all the fighting. The outcome of the Normandy battle – so goes the allegation – would have been far more conclusive if the aforesaid British and Canadians had not again been "timid" and "cautious" and "slow"… thereby allowing the German Army to escape across the Seine.[147]

Such myths are becoming increasingly engrained, particularly within the American psyche, so entrenched in fact that they are seemingly no longer susceptible to being challenged. Be it within the written word, populist documentaries, the Hollywood film industry and most alarmingly, inherent within the realms of American academia, a myth has been nurtured to the extent that the majority of today's generation of American historians fail almost completely to acknowledge any shortfall within their own contribution, and instead eagerly pass any perceived failure on to the shoulders of anyone but themsleves. Robin Neillands again describes how that myth has manifest itself within one particular book, regarded by many as the authoritative account of the battle for Normandy...

In his well-regarded book 'Decision in Normandy', Carlo D'Este devotes an entire chapter, Chapter 16 – The Price of Caution – to a highly critical appraisal of the British Second Army in Normandy. Then, on page 297, Mr D'Este, adds an explanatory footnote: 'This is not to suggest that the US forces had no problems of their own'. This brief comment is quite true... but 28 pages criticising the British Army in great detail and at every level is not balanced by a one line footnote. A balanced account has to do better than that. The Second Army certainly made mistakes in Normandy... so did all the other armies. To state or even imply that only the British Second Army was in trouble in Normandy is offensive to the veterans and a travesty of the facts... It would be perfectly easy to write a critical account of any of the armies in Normandy. A full examination of the evidence reveals that all the Allied Armies – and the German Armies – had problems during the campaign; to put the Second Army's performance in perspective you have to have put it in context. That can only be done by considering the performance of the other armies – as well as the varied strength and quality of the opposition they were facing. That takes time but the result is revealing.[148]

It is not just British academics who have identified the trend of American historians such as D'Este to over-emphasise their own nation's efforts whilst purposely detracting from this of their Allies. In the words of Michael Dolski in his book *'D-Day Remembered'* published by the University of Tennessee Press...

In a detailed discussion of the planning for Overlord, D'Este took every opportunity to fault General Montgomery for the problems Allied troops experienced in Normandy. For the majority of the book, he presented a damning assessment of British military capability, further Americanising what was really an Allied victory. D'Este echoed far more reassuring tales for American audiences that focused on their military's contributions to victory in a decisive battle against evil.[149]

Dolski went on to suggest the motivation of the likes of Ambrose, D'Este et al, were to simply offer *'stories that major segments of society sought to consume'*[150] – to tell a story that the masses wanted to hear, irrelevant of historical integrity. Such a manipulation of history, so commonplace in America, is also prominent in France. Evidence of this can be found in abundance within the work of the renowned historian and author Olivier Wieviorka (Professor of History at *École normale supérieure Paris-Saclay*), who, when commenting on Montgomery's strategy and the battle for Caen stated...

The failure of the offensive near Caen provides an excellent opportunity for the historian to examine the weaknesses of the British forces. As we have seen, the masterplan drawn up by Montgomery clearly stated that Caen should be taken within the first day, an objective the British singularly failed to achieve. In his memoirs, Montgomery turned this failure into success by arguing that his aim was to draw the bulk of German forces towards the west [sic], thereby giving the Americans room to manoeuvre in the east [sic]… This failure was due to the strategy that was adopted. British Generals put too much faith in aerial bombardments, which was something of a blunt instrument and frequently lacked precision. The British made a number of tactical errors as well. The pace of operations was, in many cases excessively slow… The obvious responsibility of the British Generals should not obscure the fact that they were deploying unmotivated troops… These weaknesses became all too apparent during the Normandy campaign. British troops seemed to be more adept at staying put than at advancing, a fact that was not helped by preparation which had emphasised 'the landings' at the expense of a subsequent ground offensive. This left soldiers inadequately prepared for the difficulties of a deadly and bloody war. On the evening of 6th June, the British were so convinced that this was the 'end' of the operation that the tendency was to stop to brew up a tea and congratulate themselves on having their objective – getting ashore.[151]

Again, in one cruel stroke, just like D'Este but this time without so much as a footnote acknowledging the problems faced by the American forces, Wieviorka defames the British and Canadian effort and regurgitates the slander which any academic in the field really should know is a complete fallacy. It is truly fantastical how a Professor of History, holding such high office within French academia, notwithstanding the fact that he obviously does not know east from west, can be so ignorant of the actual reality of the battle. Examination of pre-invasion briefings, operational orders and numerous memoirs could have avoided such ridiculous statements as those quoted above. Failure to consult these sources surely represents a neglect in implementing the most basic fundamentals of a historian's tradecraft. Indeed, just one paragraph, taken from the 1951 memoirs of General Bradley, instantly discredit the whole framework on which Wieviorka's absurd statement is based upon. Once more, to repeat the words of Bradley…

For three weeks he [Montgomery] *had rammed his troops against those panzer divisions he had deliberately drawn towards that city as part of our strategy of diversion in the Normandy Campaign… For Monty's primary task was to attract German troops to the British front that we might more easily secure Cherbourg and get into position for the breakout… In this diversionary mission Monty was more than successful, for the harder he hammered towards Caen, the more German troops he drew into that sector… Monty's success should have been measured in the panzer divisions the enemy rushed against him whilst Collins sped on toward Cherbourg… In the minds of most people, success in battle is measured in the rate and length of advance. They found it difficult to realise that the more successful Monty was in stirring up German resistance, the less likely he was to advance.*[152]

Maybe even if the pre-invasion briefings, the operational orders published during the battle or the post-war memoirs from the likes of Bradley were not deemed important enough to be taken into consideration by the likes of D'Este and Wieviorka, maybe

General Bernard L. Montgomery 1887-1976

Commander of 21st Army Group - Operational Commander of all Allied land forces for the full duration of the Battle for Normandy

Born in London in 1887, Bernard Law Montgomery endured an unsettled childhood moving from one parish to another as his family followed his father's career as a protestant missionary. From London, travelling through Ireland and Australia before moving back to Britain to complete his education at St Pauls School in London, *Monty* graduated from Sandhurst in 1908. Serving as a lieutenant in the Royal Warwickshire Regiment during the Great War, he was shot twice, once in the leg and once in the chest during the battle of Bailleul in October 1914. Having been left for dead, it has been said that a grave was dug for his seemingly lifeless body to be laid to rest. Nevertheless, he recovered from his wounds and although he would lose a lung, he did gain the Distinguished Service Order, his citation noting his 'conspicuous gallant leading... [turning] *the enemy out of their trenches with the bayonet*'. Montgomery re-joined the fight in 1916, serving in the battles of the Somme and Arras, eventually attaining the rank of Colonel. Through the successful integration of infantry and armour, Montgomery's reputation grew as his troops consistently took objectives whilst suffering a fraction of the casualties of other units.

Whilst his Great War experience was impressive, it was Monty's command of the British Eighth Army in North Africa in 1942 that led him to gain legendary status amongst the British population. Many would state that before Monty, the British Army had suffered almost nothing but defeat; under his command the Allies would go on to achieve almost nothing but victory. By the end of 1944 Montgomery held nine years of command in the field stretching over two World Wars. From Lieutenant to Field Marshal, having commanded at Company, Battalion, Regiment, Division, Corps, Army and Army Group level, very, very few would emulate Montgomery's epic journey through the ranks. However, Montgomery's achievements were matched only by his arrogance, a trait that would lead him into making many enemies, especially amongst the Americans, whom Montgomery very much saw as junior partners to the British in terms of both experience and skill. Such sentiment undoubtedly created friction during the planning and implementation of Overlord, of which Montgomery, not only planned the land battle, but commanded all land forces.

Whilst very few Allied commanders can boast the achievements of Montgomery, his legacy has undoubtedly been tarnished as a consequence of his personality. Whatever criticisms may be put against him, there is no doubt that no other individual made a greater contribution to Allied victory in Normandy. With just a little humility, the enigmatic Monty would surely have been universally revered as one of the greatest Generals of the Second World War.

After the war, Montgomery would serve as Chief of the Imperial General Staff from 1946 to 1948, a period that he found immensely frustrating by having to deal with what he perceived as being too much interference from politicians and not enough time devoted purely to military matters. He would retire in 1958, becoming increasingly reclusive up to the date of his death in 1976, aged eighty-eight. He is buried at Holy Cross Church in Binstead, Hampshire.

they may have thought of consulting the official report of the Allied Supreme Commander, to quote once more...

The resulting struggle around Caen, which seemed to cost so much blood for such small territorial gains, was thus an essential factor in ensuring our ultimate success. The very tenacity of the defence there was sufficient proof of this. As I told the press correspondents at the end of August, every foot of ground the enemy lost at Caen was like losing ten miles anywhere else.[153]

Lieutenant General George S. Patton Junior 1885-1945

Commander of the US Third Army (activated 1 August 1944)

George Smith Patton Junior was born into a wealthy Californian family in 1885. Although afforded every possible privilege, Patton's formative years would be marred through numerous learning difficulties. Although not academically talented, Patton developed a huge interest in military history, especially the American Civil War, a conflict during which both his Grandfather and Great Uncle had been killed whilst fighting for the Confederate Army. Expressing a desire for a career within the military, Patton joined the Virginia Military Institute before enrolling at West Point. Although forced to repeat his first year due to poor grades, Patton graduated from West Point in 1909 and was subsequently commissioned as a Second Lieutenant in the cavalry. A year later Patton married Beatrice Ayer, the daughter of an industrial tycoon from Boston.

In 1912 Patton represented the United States in the Stockholm Olympics, competing in the modern pentathlon and finishing in fifth place from a field of 42 competitors. Patton's interests also extended to horsemanship. The suffering of frequent head injuries during polo matches has led to speculation that this contributed to the erratic behaviour for which Patton would become infamous in later years.

As the United States entered the Great War, Patton, now a Major, became one of America's first pioneers of armoured warfare. Immersing himself in every aspect of this new concept, Patton moulded the US Army's first tank units and indeed, in September 1918, and now holding the wartime rank of Lieutenant Colonel, he led the very first American crewed tanks into battle during the Saint-Mihiel offensive. Ignoring orders and showing abandon to his objectives, not to mention displaying complete disregard for the lives of the men he commanded, Patton's armoured charge ran into an ambush. Many casualties were suffered and Patton himself would be shot in the buttocks. Despite later claims of numerous feats of glory during the Great War, the reversal at Saint-Mihiel would conclude Patton's grand total of 14 days of front line combat during the entire conflict.

The inter-war years witnessed Patton achieve steady progression through the ranks and with America now having joined the Second World War, holding the temporary rank of Major General, in November of 1942 Patton would command the westernmost of a three-pronged assault during the invasion of Morocco during Operation Torch. In March 1943, now holding

Undoubtedly the worst culprit in distorting this history is the American commentator (the author refrains from using the title of historian), Stephen E. Ambrose. A whole litany of misinformed and ignorant remarks could be chosen to discredit a man revered by so many in America yet so reviled by those who hold just the most basic knowledge of the history Ambrose so blatantly attempts to rewrite. However, the following remark, taken from Ambrose's *'Americans at War'*, is sufficient enough for the means of this example. Amongst many other ridiculous claims, Ambrose, who has been accused as a prolific plagiarist and an individual who manufactured quotes through fictional meetings that he claimed he held with Eisenhower, stated that the Germans failed to send their armour to bear in Normandy…

The panzers had started for Normandy, but now Hitler ordered them back to Calais… The panzers stayed in the Pas de Calais region all through June, all through July, while the Battle for Normandy was fought. They were still there in August.[154]

This kind of sweeping, unsubstantiated and simply inaccurate statement epitomises the work of Stephen Ambrose and can be discredited immediately with just the most the rank of Lieutenant General, Patton led the US Seventh Army into Sicily, a campaign that led to further controversy as once again he deviated from his objectives, leaving the British forces under Montgomery to deal with the main enemy force in the Sicilian mountains, as he countermanded orders and broke away on open roads in the attempt to liberate the capital city of Palermo. Achieving absolutely no strategic advantage, with very little resistance, Palermo did indeed fall to Patton. At the same time over 100,000 Axis troops escaped the clutches of the Allies, gaining an unlikely reprieve as they evacuated to Italy through the port of Messina. Patton would soon earn even greater notoriety as the story broke that he had assaulted two of his own men who had been hospitalised due to battle fatigue. Subsequently relieved of his command, Patton would miss out on D-Day and the main part of the battle for Normandy as he was left out of battle and instead used for deception purposes in the United Kingdom.

Chasing headlines if not the enemy, Patton would achieve additional fame for his rapid sweep through Brittany, Normandy and on to Paris. Whilst he indisputably gained ground, it is almost always forgotten that Patton's most famous feats were always achieved against a distinct lack of enemy presence. Indeed, the only time that Patton's forces did encounter persistently strong resistance, most notably during the Lorraine Campaign of late 1944, despite his previous claims that 'We're going to go through the enemy like shit through a tinhorn', Patton's forces became stalemated, failing to advance any considerable distance for months.

Undoubtedly, Patton's most celebrated moment occurred during the Battle of the Bulge in December 1944. However, although he would never publicly acknowledge the fact, Patton's much famed relief of the American forces encircled within the town of Bastogne was only made possible through the efforts of his operations officer. Colonel Oscar Koch had predicted the German offensive through the study of troop movements combined with transcripts of German communications, enabling Patton's forces to be placed on standby before deploying with such rapidity.

As a master manipulator of the Press, throughout his career Patton played the media in order to paint a legend of mythic neo-genius. Forgetting almost completely his many failures, and inflating his very few victories, Patton's largely unquestioned legacy has been distorted beyond any resemblance of the true history. This myth is further enhanced through the conspiracy theories suggesting that Patton's premature death, following a road traffic accident in December 1945, was as the consequence of a government sanctioned assassination, intending to silence his increasingly vocal opposition to the American stance on post-war Germany and apparent appeasement of the Soviet Union.

George Smith Patton Junior, having died at the age of 60 on 21 December 1945 is buried at the Luxembourg American Cemetery.

basic grasp of the reality of the actual battle. In the words of Michael Dolski (one American historian who does seem to be able to see the wood for the trees), *'Ambrose provided feel-good history for American society'.*[155] Ambrose's work became the equivalent of what another commentator described as *"the wartime equivalent of big fish stories",*[156] in the words once more of Michael Dolski, *'People enjoyed these stories, as evidenced in their eager consumption, which cast America as the powerful country preserving morality in a benighted world... as the city on a hill holding evil at bay'.*[157]

Indeed, Ambrose's work often portrays the complete reverse of the actual situation. In reality, by the end of August, not only had all but one armoured division in France been deployed against the Allies in Normandy (more than three-quarters of these against the British and Canadians), but an additional two had in fact been brought to the Caen front from the Soviet Union. At this time no armoured division remained within the Pas de Calais region. It does seem irrefutable that Ambrose's 'skill' was to accentuate the achievements of American forces whilst understating the role of others.

Above: *Churchill, Dempsey and Montgomery visit the ruins of Caen.*

Maybe the question has to be asked, if the likes of Wieviorka, Ambrose, D'Este etc. are either ignorant to the aforementioned core sources, or for whatever reason have simply failed to consult them, then what sources have been used in order to formulate their fantastical perspectives? Such fabrication gives credibility to growing claims that there has been an orchestrated attempt to destroy reputations and to distort the true history, to detract from the efforts of Montgomery and the Commonwealth forces, in order to purposely inflate the achievements of the Americans. Myths have not just been nurtured, but have now become so deep-rooted that they are now widely recognised as fact. Whilst it has long since become an impossible task to correct such inaccuracies, surely it is the role of historians to question such fable, especially as these falsehoods can be instantly discredited with just a modicum of understanding of the subject matter. Unfortunately, very few commentators seem to possess such basic tradecraft, meaning that the entrenched myth is simply regurgitated time and time again creating what Michael Dolski refers to *'as a depiction of the past that is widely accepted and no longer challenged'.*[158]

More and more, the battle for Normandy is being portrayed in both popular culture and even within academia as an American victory, achieved against the cream of the Nazi elite and despite the drawback of having to fight alongside and under the command of a plucky, but ultimately bungling British Ally. Despite the fact that their own official histories record, with blunt honesty, that at times the US forces displayed *'hesitation, inertia, and disorganization... Poor employment of attached units and... a particular ineptness in the realms of organization and control',*[159] despite the fact that elements of the US Army were judged by their own commanders as the very worst formations to fight in the European Theatre, despite the American advance being at times months behind the anticipated schedule, the emphasis of any perceived failure is persistently placed at the door of the British and Canadian forces. It is rarely mentioned that for the majority of the battle, the British and Canadians were facing enemy forces, in terms of both quantity and quality, that were far superior to those deployed against the Americans in Normandy, if not during the entire war.

In great contrast to such a brazen portrayal, the traditional reserve of the British leads to ultra-critical self-assessment. The self-effacing British mindset, combined with the innate self-aggrandisement, so abundant within the American psyche, has, for almost eighty years led to a great distortion of the true history, obscuring the line between fact and fiction and resulting in the Americanisation of the whole war. Whilst such defamation is unquestionably resented in the United Kingdom, it is received largely with a pinch of salt and no little satire, as Robin Neillands notes...

If this sort of thing continues it cannot be too long before some American academic reveals how the US contingent played a decisive part in beating the French at the Battle of Agincourt in 1415 while the cautious and timid British archers looked on in watchful admiration.[160]

Up to now British commentators have remained quiet, seemingly judging such slander as nothing more than an irritation emanating from an ignorant but largely harmless school of historians who really should know better. I suspect that works such as this book will never gain a mass audience, therefore I am in no way suggesting that it shall become a panacea which instantly engenders a correction of balance, but surely it is now time for the next generation of historians from every nation to challenge what has gone before them, to carry out a thorough reassessment and for the record to be set straight. The veterans themselves deserve no less than this.

Despite the ongoing criticisms, an objective and thorough examination of the conduct and performance of the Commonwealth forces during the battle for Normandy leaves surprisingly little opportunity for reproach. They fought in battles unsurpassed in ferocity against the most fanatical foe. Through, what was in the main, exemplary commitment to the cause, the Commonwealth forces made the Germans fight the way Montgomery wanted them to fight. If that meant that battles would not be launched without the build up of an abundance of material superiority, to fight with steel and not with flesh in order to avoid mass casualties, well what is wrong with that? After all, isn't that the way that modern battles are fought today? If so, then should not Montgomery be considered as a General nurturing a technique that was in fact ahead of its time - cultivating a strategy that would become the standard for generations to come? Granted, at times there were set-backs, no successful military campaign lasting the best part of three months has ever been without set-backs, but the resolve, determination and dedication of all Allied forces on the Normandy battlefield can never, in an objective way, be sincerely criticised.

In essence, in assessing the Battle of Normandy, we are concurrently assessing Montgomery. He was not just the architect of the battle, but also the main contractor who delivered what the Germans themselves assessed as their greatest loss of the Second World War. At times it did seem to those unaware of Montgomery's strategy that things were not going well but it is worth remembering that none of the criticism aimed at Montgomery during what certain present-day historians call the *'stalemate'* of late June / early July, would have had to have been endured if American forces had achieved their objectives on schedule. In facing weaker opposition, the Americans failed to keep to their own timetable in making headway in the west. In failing to position themselves ready for breakout, they prolonged the continuation of keeping the main enemy force away from the American front. The debt of gratitude owed by the Americans to the Commonwealth forces has been repaid through the defamation of reputation.

In contrast to the popular assessment of Montgomery, any failings of the American commanders are quickly forgotten. Bradley, known endearingly as *'the Soldier's General'* has been completely forgiven for his blunders during not only his preparations for battle, which led to the carnage of the initial assault at Omaha, but also for the fiasco of the pause in front of St Lo, the failure to make headway in preparation of the breakout into Brittany, the failure to take the Brittany ports and most remarkably, the failure to fully commit all available forces to the closing of the Falaise Pocket. Although in his memoirs Bradley confessed to his tardiness in setting up his breakthrough to the west, and also his long held regret in terms of his command of Patton during the end stages of the battle for Normandy, he has been forgiven to the extent that any potential misgiving does not even register in most histories of the Normandy Campaign. It is strange, considering the harsh accusations made against Commonwealth troops, that history can assess Bradley's Americans so favourably. Imagine the reaction of the American media if word got out that the British Army had been forced to establish a training camp in Normandy in order to bring up to scratch troops already committed to battle. At the same time, it is bizarre that Generals such as Dempsey, Crerar, Collins and Hodges, all of whose command could be assessed positively, are forgotten in preference to the likes of Patton who in stark reality was no more than a minor player within a much larger campaign.

It seems a real irony that if it was not for the effective leadership of Montgomery, then so many Americans whose descendants later criticised him so cruelly, would likely not have survived the battle and returned home in the first place. In the mid-Twentieth Century, America was still a young and developing power, desperate to forge an identity and express its self-proclaimed manifest destiny as leader of the Free World. American sacrifice and all that America achieved in the Second World War is an incredible enough feat, it really should not be the case that Americans distort history to purposely detract from the efforts of others in order to inflate their own legacy.

So how can we objectively assess Montgomery's command of the Normandy campaign when so much of what is perceived today is born from legend rather than

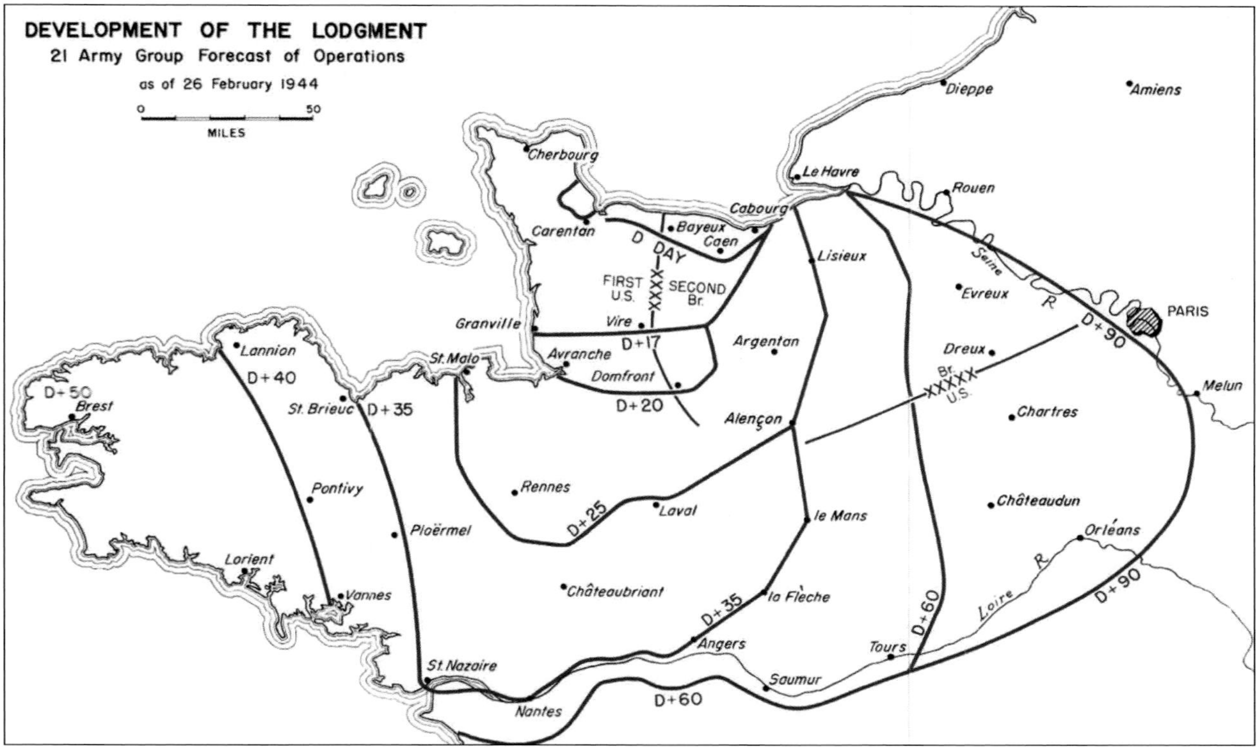

Above: *Although the Allied advance was at times behind the anticipated pre-invasion rate of advance. The overall battle concluded two weeks ahead of Montgomery's pre-invasion estimate.*

fact? Monty undoubtedly played the leading role in both the planning and execution of the World's largest ever amphibious military operation that commenced the liberation of Western Europe from the greatest tyranny it has ever faced. Armed with what was sometimes inferior weaponry, the Allies faced a German Army battling not only for its life, but for the future of its country. Monty's strategy was outlined in advance and set for completion after ninety days. It took seventy-six. During this time he deliberately manipulated the German forces to draw them onto a British and Canadian front whilst the Americans postured for position before forcing the envelopment of the Germans in Normandy.

By the end of the campaign, Montgomery had masterminded not only the successful completion of the greatest gamble of the war, but the annihilation to near extinction of thirty-eight German Divisions (to put that into context, twenty had been lost at Stalingrad). During this battle, the combined Allied effort took up to 400,000 German soldiers, 1,300 tanks and over 3,000 vehicles out of the war. For his command of this feat alone, not to mention that he had already inflicted upon Rommel in North Africa, the greatest retreat in military history, Montgomery should surely be revered as one of the all-time greats of the Second World War.

Monty's strategy was clearly defined and, although not everyone understood it at the time, was successfully applied in advance of the predicted timeframe. He was of course, an insufferable egotist and at times it must have been a real tribulation to have to work alongside him. However, many criticisms from those who were offended by the man have not revolved around the nature of his command, but instead the nature of his character. It is true to state that Monty was very much his own worst enemy in that he could have easily avoided the majority of the resentment generated against him if he had only possessed just a modicum of humility. Yet most of those who dislike Montgomery so intently today, do so through what is fundamentally nothing more than a myth. The theory goes that Monty contrived to change his objectives to suit the development of battle and that, after the fact, he never admitted any changes were made to that masterplan. Another accusation so frequently made against Montgomery is that he stopped Patton from closing the Falaise Pocket out of sheer spite. As we have heard, Bradley himself put that issue straight, stating beyond doubt that this was his decision and his decision alone. He never consulted Montgomery in making that decision and that the debate never went beyond his own headquarters. If this issue was addressed outright in Bradley's memoirs of 1951 then why do such accusations persist to this day?

Despite ongoing accusations, Monty's plan was formulated months before the invasion was launched and the basic principle of that strategy was adhered to throughout the three month campaign. Such facts are endorsed by two volumes of autobiography from Bradley and General Eisenhower's official report of 1946 and were doubted only by those with an axe to grind. Montgomery is often quoted as stating, *'I never once had cause or reason to alter my master plan'.*[161] – such words are often used in highlighting the arrogance of the man but are almost always quoted in isolation of what Monty wrote next…

Of course we did not keep to the times and phase lines we had envisaged for the benefit of administrative planning, and of course, too, we didn't hesitate to adjust our plans and dispositions to the tactical situation as it developed – as in all battles. Of course we didn't. I never imagined we would. But the fundamental design remained unchanged; it was to that that I pinned my hopes and clung so resolutely, despite increasing opposition from the fainter-hearted.[162]

There is indeed a fine line between supreme self-confidence spilling over into arrogance, but then there is also a line between those who understand, and those who do not, that although a campaign may suffer numerous tactical setbacks, an overall strategy can remain intact. Those who knew Monty best recognized that his greatest strengths were born of *'single minded obstinacy to forward his own clearly perceived plan with sincerity, simplicity and unfaltering, infuriating, reassuring self-confidence'.*[163] This was often perceived, rightly or wrongly, as arrogance, especially when Montgomery had dealings with the Americans, whom he measured, principally due to their almost universal lack of experience compared to that which he himself possessed, very much as junior partners. Monty could certainly have done more to reassure the concerns being addressed by the likes of Eisenhower during the battle itself, but then Eisenhower himself can be assessed as not holding an appreciation of the complexities of such battles on a scale of which he himself had no previous experience. Eisenhower certainly did not help himself with his detachment from the battlefield, not to mention his *'honours and sacrifices equally shared'* statement, nor did his subsequent management of the North West European Campaign after he took the reins from Montgomery on 1 September 1944, instill great confidence in Eisenhower as a commander in the field.

When comparing Montgomery against those who are regularly misrepresented as his peers, it is indeed ironic that that with regard to character traits, Monty and Patton were very similar. Both were at times insufferably arrogant, and sometimes close to

Above: *The Big Three – Generals Bradley, Montgomery and Dempsey.*

impossible to work with. However, where Patton's legacy has been greatly enhanced due to the brash bluster and bravado of his character, rather than as a consequence of his actual achievements on the battlefield, Monty's actual achievements have in contrast been diminished by his personality; even one of his own admirers once called him an *"efficient little shit."*

What is habitually forgotten is that Patton never reached the level of Montgomery's command. To compare an army commander to that of the role of Montgomery who not just planned, but executed one of the greatest military operations ever undertaken, is like trying to compare night and day or chalk and cheese. Patton was undoubtedly a resourceful leader at a certain level and whilst facing favourable circumstances. As a Corps Commander, in some, albeit not the majority of his campaigns, Patton could potentially be rated favourably amongst the likes of Generals Joe Collins and possibly even Guy Simonds. However, at anything above Corps level, he displayed a lack of sophistication and excelled only during operations fought against a distinct lack of enemy resistance. As the near 100,000 casualties of Patton's ill-fated Lorraine Campaign proved, he was consistently found lacking when moved up the chain of command. There is a reason why, in a campaign of such magnitude which cried out for an outstanding commander, Montgomery remained at the top and Patton's repeated pleas for a greater role were consistently supressed by Eisenhower and Bradley, both of whom had at times evaluated Patton in terms only just short of a liability. Patton's legend is one of *could have, would have, should have.* To compare the imaginable achievements of Patton against the actual achievements of Montgomery is a laughable proposition, yet one which still exists within the work of a certain breed of popular historian.

Maybe if Monty had been perceived as being a little less uptight and more media savvy, and just maybe if he had been an American, then potentially his legacy would be that of one of the greatest Generals of all time. Instead his reputation has been cruelly tainted in no small part by his nationality and in a large way by his more than infrequent bouts of arrogance, a legacy as explained by the British comedian, author and historian, Al Murray...

His negatives are all marshalled against him. His positives are blindly ignored. His personal failings are refracted as greater than his successes. His errors brought to overshadow the things that he got right. So, the Monty conundrum is this. If he was so slow, tactless, ponderous, spiteful, boastful and so on, how did he get the job, how did he retain it and how of course did he win? ... In short if the German Army is the greatest army the world has ever seen, how did Monty beat it? If he was such a terrible General, how did he win?[164]

If only Montgomery had heeded the words of Alanbrooke which were sent to him on the day of his promotion to Field Marshal...

You may perhaps have thought during the last five years that I was occasionally rude to you. If I was then I can assure you that it was only because I wanted to guard you against the effect of some of your actions which are incorrectly judged by others and lead to criticism which might affect your progress, a matter which has been of great concern to me. I should like at this moment of your triumph to offer you one more word of advice. Don't let success go to your head and remember the value of humility.[165]

At the same time that we attempt to assess the hierarchy of Allied command, it is also very much worth remembering that for every general who became a household name, indeed for every individual recipient of the Medal of Honor or Victoria Cross, the final victory was only delivered through the efforts of millions of individuals who took part in the greater struggle, putting their lives on the line in order to enable the final victory.

Constant bickering about which nation played the greater role in this victory is, of course, futile. Without the Commonwealth forces, the Americans would never had gained the opportunity to break out, and without the Americans the Commonwealth forces would never have been able to advance. What is inescapable is the fact that history has neither been kind to Montgomery, nor the Commonwealth forces who fought in Normandy. Popular history has judged D-Day and the Battle of Normandy as a predominantly American affair; of course it was not. It is about time that this popular misconception was put to bed and that greater emphasis be given to the vital achievements of British and Canadian forces, recognised at least as equals, and certainly not behind their American Allies. Let us never forget what the whole coalition, together, actually achieved. From facing head on a regime which had dominated mainland Europe within a vice-like grip of death and terror, Operation Overlord had reduced the Germans in France to a shattered shell in full retreat. As recorded in the German archives...

On August 29th, as the last of his troops were crossing the river, Model reported to Hitler on the state of the Wehrmacht in the west. The average strength of the panzer and panzer grenadier divisions which had fought in Normandy was, he said, '5-10 tanks each.' From these eleven divisions he might form 11 battlegroups of regimental strength, but could do this only if he were to receive prompt replacements of men and equipment. From the 16 infantry divisions which had been brought back across the lower Seine he could raise sufficient men to form 4, but he could not equip them (in addition to the sixteen infantry divisions mentioned here, there were another 7 which had been wiped out in the Normandy fighting and were no longer included by Model in the German Order of Battle). *These troops, he said... 'have only a few heavy weapons and for the most part are equipped with nothing more than small arms... the supply of replacements in men and material is utterly inadequate... there is no reserve whatever of assault guns and other heavy anti-tank equipment'.*[166]

Below: *With thousands dead and countless more made homeless - the civilian losses during the Battle for Normandy were immense.*

In summarising the success of the battle for Normandy, on 26 August, Monty noted in his diary… *'The Battle of Normandy is over… And they were destroyed… we are well ahead of our forecast'.*[167] Eisenhower reported that by 25 August, the enemy had lost, in round numbers, 400,000 killed, wounded or captured, of which 200,000 were prisoners of war. Thirteen hundred tanks, 20,000 vehicles, 500 assault guns, 1,500 field guns and heavier artillery had been captured or destroyed, aside from the destruction inflicted upon the Normandy coastal defences - if this was an incomplete victory, then maybe the Allies could be better served realising more of them.

Without doubt the likes of Montgomery or Eisenhower would have liked the final word, I have however chosen the words, not of one of the commanders, not of any of the pundits who, like myself, are so detached from the realities of the true horrors of such a struggle. Instead I wish to conclude by quoting from the memoirs of one who witnessed first-hand, what was for anyone who was not there, the unimaginable brutality of the battle for Normandy. In the words of the Canadian Normandy veteran George Blackburn…

No one can properly appreciate the valour and judge the effectiveness of the front line soldiers… who does not fully appreciate the severity of the fighting in Normandy… the high tension overlaying every minute of every hour of every day for weeks on end, when massive opposing forces were committed to endless offensive operations designed to overwhelm and destroy each other in a bloodbath that was pursued with unabated fury for almost 3 months, with neither side allowed any flexibility of manoeuvre – the Allies confined by their perimeters of the bridgehead, and the enemy denied any planned withdrawal by the Fuhrer.

There is little recognition of the conditions under which the fighting soldier existed… none of the sparse unit diaries or post battle intelligence reports make any serious attempt to describe what was entailed in simply staying alive during those terrible days and nights… This deficiency… has led to inaccurate, irresponsible conclusions bordering on outright dishonesty... these inaccuracies, insulting to the memory of all those who died facing the enemy… are perpetuated by writers and even built upon by some domestic revisionists… It is irritating to the point of enraging to read critical analysis of the shortcomings of men and officers engaged at the spearhead of operations by critics with not a single day of frontline experience… with no responsibility for men's lives resting on their decisions, they are sickeningly arrogant. Clearly, when all the sinister mystery is removed from any battlefield as to what the enemy has over there beyond those trees, or amongst the silent rubble of that village, or in the dead ground just over that ridge, any fool can decide what should have been done and the best way of doing it.

There is something particularly obscene about the works of historians who conduct cold blooded analysis and write without emotion of the accomplishments of units and the 'fighting qualities' of men while never giving any indication they recognize and understand the frailty of the human spirit and the resolve of all men, regardless of training or background, when forced to live for days without end in a continuing agony of fear made manageable only by the numbing effects of extreme fatigue… I think I would have keeled over in shock had I come across one historian purporting to describe the battles on the road to Falaise, who once acknowledged that those battles (like those in every major operation extending over several weeks) were not fought by alert, well rested, well fed, healthy men but by men suffering utter exhaustion, from heat and

dysentery and the never ending itching induced by lice and sand fleas, from never being allowed to stretch out and get a night's sleep, and from continuously living with grinding tension arising from the irrepressible dread of being blown to pieces or being left mangled and crippled.

What a hellish nightmare it must have been for foot soldiers with dysentery just to drag themselves over hill and dale, let alone dash here and there for cover when on the attack, and then dig in on the objective to meet the inevitable counterattack. I wondered then and I wonder still how men found the will to move out from cover and risk death and crippling wounds day after day until they were wounded or killed. I saw them do it when they were so stunned by fatigue they scarcely flinched when an 88mm whacked an air burst above them. And I saw them do it shortly after some opening rounds of a fire plan fell short, causing a few overwrought with tension, to cry like babies…

Armchair strategists writing of those days – whether British, American or Canadian – have all spent too much time wondering why they were so slow… they should have spent more time wondering how men ever summoned up the necessary moral courage and physical stamina to get there at all.[168]

Above: *US troops in Chambois following the battle for the Falaise Pocket.*

PART FIVE

Appendix 1

Visiting the Battlefield

Travelling to Normandy

By Air

The closest international airports which serve Normandy are those located in Paris. At the time of publication there are also flights from various airports in the UK to Caen / Carpiquet, to Deauville (located less than an hour from Caen) and to Dinard in Brittany (which is approximately a two-hour drive from the Normandy battlefields).

By Train

To get to Normandy from Paris the most popular method is to catch a train from Paris St Lazare (direct line to Caen, Bayeux, Carentan and Cherbourg).

By Car

The main Paris to Cherbourg highway, the A13 / RN13 offers good access to the whole region.

By Sea

At the date of publication, Brittany Ferries operate a cross-channel ferry service from Poole or Portsmouth to Cherbourg, Caen and Le Havre. Such crossings vary in duration from anything between four and eight hours.

Staying in Normandy

If you intend to visit the Normandy battlefields without a guide, the best location to base your stay is right in the heart of where the battle took place. 1 Le Port is a seventeenth century farm cottage located close to the town of Ste Mere Eglise and less than twenty miles away from where no fewer than ten of the featured actions which led to the award of the Medal of Honor took place (three of which are less than seven miles away). The house, recently renovated into a comfortable self-catering cottage, features four bedrooms and four bathrooms and can sleep up to eight people. Along with every necessity you may need the house also features a library of books and DVDs relevant to the military history of the area. For more information you can email *enquiries@normandybattletours.com.*

Left: *A B26 Marauder – the main exhibit at the excellent Utah Beach museum.*

Battlefield Tours

Although there are a growing number of excellent reference books being published on the subject of the Battle for Normandy, maximum insight into the Normandy battlefields can only ever be achieved by visiting the region and by physically walking the battlefields with a specialist guide. The author is one of the foremost battlefield guides in the region and offers award winning tours inclusive of accommodation. More information on these tours can be found on the author's website www.normandybattletours.com

Visiting the Battlefields

The Medals of D-Day

With so much emphasis dedicated to the story of D-Day, as opposed to the wider battle, it may be no surprise that the D-Day sites, and the stories associated with these locations, are memorialised in greater proportion to the struggles faced during the subsequent inland campaign. Even with this in mind, it is remarkable that relatively few of the twenty-two individuals to receive either the Victoria Cross or Medal of Honor have memorials dedicated to them. Indeed, in regard of the five highest status medals awarded for actions taking place on D-Day, only the Victoria Cross awarded to CSM Stanley Hollis is commemorated. It is regrettable that there is a great lack of consistency with regard to the commemoration of these actions. This inevitably leads to a disparity of coverage within the following pages which is a direct consequence of either an abundance, or indeed a lack of, existing monuments and in no way is it a reflection of any other factor.

Although there is no specific memorial dedicated to the award of the medal, to visit sites associated with the story of the Medal of Honor awarded to Brigadier General Theodore Roosevelt Jnr, there is ample parking available at Utah Beach. This can be found by setting your GPS to locate the **Musee du Debarquement Utah Beach, 50480, Ste Marie du Mont (GPS Coordinates - 49.414793, -1.176917).**

The highlight of any visit to Utah Beach must be the excellent museum which is located within the remnants of the Widerstandsnest 5 complex. This beachfront strongpoint was subjected to the most accurate aerial bombardment to be placed against any German fortification overlooking the entire invasion coastline. Although there has been a museum located at this site since the 1960s, €6,000,000 of investment was made in preparation for the 70th anniversary of D-Day in 2014 transformed the museum from what was once admittedly a mediocre site, to what is now undoubtedly the best 'beach' museum in Normandy. Amongst the many superb exhibits, there is a LCVP (Landing Craft Vehicle Personnel - more commonly known as a Higgins Boat), a B26 Bomber and a very informative film. The Utah Beach museum features a profile of Teddy Roosevelt and is home to the Medal of Honor awarded to Lieutenant John Butts, who received his award for actions during the battle of the Fort du Roule strongpoint in Cherbourg.

Alongside the museum stands the Roosevelt cafe bar. Within just a few yards of here General Roosevelt established his D-Day HQ within the sand dunes. The house itself, whilst having been substantially redeveloped since the war, existed as a single storey fisherman's cottage prior to being requisitioned by the Germans. It then became an integral component of the enemy strongpoint which bore the wrath of the first wave assault at Utah Beach. Also within close proximity to the museum and the Roosevelt Cafe are memorials dedicated to the US Army VII Corps, the 4th and 90th Infantry Divisions, the US Navy, the 1st Engineer Special Brigade and other elements of the Allied naval forces that assisted the Utah Beach landings.

The draw which leads to the beach through the sand dunes located immediately to the front of the Roosevelt café, is the same as was developed by US Engineers on D-Day. There had been an existing gap built through the sand dunes here prior to the occupation which had been used by local fishermen as they moved their boats to and from the beach. This initial gap had been blocked by the Germans through the construction of a concrete wall, however American bulldozers widened the draw to create a crucial link connecting the beach to the adjacent causeway which leads inland.

Located between the Roosevelt Cafe and the draw that leads through the sand dunes is a memorial dedicated to the designer and constructor of the famous LCVP landing craft. Inaugurated in 2015, the Andrew Higgins Memorial features statues of three infantrymen disembarking from a full-scale model of such an assault craft. Although the Andrew Higgins factory in New Orleans constructed over 20,000 of this variation of assault craft, with the majority of the US Navy operating in the Pacific Theatre of Operations, well over three-quarters of the D-Day Naval Force were of British Royal Navy descent, meaning most assault craft used on D-Day were the British LCA (Landing Craft Assault) variant and only a fraction were the LCVP. However, here at Utah, the whole of the first wave of twenty assault craft were Higgins Boats, in this instance manned by personnel of the US Coast Guard.

Located in front of the road which runs directly inland is a marker commemorating the starting point of what is known as the Route du Voie de la Libertie (The Route of Liberty). Commencing here, and then distanced every kilometer from Utah Beach to Bastogne in Belgium (scene of one of the most famous battles fought during the Battle of the Bulge in December 1944), are 1,146 road markers which follow the approximate route taken by American forces from their first landing in Normandy, to their battles fought on the German border some six months later. Brigadier General Theodore Roosevelt Jnr died of a heart attack in a small village called Meautis on 12 July 1944. Within the village there is a plaque dedicated to him **(GPS -49.278993, -1.300644)**. There is also a small plaque upon the village's war memorial located within the nearby churchyard **(GPS - 49.279556, -1.302028)**.

All three of the Medals of Honor awarded for actions during the Omaha Beach assault were presented to men of the 1st Infantry Division who disembarked on the eastern half of the beach. When visiting this area the most practical place to park is the car park of the American Cemetery and Memorial located at the top of the bluff overlooking the eastern half of Omaha Beach at Colleville sur Mer **(American Cemetery, Colleville sur Mer, 14710 - GPS Coordinates - 49.357799, -0.852449 - be aware that the car park is locked beyond the opening hours of the cemetery, which depending upon the time of year opens at 9am and closes at either 5pm or 6pm)**. Whilst it would be easy to spend at least half a day visiting solely the 172 acres of the American Cemetery and the excellent accompanying Visitor's Centre, there follows a walking tour which itself could last up to three hours and involves traversing a distance of up to four miles on what can be steep and uneven ground.

The cemetery itself is the final resting place of three Medal of Honor recipients: Brigadier General Theodore Roosevelt Jnr (Burial Reference: Block D, Row 28, Grave 45), Lieutenant Jimmie Monteith Jnr (Burial Reference: Block I, Row 20, Grave 12) and Technical Sergeant Frank Peregory (Burial Reference: Block G, Row 21, Grave 7). General Leslie McNair, the highest ranking American officer to be killed in the Second World War, is also buried here (Burial Reference: Block F, Row 28, Grave 42).

Having visited the cemetery, you can leave on foot through the side exit of the car park located to the east of the Visitor's Centre. Having walked approximately 100 yards to the east, following the sight of the obelisk-like memorial dedicated to the 1st Infantry Division which is visible along the track heading north, you can now cut down onto the beach through the site of Widerstandsnest 62 - the largest and best preserved of the fifteen strongpoints built to protect Omaha Beach. Having reached the beach walk in a westerly direction to the area overlooked by the cemetery. This is Easy Red Sector where Medal of Honor recipient Carlton Barrett disembarked. Having reached the section of beach overlooked by the western limit of the American Cemetery, turn around and retrace your route to the point where you first stepped down onto the beach. Now continue walking along the beach heading east. You are now walking upon Fox Green Sector where John Pinder was fatally wounded on D-Day.

Continue walking in an easterly direction along the beach until you reach the area where the sand dunes give way to cliffs. At the commencement of these cliffs, Lieutenant Jimmie Monteith led two Sherman tanks through a minefield to a position where they could provide supporting fire for Monteith himself to lead a force from the beach and up the F1 Draw. Following in his footsteps, you can retrace his route through the steep F1 Draw which commences from the beach **(GPS -49.359176, -0.836115)** before, having reached the top of the road, you take a sharp left turn through the wooden gate which leads to the WN60 strongpoint **(GPS - 49.356716, -0.832047)**. It was close to here that Jimmie Monteith was killed at approximately 1600 hours D-Day. Having explored the remnants of the WN60 strongpoint, you can conclude your visit by retracing your route back down to the beach and to the parking lot of the American Cemetery.

For those who wish to achieve an overview of the Commonwealth Sector, the Pegasus Memorial **(Avenue du Major Howard, 14860, Ranville. GPS Coordinates - 49.242447, -0.272032)**, the Merville Battery **(Place du 9ème Bataillon, 14810, Merville-Franceville, GPS Coordinates – 49.270124, -0.196289)**, the Grand Bunker at Ouistreham **(Avenue du 6 juin, 14150, Ouistreham. GPS Coordinates – 49.287383, -0.252568)**, the Hillman Complex **(64 rue du Suffolk Regiment, 14880, Colleville Montgomery. GPS Coordinates- 49.264796, -0.310147)** and the Juno Beach Centre (which was built in front of the sector where 'B' Company of the Royal Winnipeg Rifles lost eighty per cent of their force during the initial assault) – **(Voie des Français Libres, 14470, Courseulles sur Mer. GPS Coordinates - 49.336189, -0.460951)**, would be useful locations to visit before following the suggested itinerary which takes in sights relevant to the story of the Victoria Cross awarded to Company Sergeant Major Stanley Hollis.

Hollis was amongst the leading elements of the 6th Battalion of the Regiment of the Green Howards which led the first wave assault ashore upon King Sector of Gold Beach, a location which is today overlooked by a road named the **Voie du Debarquement, 14114, and is located close to the town of Ver sur Mer (GPS Coordinates - 49.345348, -0.528095)**. Overlooking this sector of beach is a pre-war tram hut which the man himself supposedly fired upon as he mistook the structure for an enemy pillbox during his final approach to the beach. Today the hut can be found to the north east of where the Voie du Debarquement meets the Voie de la 50eme Divi-

sion d'Infanterie. This structure was recently purchased by the Association of the Regiment of the Green Howards which has mounted an information panel on the side of the hut. Moving away from the beach, on the Voie de la 50eme Division d'Infanterie, you are now following in the footsteps of Stan Hollis and his men, a journey as explained within his personal testimony. Crossing over the main D514 road you now join Avenue Franklin D. Roosevelt. Take the first right turn which leads you onto Rue Claude Debussy. The high stone wall to your left **(GPS – 49.341216, -0.527482)** is the wall which ran around the only property standing here on D-Day, and was nicknamed *The Lavatory Pan Villa,* due to the appearance of its former circular driveway which was observed by aerial photograph reconnaissance prior to the invasion. It was at the junction of what is today the Avenue Franklin D. Roosevelt and the Rue Claude Debussy that Hollis' men made first contact with the garrison of the Mont Fleury Gun Battery.

Having identified two pillboxes located directly to the west of the stone wall, Stan Hollis ran along this position before infiltrating German trenches which ran along the line of what is today the Rue Claude Debussy and Rue Mozart. Rejoining Rue Claude Debussy from Rue Mozart, follow this road to the right, until you reach the Rue Hector Berlioz. At the junction ahead, you can observe remnants of the Mont Fleury Battery **(GPS – 49.338480, -0.528527)** which are visible to your front and right (do not venture onto the private land beyond the Rue Hector Berlioz).

The second action of the Hollis Victoria Cross took place on the southern edge of the small town of Crepon, located two miles inland from Ver sur Mer on the D112. Although this area is today located upon private land, and therefore inaccessible to the public, there is an impressive memorial to both Stan Hollis and the Regiment of the Green Howards located a few meters to the left of the junction of the D65 and the D112 which leads to Le Bourg **(Place de l'Eglise, 14480, Crépon. GPS – 49.315628, -0.550018)**.

Sites associated to the Medals of Honor awarded to Frank Peregory, Robert Cole, Charles DeGlopper and Joe Gandara.

The location of the action which led to the award of Frank Peregory's Medal of Honor can easily be located upon the D514 road at the eastern approach to the town of Grandcamp Maisy. It is here where the main road crosses the small river at La Carriere, close to **Le Pont du Hable, 14450, Grandcamp Maisy (GPS - 49.389513, -1.019667)**, that the advance of the 29th Division came to a halt. Across this bridge, Peregory made a solo charge heading west through the fortifications which existed around what is now a modern housing estate and extending to a position as far as where the Peregory memorial stands today **(located at the junction of the D514 and Avenue du Commandant Keiffer, 14450, Grandcamp Maisy. GPS - 49.387958, -1.030970)**. Frank Peregory's monument is located at the side of a machine-gun nest, which once formed part of the strongpoint he defeated. The memorial is also located next to the striking sculpture; a gift to the people of Normandy from the government of the Republic of China. There is also a plaque dedicated to Peregory located outside the church in the town of Couvains, close to where he was killed on 13 June **(Le Bourg, 50680, Couvains. GPS - 49.164930, -1.007155)**.

On a separate but related point of interest, particularly for those who have already visited the Grand Bunker complex at Ouistreham, the civilian churchyard, to the north of the memorial, is home to the final resting place of Commandant Phillipe Kieffer. A Frenchman born in Haiti, Kieffer volunteered to join the British Special Forces after the defeat of France in 1940 and led a force of Free French Commandos against the *Stutzpunktgruppe Riva Bella* (the largest individual coastal defence in Normandy) located at Sword Beach. This position was defeated by elements of the 1st Special Service Brigade under the command of Lord Lovat. Of the 2000+ men of Lovat's force, 177 of these Commandos were French volunteers commanded by Keiffer.

Colonel Robert Cole's infamous bayonet charge can be retraced, commencing within the hamlet of **Vierge de L'Almont, 50500 St Come du Mont. (GPS - 49.328437, -1.268615)**. Positioned here, at the junction of the D913 and D974, is the D-Day Experience Museum (also known as Dead Man's Corner) which is dedicated to the airborne assault and subsequent battles fought by the 101st Airborne Division. Heading south from the museum, you can follow Cole's charge along the road which became known as 'Purple Heart Lane'. The original bridge over the River Jourdan **(GPS - 49.320938, -1.264846)** can be seen to the right of the modern crossing, before continuing for a further 100 metres, you will reach the River Douve. This is the crossing that had been destroyed by the Germans, the loss of which resulting in the failure of the first attempt to move against Carentan.

After crossing the River Douve, the road continues over the Rivers Groult and Madeleine before reaching a modern roundabout. Overlooking this roundabout, inaugurated during the commemorations of the 70th Anniversary of D-Day in 2014, is a memorial dedicated to the action that became commonly known as 'Colonel Cole's Bayonet Charge' **(GPS - 49.314382, -1.259751)**. Three hundred meters to the south west is the farm complex that Cole made his temporary HQ during the assault which led to the final engagement against the German lines. This is also the location where he was famously photographed after the battle **(GPS - 49.312477, -1.260990)**. The final phase of the battle for Carentan, known as 'the cabbage patch', fought by the 1st Battalion of the 502 PIR, is commemorated by a memorial located close to the retail park which has been built on top of the battlefield at the side of the D974 main road that leads into Carentan from the north **(Avenue du 101eme Airborne, 50500, Carentan. GPS - 49.311091, -1.256684)**.

To visit locations relevant to the Medals of Honor awarded to Charles DeGlopper and Joe Gandara, the best starting point is the Iron Mike memorial overlooking the bridge which spans the River Merderet close to the hamlet of **La Fiere, 50480 (GPS - 49.401125, -1.363418)**. Here you will find memorials and information panels dedicated to the three-day siege which took place as elements of the US Airborne forces, primarily drawn from the 1st Battalion of the 505 PIR of the 82nd Airborne Division, secured the ground around you before fending off ferocious counterattacks. German attempts to break the tenuously-held line emanated from across the causeway which spanned the inundated low-lying marshlands that separated La Fiere from the hamlet of Cauquigny, 680 yards to the west. Amongst the memorials located here is a plaque dedicated to PFC Charles DeGlopper. This, the first memorial to be inaugurated in honour of DeGlopper, is not located in proximity to the action that led to the award, and ultimately DeGlopper's demise, but was one of a number of generic memorials unveiled in 2003 by members of the various associations of the veterans of the 82nd Airborne Division.

The precise location where DeGlopper's heroics took place is not conclusively known and to this day is still subject to much discussion and speculation. A local history association have erected a memorial to DeGlopper close to the location where they believe he was killed. This memorial can be found one kilometre to the west of La Fiere on the **Route du Hameau Flaux, 50480, Amfreville. (GPS - 49.401979, -1.375892)**.

Once again, the precise location of the action that led to Joe Gandara receiving the Medal of Honor was never precisely recorded but took place in close proximity to the village of Amfreville, a picturesque village which is today home to a splendid memorial dedicated to the 507th Parachute Infantry Regiment. This can be found on the D126 where the **Rue du Motey meets the Rue du Moulin, 50480, Amfreville. (GPS - 49.405446, -1.386707)**. Although at the time of publication there is no memorial specifically dedicated to Joe Gandara, there have been in recent times calls amongst the locals for a monument dedicated to him to be placed within close proximity to the existing memorial in Amfreville.

Sites associated to the Medals of Honor awarded to Matt Urban, John Butts, John Kelly and Carlos Ogden during the battle for Cherbourg.

One of the several actions, spread over many months and numerous campaigns, that eventually led to Matt Urban receiving the Medal of Honor, took place close to the small village of Orglandes. Although there are no memorials dedicated specifically to Captain Urban, Orglandes is home to a German military cemetery that holds 10,152 burials **(42 Rue Pierre Devouassoud, 50390, Orglandes. GPS - 49.425248, -1.448369)**. As you enter the village, notice the memorial plaque dedicated to the US Army's 9th and 90th Infantry Divisions who, with Urban amongst their number, liberated Orglandes on 17 June 1944.

Amongst the most notable burials in the German cemetery is a mass grave of twenty-two prisoners of war who were killed in an accidental explosion as they deactivated mines in the village of Asnieres en Bessin in October 1945 (Block 27, Row 13, Grave 420/421). General Wilhelm Falley, (Commanding 91st Luftlande Division) who was killed in the early morning of D-Day as his command car was ambushed by mis-dropped paratroopers, is also buried here (Block 10, Row 2, Grave 207).

If you wish to continue your journey to the west, following the line taken by Matt Urban and his comrades of the 9th Infantry Division, there are also memorials dedicated to the 9th Division close to **Le Ronceray, 50270, St Maurice en Cotentin (GPS - 49.399257, -1.691822)** and at the point where the objective of splitting the peninsula was completed at Barneville Carteret **(Junction of the D903E and the Rue Breissand, 50270, Barneville-Carteret. GPS - 49.379348, -1.747617)**. To resume the drive for Cherbourg, there are some excellent opportunities to compare photographs taken immediately after the battle within the towns of Montebourg **(Place Jeanne d'Arc, 50310, Montebourg. GPS - 49.487563, -1.380431)** and Valognes **(Rue de la Poterie, 50700, Valognes. GPS - 49.511086, -1.469267)**.

Regrettably, there are no specific memorials dedicated to the Medals of Honor awarded to John Butts, John Kelly or Carlos Ogden. There is also little reminder of the struggles in which these men partook. However, one obvious location, very relevant to the overall story, and very much worth seeing today is the **Fort du Roule complex located at Mont Resisters, 50100 Cherbourg-Octeville (GPS - 49.630349, -1.613725)**. Here you will find the Musee de la Liberation, a museum holding exhibits relating to the experiences of civilians living under German occupation, the emphasis very much being on propaganda used by both the Germans and the Free French Forces of the Interior.

Upon the approach to Cherbourg there is another wonderful opportunity to compare photographs taken during the immediate aftermath of the surrender of Fort du Roule at **219 Avenue de Paris, 50100, Cherbourg. (GPS - 49.627625, -1.617474)**.

For those wishing to undertake a more detailed battlefield tour of both the Cutting of the Peninsula and the Battle for Cherbourg, then an excellent guidebook entitled *Battle for Cherbourg* by Robin Havers (ISBN 0750930063) would be of great help for those planning a more intricate visit to this particular phase of the Battle for Normandy.

Sites associated to the Medals of Honor awarded to Walter Ehlers and Arthur DeFranzo during the battle for St Lo.

There are no specific memorials dedicated to the Medals of Honor awarded to either Walter Ehlers or Arthur DeFranzo. However, both names are listed on the memorial dedicated to the 1st Infantry Division overlooking Omaha Beach. For those wishing to undertake a more detailed tour of the approach to St Lo, then an excellent guidebook entitled *Battle for St Lo* by Peter Yates (ISBN 0750930187) would be of great help for those planning a more intricate visit to this particular phase of the Battle for Normandy.

Sites associated to the Medal of Honor awarded to Hulon Whittington and the Victoria Cross awarded to Sydney Bates during Operations Cobra and Bluecoat.

The start line of Operation Cobra is commemorated by a memorial located **at the junction of the D900 and D189 at the Rue de Mercure, 50570, La Chappelle en Juger (GPS - 49.143632, -1.199110)**. Although there is no monument dedicated specifically to Hulon Whittington, the site of the battle for which his medal was awarded is commemorated by a memorial located at **Le Chapitre, 50660, Trelly (GPS - 48.959554, -1.389131)**. This memorial stands at the position of the forward roadblock which was overrun by the Germans before their approach towards the high ground was stopped by the actions of Whittington and his comrades. Ironically, this area, known as the Land of the Dead, is named after a battle that took place here in the Fifteenth Century, during The Hundred Years War.

For those wishing to undertake a more detailed tour of the battlefields of Operation Cobra and the Battle for Mortain, then an excellent guidebook entitled Operation Cobra by Christopher Pugsley (ISBN 0750930152) would be of great help for those planning a more intricate visit to this particular phase of the Battle for Normandy.

A memorial dedicated at the site of the action that led to the award of the Victoria Cross to Sydney Bates can be found close to the hamlet of **Pavee, 14410, Viessoix (GPS - 48.852722, -0.784353)**. Sydney Bates is the only recipient of the Victoria Cross to be killed during the Battle for Normandy. His burial can be found at **Plot 20 (XX), Row E, Grave 19 at the Bayeux Commonwealth War Graves Cemetery, Boulevard Fabian Ware, 14400, Bayeux (GPS - 49.274206, -0.713820)**. A museum dedicated to the story of Operation Bluecoat (the Musee 44 La Percee du Bocage) can be found at **5 rue du 19 Mars 1962, 14350 St Martin des Besaces (GPS - 49.011217,**

-0.850059). A vital objective of the battles fought within this area, and in fact the highest ground in Normandy, is Mont Pincon which can be found at **14770, Le Plessis-Grimoult (GPS - 48.971264, -0.630728)**. For those wishing to undertake a more detailed tour of the battles fought during Operation Bluecoat, an excellent book entitled *Over the Battlefield - Operation Bluecoat* by Ian Daglish (ISBN 1848840497) would be of great help for those planning a more intricate visit to this particular phase of the Battle for Normandy.

Sites associated to the Victoria Crosses awarded to David Jamieson, Tasker Watkins, David Currie and the Medal of Honor awarded to John Hawk during the battles upon the approach to the city of Falaise and the subsequent battle of the Falaise Pocket.

Unfortunately, there are no specific memorials dedicated to the award of the Victoria Crosses to either David Jamieson or Tasker Watkins, nor is there any memorialisation of the battles that led to these awards. Although not part of the Operation Totalize battle, there is a monument dedicated to the Canadian forces who partook in the previous struggles fought in this area in the days and weeks immediately prior to the launch of Totalize. Occupying a position of high ground, looking to the south-east, the start line for Totalize can be observed from **La Grand Barberie, 14320, St Martin de Fontenay. (GPS - 49.127713, -0.374544)**.

Joining the N158, a dead straight road that runs from Caen to Falaise, this is the same road which was the central axis of the Totalize Assault. Upon this road, six miles to the south of the City of Caen, a Canadian Cemetery can be found close to the village of **Cintheaux, 14680. (GPS - 49.060595, -0.291720)**. Although holding almost 3,000 Canadian burials, those buried here whose date of death is recorded between the dates of 8 and 22 August were mostly killed during the struggles faced between the commencement of Operation Totalize and the closing of the Falaise Pocket. Notable burials include 16-year-old Gerard Dore (Grave XVI G 11) and Colonel Donald Worthington (Grave XIX F 1) whose story is told two paragraphs below.

A little further along the N158, a Polish Cemetery can be found upon the **D131, 14190 Urville. (GPS - 49.023083, -0.270167)**. A large proportion of over 600 burials within this cemetery were men under the command of General

Maczek who were positioned upon the high ground known as The Mace and faced the most furious attempts of the enemy forces fleeing the horrors of the Falaise Pocket.

Upon the **D131 close to the village of Soignolles (GPS - 49.017492, -0.199209)** is a memorial dedicated to a battlegroup of Canadian troops who, during the second phase of Operation Totalize, on the night of 9 August, attempted to occupy a position of high ground known as Hill 195. Moving into enemy-held territory, in the dead of

Left: *Although very rarely in their original positions, there are still remnants of the German beach obstacles to view along the invasion coastline.*

night and in the chaotic immediate aftermath of the shortfall of the supporting bombardment, this improvised battlegroup under the command of Colonel Donald Worthington, drifted off course some six miles from their intended position. Alone and disorientated, Colonel Worthington's force would be subjected to a brutal attack by elements of the 12th SS Hitler Jugend Division. Cut off from reinforcements, very few survived this engagement to return to friendly lines. Colonel Worthington himself was killed, another 239 of his men would be killed, wounded or taken prisoner.

Two memorials dedicated to the actions that led to the award of the Victoria Cross to Major David Currie can be found in close proximity to St Lambert sur Dives (61160). The first, occupying a position on the high ground from which Currie's force entered St Lambert, can be found on the D13, a few hundred metres north west of the village **(GPS - 48.824381, 0.069751)**. The second memorial is on the north western limit of the village at **Le Bourg, 61160, St Lambert sur Dives (GPS -48.822540, 0.071956)**.

One kilometre to the south east of St Lambert sur Dives is a shallow crossing of the River Dives. Known as the Moissy Ford, located at **La Droitiere, 61160, Chambois. (GPS - 48.811653, 0.090759)**, the road which runs from this point to the north east was one of the very last routes of escape left open to the fleeing German forces as they attempted to flee the horrors of the Falaise Pocket. By following this road to the memorial located at **8 Boisjos, 61160, Coudehard. (GPS - 48.848583, 0.140711)**, a position that became known to the Polish soldiers occupying it as The Mace, you can retrace one of the few tracks which combined became known as the corridor of death. Close by is an excellent museum dedicated to the struggle faced by all those caught up within the bitter struggle of the Falaise Pocket, this can be found at Mont Ormel **(Les Hayettes, 61160, Coudehard. GPS - 48.837882, 0.142752)**.

A memorial dedicated to the link up of American and Polish troops on 21 August, a meeting which signalled what many class as the conclusion of the Battle for Normandy can be found next to the Eleventh Century Norman Keep in the town of Chambois **(Rue des Polonais, 61160, Chambois. GPS - 48.805271, 0.105894)**.

For those wishing to undertake a more detailed tour of the battles fought between Caen and Falaise and the subsequent Battle of the Falaise Pocket, two excellent guidebooks entitled *Road to Falaise* by Stephen Hart (ISBN 0750930160) and *The Falaise Pocket* by Paul Larawski (ISBN 0750930152) would be of great help.

Appendix 2

German Order of Battle

Elite Armoured and SS Formations highlighted in red

Date First Deployed	Name of Formation	Strength of manpower	Location on 6/6/44	Sector Majority of Strength First Deployed Against	Approximate Location of First Deployment if known
6 June 1944	21 Panzer Division	16297	Caen	Commonwealth	Caen
6 June 1944	352 Infantry Division	12734	Molay Littry	US/Commonwealth	Omaha / Gold
6 June 1944	709 Infantry Division	12320	Cotentin	American	Cotentin
6 June 1944	711 Infantry Division	7242	Cabourg	Commonwealth	Caen
6 June 1944	716 Infantry Division	7771	Caen	Commonwealth	Gold / Juno / Sword
6 June 1944	91 Luftlande Division	7500	Cotentin	American	Cotentin
7 June 1944	12 SS Panzer Division	20516	Lisieux	Commonwealth	Caen
8 June 1944	243 Infantry Division	11529	Cotentin	American	Cotentin
8 June 1944	346 Infantry Division	9816	Le Harvre	Commonwealth	Caen
8 June 1944	Panzer Lehr Division	14699	Chartres	Commonwealth	Caen
9 June 1944	3 Flak-Korps	12000	Somme	Commonwealth	Caen
10 June 1944	17 SS Panzer-Gren Div.	17321	Loire Valley	American	Carentan
11 June 1944	265 Infantry Division	9726	Brittany	American	St Lo
11 June 1944	7 Werfer Brigade	3785	Picardie	Commonwealth	Caen
11 June 1944	77 Infantry Division	9095	St Malo	American	Coutances
12 June 1944	275 Infantry Division	12328	Western France	American	St Lo
12 June 1944	3 Para Division	17420	Brittany	American	St Lo
13 June 1944	101 SS Heavy Tank Btn	1000	Picardie	Commonwealth	Villers Bocage
13 June 1944	2 Panzer Division	16762	Amiens	Commonwealth	Caumont
17 June 1944	353 Infantry Division	13330	Brittany	American	St Lo
18 June 1944	9 Werfer Brigade	3800	Germany	Commonwealth	Caen
25 June 1944	5 Para Division	12253	Brittany	American	St Lo

Date First Deployed	Name of Formation	Strength of manpower	Location on 6/6/44	Sector Majority of Strength First Deployed Against	Approximate Location of First Deployment if known
28 June 1944	8 Werfer Brigade	3800	Germany	Commonwealth	Caen
29 June 1944	10 SS Panzer Division	16011	Russian Front	Commonwealth	Caen
29 June 1944	2 SS Panzer Division	18108	Toulouse	Commonwealth	Caen
29 June 1944	9 SS Panzer Division	20910	Russian Front	Commonwealth	Caen
30 June 1944	1 SS Panzer Division	19618	Belgium	Commonwealth	Caen
1 July 1944	16 Luftwaffe Field Division	9354	Holland	Commonwealth	Caen
5 July 1944	276 Infantry Division	11658	South of France	Commonwealth	Caen
9 July 1944	102 SS Heavy Tank Btn	1000	Holland	Commonwealth	Caen
11 July 1944	277 Infantry Division	9136	South of France	Commonwealth	Caen
11 July 1944	503 Heavy Tank	1000	Germany	Commonwealth	Caen
13 July 1944	5 Para Division	12253	Brittany	American	Cobra
17 July 1944	272 Infantry Division	11211	South of France	Commonwealth	Caen
22 July 1944	271 Infantry Division	11617	Montpellier	Commonwealth	Caen
24 July 1944	116 Panzer Division	13621	Germany	American	St Lo
25 July 1944	326 Infantry Division	11533	Pas De Calais	Commonwealth	Caumont
1 August 1944	363 Infantry Division	11000	Denmark	US/Commonwealth	Vire / Flers
2 Aug. 1944	266 Infantry Division	8852	Brittany	American	Avranches
4 Aug. 1944	9 Panzer Division	14459	South of France	US/Commonwealth	Falaise
5 Aug. 1944	708 Infantry Division	8123	Biscay	American	Le Mans
5 Aug. 1944	84 Infantry Division	8437	Northern France	US/Commonwealth	Falaise
5 Aug. 1944	89 Infantry Division	8500	Norway	US/Commonwealth	Falaise
7 Aug. 1944	343 Infantry Division	11021	Brest	American	Cobra
9 Aug. 1944	85 Infantry Division	8393	Northern France	US/Commonwealth	Falaise
10 Aug. 1944	331 Infantry Division	10543	Refit after Russian Front	US/Commonwealth	Falaise
12 Aug.t 1944	6 Para Division	4000	Brittany	American	L'Aigle - Moulins
15 Aug. 1944	348 Infantry Division		Dieppe	US/Commonwealth	Falaise
16 Aug. 1944	344 Infantry Division	10000	Northern France	US/Commonwealth	Trun

Appendix 3
Bibliography / Suggested Reading

Electronic Resources

All Medal of Honor citations are taken from the U.S. Army Centre of Military History website:

http://www.history.army.mil/moh/index.html

http://webarchive.nationalarchives.gov.uk/+/http://www.operations.mod.uk/honours/honours.htm

http://www.29infantrydivision.orghttp://www.warchronicle.com/ksli/historiantales_wwii/normandyreg.htm

Books

There are a huge number of books available on the subject of D-Day and the Battle for Normandy. Here are the author's suggestions for further reading.

General D-Day

W Buckingham *D-Day; the first 72 hours*
D Howarth *Dawn of D-Day*
R Kershaw *D-Day: Piercing the Atlantic Wall*
J Levine *Operation Fortitude*
B MacIntyre *Double Cross*
R Neillands & R De Normann *D-Day 1944*
Robertson and Booth *Following in the Footsteps of Heroes: D-Day; June 6th 1944*
C Ryan *The Longest Day*
D Stafford *Ten Days to D-Day*
S Trew *D-Day and the Battle for Normandy*
Various *D-Day: Then and Now (2 Volumes)*

American Airborne

N Crookenden *Drop zone Normandy*
I Gardner & R Day *Tonight We Die As Men*
G Koskimaki *D-Day with the Screaming Eagles*
P Nordyke *All American All the Way*
C Shilleto Utah Beach / Ste Mere Eglise

Utah Beach

S Badsey *Utah Beach*
J Balkoski *Utah Beach*

Pointe du Hoc

RW Black *The Battalion*
J MacDonald *The Liberation of Pointe du Hoc*
S Zaloga *Rangers Lead the Way*

Omaha Beach

Badsley and Bean *Omaha Beach*
J Balkoski *Omaha Beach*
F Whitlock *The Fighting First*
J MacManus *The Dead and those about to Die*

Gold Beach

G Bernage *Gold Juno Sword*
G Hartcup *Code Name Mulberry*
S Trew *Gold Beach*

Juno Beach

K Ford *Juno Beach*
M Zuehlke *Juno Beach*

Sword Beach

P Delaforce *Monty's Iron Sides*
K Ford *Sword Beach*
N Scarfe *Assault Division*

British Airborne

N Barber *The Day the Devils Dropped In*
N Barber *The Pegasus and Orne Bridges*
L Clark *Orne Bridgehead*
C Shilleto *Pegasus Bridge and Horsa Bridge*
C Shilleto *Merville Battery & The Dives Bridges*
D Tibbs *Parachute Doctor*

Commando Operations

K Ford *D-Day Commando*
J Forfar *From Omaha to the Scheldt*
S Scott *Fighting with the Commandos*

Post D-Day - The Battle for Normandy/ General Reading

M Blumenson *Breakout and Pursuit*

G Blackburn *The Guns of Normandy*
O Bradley *A Soldier's Story*
J Buckley (Ed.) *The Normandy Campaign 1944; Sixty Years On*
J Buckley *Monty's Men*
J Buckley *British Armour in the Normandy Campaign*
L Clark *Operation Epsom*
T Copp *Fields of Fire*
Curruthers / Trew *The Normandy Battles*
D Eisenhower *Crusade in Europe*
Major Ellis *Victory in the West*
G Forty *Villers Bocage*
G Harrison *Cross Channel Attack*
R Hargreaves *The Germans in Normandy*
S Hart *Road to Falaise*
S Hart *Montgomery and Colossal Cracks*
S Hart *Colossal Cracks*
S Hart *Operation Totalize*
RPW Havers *Battle for Cherbourg*
J Holland *The War in the West Volume 1 – Germany Ascendant 139-1941*
J Holland *The War in the West Volume 2 – 1941-1943*
Col G Johns *The Clay Pigeons of St Lo*
J Keegan *Six Armies in Normandy*
P Latawski *Falaise Pocket*
N de Lee *Battle for St-Lo*
A McKee *Caen: Anvil of Victory*
BL Montgomery *Memoirs*
R Neillands *The Battle for Normandy 1944*
C Pugsley *Operation Cobra*
M Reynolds *Steel Inferno: 1 SS Panzer Corps in Normandy*
M Schulman *Defeat in the West*
Tombs / Chabel (Ed) *Britain and France in Two World Wars – Truth, Myth and Memory*
K Tout *The Bloody Battle for Tilly*
K Tout *A Fine Night for Tanks*
K Tout *Roads to Falaise*
S Trew *Servants of Evil*
Trew / Badsey *Battle for Caen*
R Weiss *Fire Mission*
D&S Whitaker *Victory at Falaise*
C Wilmot *The Struggle for Europe*
P Yates *Battle for St-Lo*
M Zuehlke *Holding Juno*
M Zuehlke *Breakout from Juno*
M Zuehlke *Forgotten Victory*

General VC

R Bailey *Forgotten Voices of the Victoria Cross*
J Laffin *British VCs of World War 2: A Study in Heroism*
M Morgan *D-Day Hero – CSM Stanley Hollis VC*
Mulholland and Jordan *Victoria Cross Bibliography*

Endnotes

1 Definition as defined by the American 'Institute of Heraldry', a department of the 'Office to the Administrative Assistant to the Secretary for the Army'.

2 Definition as defined by the American 'Institute of Heraldry', a department of the 'Office to the Administrative Assistant to the Secretary for the Army'.

3 Many commentators have incorrectly identified Montgomery's role during the Battle for Normandy as solely the Commander in Chief of British forces. Throughout the entire Battle for Normandy, Montgomery was the commander of all Allied land forces. This means of course that the highest ranking American officers, names such as Bradley and Patton, were subordinate to Montgomery through the whole campaign. Not until 1 September 1944, when Eisenhower took command of all ground forces, did the American forces on the ground revert to American command. Maybe the origins of any confusion lies within the way figures as Bradley refer to his own battles to the west, separating these from 'Monty's' battles around Caen. In actual fact, Bradley's own operations were just as much 'Monty's' as those operations fought around Caen, these battles commanded not by 'Monty' but rather General Dempsey. Although Bradley would maybe wish the reader believe that he was commanding at an equivalent level to that of Montgomery, until 1 September 1944, Bradley, and all other land commanders were in actual fact subordinate to Montgomery – the supreme commander of all Allied land forces.

4 General Omar Bradley as quoted in Gelb - 'Ike and Monty; Generals at War'. P331.

5 V Corps Summary, Overlord Conference – 3 February 1944. As quoted in Balkoski – Omaha Beach. P72.

6 Balkoski - Omaha Beach. P73.

7 Capt. Harry Butcher (US Navy Aide to Eisenhower) as quoted in Balkoski – Omaha Beach. P72

8 Major Sidney Bingham, Commanding 2nd Battalion of the 116th Regiment of the 29th Infantry Division quoting General Bradley during his visit to the Battalion in late May 1944 as quoted in Balkoski – Omaha Beach. P72

9 Balkoski - Omaha Beach. P86-87.

10 Major General James Raaen (5th Ranger Battalion) as quoted during the Veteran's Q&A session at the WW2 Museum Conference, New Orleans, 5 December 2014.

11 Balkoski – Omaha Beach. P129.

12 Wilmot – Struggle for Europe P291

13 Dwight D. Eisenhower (Cited in: B. H. Liddell Hart, The Tanks (Praeger, 1959), vol. II, p. 332).

14 McManus – The Dead and Those About to Die. P136.

15 Balkoski – Omaha Beach. P187-88.

16 McManus – The Dead and Those About to Die. P138.

17 Balkoski – Omaha Beach. P200.

18 Balkoski – Omaha Beach. P292-293.

19 Captain Synge (6th Battalion, Green Howards) as quoted in Morgan – D-Day Hero: CSM Stanley Hollis VC. P27.

20 Ernie Roberts (6th Battalion, Green Howards) as quoted in Morgan – D-Day Hero: CSM Stanley Hollis VC. P28-29.

21 Jack Strachan (6th Battalion, Green Howards) as quoted in Morgan – D-Day Hero: CSM Stanley Hollis VC. P31-32.

22 CSM Hollis personal testimony as quoted in Morgan – D-Day Hero: CSM Stanley Hollis VC. P61-62.

23 CSM Hollis personal testimony as quoted in Morgan – D-Day Hero: CSM Stanley Hollis VC. P65-66.

24 Morgan – D-Day Hero: CSM Stanley Hollis VC. P7.

25 Harrison – Cross Channel Attack. P332.

26 Virginia Military Institute Archive Digital Collection – Interview with Carl Proffitt - http://digitalcollections.vmi.edu/cdm/ref/collection/p15821coll13/id/434

27 Omar Bradley as quoted in Breuer - Hitler's Fortress Cherbourg. P103.

28 PFC Raymond T. Burchell as quoted in Nordyke – All American, All the Way. P336.

29 Speech made on the occasion of the 70th anniversary of D-Day by Major General John W. Nicholson, Jr. of the 82nd Airborne Div. As quoted on http://smdp.com/letter-metro-board-honor-joe-gandara/145048

30 Bradley – A Soldier's Story. P297.

31 ETHINT66-(ML1079). Interview with General Fritz Bayerlein held on 7-9 August 1945 by the Department of the Army Historical Division, Washington DC. As Published in Steinhardt (Ed)– Panzer Lehr Division 1944-45. P68.

32 Whitaker – Normandy, the Real Story. P12.

33 Harrison - Cross Channel Attack. P404.

34 Blumenson – Breakout and Pursuit. P47. 35 Bradley – A Soldier's Story. P297.
36 Colonel Kauffman as quoted in Havers - The Battle for Cherbourg. P54.
37 Major Harry Herman as quoted in Max Hastings - Overlord. P160.
38 US Army Historical Section - Utah To Cherbourg. P164-165.
39 New York Times Obituary – 6 April 2001.
40 ETHINT66-(ML1079). Interview with General Fritz Bayerlein held on the 7-9 August 1945 by the Department of the US Army Historical Division, W ashington DC. As Published in Steinhardt (Ed)– Panzer Lehr Division 1944-45. P56-59.
41 Ambrose – Citizen Soldiers. P21.
42 Atkinson – The Guns at Last Light. P101.
43 Wieviorka – The British and the Liberation of France as published in Tombs / Chabel (Ed) – Britain and France in Two World Wars: Truth, Myth and Memory. Page 142.
44 French production 'La lumière de l'aube' (The Light of Dawn). 2014.
45 Fritz Bayerlein (Commanding Panzer Lehr Division) as quoted in Milton Schulman – Defeat in the W est. Pages 124-125.
46 Helmut Ritgen – Die Geschichte Der Panzer Lehr Division Im Westen: 1944 1945. P112 as quoted in Steinhardt (Ed) – Panzer Lehr Division 1944-45. P42.
47 Bradley – A Soldier's Story Page 325-327.
48 Eisenhower – D-Day to VE Day: General Eisenhower's Report 1944-45. P107.
49 Official Correspondence of C in C 21st Army Group, PRO London. Quoted in M. Reynolds - Steel Inferno P83.
50 Official Correspondence of C in C 21st Army Group, PRO London. Quoted in M. Reynolds - Steel Inferno P83.
51 Montgomery personal diary – 26 May 1944. IWM – Montgomery Papers Part II, LMD 59/1 as quoted in Brooks – Montgomery and the Battle for Normandy. P136.
52 Messenger – Hitler's Gladiator. P126.
53 Meyer – Grenadiers. P242.
54 Zetterling – Normandy 1944: German Military Organization, Combat Power and Organizational Effectiveness. P373.
55 Zetterling – Normandy 1944: German Military Organization, Combat Power and Organizational Effectiveness. P351.
56 Zetterling – Normandy 1944: German Military Organization, Combat Power and Organizational Effectiveness. P384.
57 Generalmajor Fritz Kramer (Deputy 1 SS Panzer Corps), as quoted in Isby (Ed) – Fighting in Normandy (The German Army from D-Day to Villers Bocage). P134.
58 Bradley – A Soldier's Story. P291.
59 Spiedel – We Defended Normandy. P101.
60 Spiedel – We Defended Normandy. P112.
61 BLM 216/16 – Taken from Whitaker – Normandy, the Real Story. P17.
62 Bradley – A Soldier's Story. P325-327.
63 Hastings – Overlord. P358.
64 Belfield / Essame – The Battle for Normandy. P172.
65 Letter (M513) from Eisenhower to Montgomery dated 21 July as quoted in Brooks – Montgomery and the Battle for Normandy. P230.
66 Letter from Alanbrooke to Montgomery, 28 July 1944 as quoted in Brooks – Montgomery and the Battle for Normandy. P253-54.
67 Montgomery personal diary – 19 July 1944. IWM – Montgomery Papers Part II, LMD 60/1 as quoted in Brooks – Montgomery and the Battle for Normandy. P222-23.
68 Letter from Sir James Grigg (Secretary of State for War) to Montgomery, 1 August 1944 as quoted in Brooks – Montgomery and the Battle for Normandy. P261.
69 French – Raising Churchill's Army. P147.
70 Letter from Montgomery to Eisenhower – 8 July 1944 as quoted in Brooks – Montgomery and the Battle for Normandy. P191.
71 Walter Ehlers MOH interviewed by Flint Whitlock on the 27 April, 2002. As quoted in Flint Whitlock - The Fighting First. P260-261.
72 Walter Ehlers MOH interviewed by Flint Whitlock on the 27 April, 2002. As quoted in Flint Whitlock - The Fighting First. P260-261.
73 Harrison - Cross Channel Assault. P365.
74 Harrison - Cross Channel Assault. P377.
75 Harrison - Cross Channel Assault. P377.
76 Schimpff - Operations of (German) 3rd Parachute Division (US National Archives) as quoted in Buckley (Ed) The Normandy Campaign 1944; Sixty Years on. P65.
77 Letter from Montgomery to Alanbrooke – 27 June 1944 as quoted in Brooks – Montgomery and the Battle for Normandy. P166.
78 Bradley – A Soldier's Story. P319-320.

79 Balkoski - Beyond the Beachhead. P212.
80 Bradley – A Soldier's Story P325-327.
81 Montgomery of Alamein – The Memoirs of Field Marshal Montgomery. P262.
82 Hart – Montgomery, Morale, Casualty Conservation and Colossal Cracks: 21st Army Group's Operational Technique in North-West Europe, 1944-45. Article in the Journal of Military History. 65(2) April 2001.
83 Hart – Montgomery, Morale, Casualty Conservation and 'Colossal Cracks': 21st Army Group's Operational Technique in North-West Europe, 1944-45. Article in the Journal of Military History. 65(2) April 2001.
84 Bradley – A Soldier's Story. P320-321.
85 Montgomery's Directive (M510) to Lt. Gen O.N. Bradley, First US Army, Lt. Gen Sir Miles Dempsey, Second British Army, Lt. Gen G. Patton, Third US Army, and Lt. Gen H.D. Crerar, First Canadian Army. 10 July 1944 as quoted in Brooks – Montgomery and the Battle for Normandy. P194.
86 Wilmot – The Struggle for Europe. P354
87 Ellis – Victory in the West. P329-330
88 The Memoirs of Field-Marshal Montgomery. P254-56.
89 Wilmot – The Struggle for Europe. P352
90 NA (Kew) CAB 106/1061. Quoted in Richard Doherty – Normandy 1944; The Road to Victory. P224.
91 Maule – Caen: The Brutal Battle and the Breakout from Normandy. P80
92 Blumenson – Breakout and Pursuit. P188.
93 Bradley – A Soldier's Story Page 325-327.
94 Bradley – A Soldier's Story. P319.
95 Letter (M513) from Eisenhower to Montgomery dated 21 July as quoted in Brooks – Montgomery and the Battle for Normandy. P229.
96 Whitaker – Normandy, the Real Story. P17.
97 Blumenson - Breakout and Pursuit. P72.
98 Blumenson - Breakout and Pursuit. P125.
99 General R Barton, Commanding 4th Infantry Division : NA II 407/427/6431 as quoted in A Beevor – D-Day. P249.
100 Bradley – A Soldier's Story. P332.
101 Generalmajor von Gersdoff – The Situation Prior to 25 July. Taken from Isby (Ed) – Fighting the Breakout. P25.
102 Bradley – A Soldier's Story. P369.
103 Zetterling - Normandy 1944: German Military Organization, Combat Power and Organizational Effectiveness. P384.
104 General Heinz Guderian as quoted in Steinhardt (Ed) - Panzer Lehr Division. P81-82.
105 Von Kluge had taken command of all German forces in Normandy following the loss of Rommel who had suffered severe wounds as his staff car had been shot off the road by a RAF fighter on the 17 July.
106 General Bayerlein as quoted by Hastings – Overlord. P256.
107 Daglish - Operation Bluecoat. P237.
108 Bailey – Forgotten Voices Victoria Cross. P262-64.
109 Bailey – Forgotten Voices Victoria Cross. P265.
110 Blumenson – Breakout and Pursuit. P177.
111 Geyr von Schweppenburg ETHINT 13 as quoted in A Beevor – D-Day. P413
112 National Archives – MSB840, 981SOM (D123). Eberbach; Panzer Group Eberbach and the Falaise Encirclement, Feb 1, 1946 as quoted in Whitaker – Normandy; The Real Story. P130.
113 Copp – unpublished article entitled 'The Canadians in Normandy; A Reassessment' as quoted in Normandy – The Real Story. P135.
114 Bailey – Forgotten Voices of the Victoria Cross. P266-270.
115 Eisenhower – D-Day to VE Day: General Eisenhower's Report 1944-45. P146.
116 The Patton Papers P464 as quoted in Beevor – D-Day. P282.
117 Beevor – D-Day. P292.
118 Montgomery's Directive (M512) to Lt. Gen O.N. Bradley, First US Army, Lt. Gen Sir Miles Dempsey, Second British Army, Lt. Gen G. Patton, Third US Army, and Lt. Gen H.D. Crerar, First Canadian Army. 21 July 1944 as quoted in Brooks – Montgomery and the Battle for Normandy. P227.
119 Letter (M513) from Eisenhower to Montgomery dated 21 July as quoted in Brooks – Montgomery and the Battle for Normandy. P228.
120 Bradley – A General's Life – p285.
121 Bradley – A Soldier's Story. P355.
122 Bradley – A Soldier's Story. P362-63.
123 Bradley – A Soldier's Story. P 365-67.
124 Patton – War As I Knew It. P104.
125 Eisenhower – D-Day to VE Day: General Eisenhower's Report 1944-45. P136-37.
126 Hastings – Overlord. P281.
127 Bradley – A Soldier's Story. P353.
128 Tony Triumpho as quoted in Henry Maule – Normandy Breakout. P132.
129 In fact Argentan would not be taken by Patton's forces until the 20 of August.

130 Bradley – A Soldier's Story. P376.
131 Bradley – A Soldier's Story. P377.
132 Bradley – A Soldier's Story. P379.
133 Letter from Montgomery to Alanbrooke – 14 August 1944 as quoted in Brooks – Montgomery and the Battle for Normandy. P298.
134 Montgomery's personal diary – 17 August 1944. IWM – Montgomery Papers Part II, LMD 61/1 as quoted in Brooks – Montgomery and the Battle for Normandy. P306.
135 David V. Currie VC. 'In my own words'. As published in After the Battle magazine, Volume 8. 1975.
136 Colonel McHugh, 317 Infantry Regiment, 80th Infantry Division. NA II 407/427/24242 as quoted in Beevor P438.
137 NAC. RG24, Vol 13, 751. Lt. Gen G. Simonds, Notes on Corps Commanders Talk, 13 August 1944. As quoted in Whitaker – Normandy; the Real Story. P212.
138 90th Infantry Division Combat Interviews, RG407, Box 24065, Folder 194, US National Archive.
139 NA. RG94, The Gap at Chambois 194. As quoted in Whitaker / Whitaker / Copp – Normandy; the Real Story. P274.
140 1995 Boston Globe interview as quoted at http://www.nytimes.com/2013/11/09/us/john-hawk-hero-of-normandy-battle-dies-at-89.html
141 Article by Ed Friedrich, published in the Kitsap Sun on 7 April 2008 entitled 'War Hero John Hawk Receives Medal of Honor Flag'.
142 General von Luttwitz, Commanding 2nd Panzer Division as quoted in M. Shulman – Defeat in the W est. P181-182.
143 Belfied & Essame – The Battle for Normandy. P216.
144 Belfied & Essame – The Battle for Normandy. P215.
145 Neillands – The Battle of Normandy. P385.
146 Eisenhower – Crusade in Europe. P306.
147 Neillands – The Battle of Normandy 1944. P18-19.
148 Neillands – The Battle of Normandy 1944. P22.
149 Dolski – D-Day Remembered. P120.
150 Dolski – D-Day Remembered. P120.
151 Wieviorka – The British and the Liberation of France as published in Tombs / Chabel (Ed) – Britain and France in Two World Wars: Truth, Myth and Memory. Page 142-144.
152 Bradley – A Soldier's Story Page 325-327.
153 Eisenhower – D-Day to VE Day: General Eisenhower's Report 1944-45. P107.
154 Ambrose - Americans at War. P89.
155 Dolski – D-Day Remembered. P161.
156 Torgovnick – The War Complex. P2-3.
157 Dolski – D-Day Remembered. P179-80.
158 Dolski – D-Day Remembered. P5.
159 Blumenson – Breakout and Pursuit. P125.
160 Neillands – The Battle of Normandy 1944. P22.
161 Montgomery of Alamein – The Memoirs of Field Marshal Montgomery. P254.
162 Montgomery of Alamein – The Memoirs of Field Marshal Montgomery. P254-55.
163 Kirby – 1100 Miles with Monty. P223.
164 Al Murray lecture entitled 'Monty' given at Chalke Valley History Festival, 26 June 2017.
165 Horne – The Lonely Leader. P271.
166 Extracts of a teleprinter message, Model to Jodl, 29 August 2400hrs. (Templhoff Papers), taken from; Chester Wilmot – The Struggle for Europe. P434
167 Horne – The Lonely Leader. P256. 168 Blackburn – Introduction to the Guns of Normandy.

Index

T

U

V

W

Z

FOR VALOUR